The most amazing places to visit in London

PUBLISHED BY
THE READER'S DIGEST ASSOCIATION, INC.
LONDON • NEW YORK • SYDNEY • MONTREAL

The most amazing places to visit in London

More than 400 unusual, surprising and captivating spots in London

Contents

Introduction

Discover the most amazing places the capital has to offer with this insider's guide to the city. All the famous sites are here, together with the best of the rest – the closely-guarded secrets, the cherished local treasures and the hidden oases of greenery.

London is a glorious, sprawling, patchwork city like no other. What began as a Roman trading port, Londinium, nearly 2,000 years ago, and grew into a miniature Rome protected by a two-mile wall, today spans 20 miles and has subsumed a thousand villages, hamlets and settlements, woodlands, forests and pastures. Two millennia of fortune and disaster, devastation and renewal have resulted in incredible diversity – London was not built to one grand design but grew up piecemeal over centuries according to the affluence, philanthropy, power and whim of its citizens. Its grander buildings are monumental, its parks magnificent and its boulevards stately. But it is also a city crammed with hidden gems and curios – tiny museums, specialist shops and eccentric architecture.

Experience the best
Each destination in this book has been chosen for its special appeal to visitors. Every one is amazing, whether world famous or locally known. Discover Temple Church with its life-sized effigies of nine medieval knights, or marvel at the City's spectacular and ecologically designed No 30 St Mary Axe, otherwise known as the Gherkin. Climb the 311 steps of the world's tallest freestanding stone column – the Monument – erected to commemorate the Great Fire of London or skate on the magnificent floodlit ice rink in the courtyard of the 18th century Somerset House. Take a bracing walk on Hampstead Heath among the kite-flyers, dog walkers and London locals and admire the view, or stroll along The Terrace at Barnes (below), a Domesday settlement with some of the oldest riverside housing in the city. Whether you're a first-time visitor, a regular day tripper or a Londoner born and bred, you will find so much to excite, fascinate, intrigue or divert you.

Extraordinary history
More than a visitors' guide, this book is also a great armchair read, bringing the capital vividly to life. Entries tell the story of each place, revealing the vision of architects, engineers and landscapers, the greed and ambition of kings, the vanity of queens, national power and aspiration, law and order, work and play, trade and industry, grandiosity, human creativity and caprice. Here is London in all its grime and glory. Samuel Johnson, who wrote extensively on the city, declared: 'By seeing London, I have seen as much of life as the world can show.' If he could return to his beloved city today, the great 18th century lexicographer would be lost for words.

How to use this book

This guidebook is divided into ten chapters, each featuring a distinct area of the capital: City, Central, West End, Westminster & St James's, South Bank & Beyond, Kensington, North, Southeast, and East. Each chapter opens with a map of the area, as shown above. Numbers on the map show the geographical location of each entry listed within the chapters and act as an at-a-glance guide when planning tours or days out. Nearest tube or rail stations are included, together with addresses and postcodes. Opening times are shown where relevant, though always check these before visiting as they may be subject to change.

Useful websites

www.visitlondon.com
The official visitor organisation for the capital.
www.cityoflondon.gov.uk
For sites, ceremonies, history and heritage.
www.tfl.gov.uk
Transport for London offers all the information you need for getting around the city.
www.english-heritage.org.uk
www.nationaltrust.org.uk
Both organisations have properties in the capital.
www.londonopenhouse.org
Lists buildings open to the public each September.
www.timeout.com/london
Online guide to culture, eating out and entertainment.

KING'S
CROSS

Pentonville Road

Swinton St

Acton St

King's Cross Road

Gray's Inn Road

Rosebery Avenue

St John Street

Spencer Street

City Road

Goswell Road

Old Street

OLD STREET

Great Eastern Street

10

Farringdon Rd

Clerkenwell Road

11

12

13

FARRINGDON

BARBICAN

44

45

43

City Road

Bishopsgate

Houndsditch

Bevis Marks

CHANCERY
LANE

8

9

Farringdon Road

17

16

14

15

21

18

20

22

25

24

MOORGATE

41

London Wall

42

LIVERPOOL
STREET

Holborn   Viaduct

Fetter Lane

26

19

Newgate St

23

33

34

40

CITY
THAMESLINK

New Bridge St

5

4

6

3

27

31

29

30

ST PAUL'S

28

32

39

38

35

46

47

BANK

ALDGATE

48

49

2

7

MANSION
HOUSE

37

36

CANNON
STREET

FENCHURCH
STREET

Minories

1

BLACKFRIARS

Victoria Embankment

Upper Thames Street

MONUMENT

TOWER
GATEWAY

TEMPLE

Blackfriars
Bridge

Thames

Southwark
Bridge

London
Bridge

Lower Thames Street

50

TOWER HILL

51

52

Tower Bridge

53

BATEAUX   LONDON

City

Wren churches and famously cosy old pubs characterise the City of London, which now lies at the centre of the financial and legal world; but a closer look uncovers remnants of an even more distant past, intermingled with 21st century pizzazz.

FLEET STREET

❶ Middle Temple

Beneath a spreading mulberry tree, Fountain Court in Middle Temple is a most beguiling backwater, described by the author and diarist James Boswell (1740–95) as 'a pleasant academical retreat'. Reached through Gate House in Fleet Street, Middle Temple stretches down to the Embankment, with mellow brickwork and shadowy lamps that make it seem unchanged since Boswell's day. It is the only one of the four Inns of Court that is regularly open to the public.

Beside Fountain Court is Middle Temple Hall, one of the finest Elizabethan halls in Britain. Dating from 1562, it has barely been altered in the intervening years. Beneath the massive double hammerbeam roof the 31m (101ft) long space is occupied during term time, serving as a dining room for students and barristers. Half a dozen royal portraits include one of Elizabeth I, who dined there often. Her gift of oak from Windsor was used to make the 9m (29ft)-long high table. Sir Francis Drake, feted here on his return from the Indies, donated wood from the hatch of the *Golden Hind* to make the 'cupboard', a ceremonial table where members sign a book when called to the Bar.

Middle Temple Lane, EC4Y 9AT. Temple tube. Viewing of Middle Temple Hall by appointment.

❷ Temple Church

Life-sized effigies of nine medieval knights in this church bring the story of the Crusades to the heart of the City. Lying in the Round – the original circular church, with battlements added by Wren – they look particularly dramatic when sunlight streams through the stained-glass windows. They have lost all their colour, and nobody is quite sure why some should have their legs crossed, others not.

The Knights Templar were founded after the First Crusade to protect pilgrims travelling to the Holy Land, and the monastery church consecrated here in 1185 was inspired by the Church of the Holy Sepulchre in Jerusalem. Stone grotesques are a noticeable feature in the Round, and the pointed arches are a breakthrough in otherwise Romanesque style. A Norman nave was added to the east end, as well as a small chapel against the south side of the Round, now lost, although its crypt remains. Initiation ceremonies took place there. By the west entrance, a small set of stairs leads to a penitential cell, about half a metre by little more than a metre (2 x 4ft), where Walter le Bacheler, Grand Perceptor of Ireland, was starved to death for going against the Master of the

TEMPLE CHURCH

Order. In 1324, after the Order of Knights Templar had been suppressed, the property was taken over by the Knights of St John and some of the monastery was leased to accommodate law students, which began Temple Inn as one of the Inns of Court. Badly damaged by Second World War bombing, the Temple has been faithfully repaired. *Temple Place, EC4Y 7HL. Temple tube.*

❸ El Vino

It was not until 1983 that women were allowed to buy drinks at the bar of London's oldest wine bar, and it still has a clubby aura. The sign hanging outside advertises wine from France, Portugal, Spain and Germany, but the choice today is world wide, although the large sherry barrels at the back of the bar are now only for show. Cigars as well as wine are for sale, and a television for major sporting events has the sound turned down. On a wall opposite the bar, an Edwardian telephone, with connecting wires hanging free, is a reminder that this was a hub of gossip for Fleet Street journalists. Lawyers and finance men have taken their place now that the newspaper presses have moved out.
47 Fleet Street, EC4Y 1BJ. Temple tube. Monday 8.30am–9pm; Tuesday–Friday 8.30am–10pm; closed at the weekend.

❹ Ye Olde Cheshire Cheese

Sawdust on the floor, coal fires, high-backed settles, snug booths and a warren of oak-dark rooms on half a dozen levels... there is no pub in London that feels as 'Olde' as Ye Olde Cheshire Cheese. Rebuilt in 1667 after the Great Fire, it dates from 1538. The earliest rooms are just inside the main door, which is to be found in an alley leading off Fleet Street. 'Gentlemen only served in this bar' reads the sign above the doorway to the small wood-panelled room on the right, while on the left is the Chop Room, a small restaurant with a portrait of Dr Johnson, who lived nearby. Rooms and passageways tumble around and down to the vaulted stone cellar, once part of a Carmelite monastery that occupied the site. Narrow stairs lead to an upstairs bar and smaller rooms for hire. Glass cases contain visitors' books, with comments and signatures going back to the 19th century. Voltaire, Charles Dickens and Mark Twain all drank here, and in the 1890s it was the meeting place for the Rhymers Club, which included W.B. Yeats and Oscar Wilde.
Wine Office Court, 145 Fleet Street, EC4A 2BU. Temple tube. Closes 7pm Sunday.

⑤ Dr Johnson's House

The most telling part of this literary figure's home is the front door. A narrow window above the solid black entrance is barred to prevent small children climbing in, while a chain across its middle is attached to a spiral post so that, reaching in, nobody could lift it off. This state of siege is in complete contrast to the stories of great sociability that surrounded Dr Johnson, whose first-floor reception room was so often full of conversation. Authors, artists and thinkers of the day, including Joshua Reynolds, Charles Burney, Oliver Goldsmith, Edmund Burke and James Boswell, visited the house, which Dr Johnson rented from 1748 to 1759. A copy of his two-volume dictionary graces the library; the well-lit garret is where six amanuenses helped in its compilation. Built in 1700, the house is one of the few surviving residential properties of its age. Dr Johnson fed his cat, Hodge, on oysters, and there is a statue of the great man's companion, sitting on a copy of the dictionary, with an empty oyster shell, outside in Gough Square.

17 Gough Square, EC4A 3DE. Temple tube. Open daily. A Dr Johnson walk leaves from the house at 3pm every Wednesday.

⑥ Fleet Street Newspapers

The best time to see the Art Deco Express building is after dark, when the gold and silver lobby glisters like the interior of a 1930s ocean liner awaiting passengers to embark. It was designed for the paper's Canadian-born proprietor Lord Beaverbrook by Sir Owen Williams just after he had completed the Dorchester Hotel. Within five years of moving into the building, the *Daily Express* became the best-selling newspaper in the world, and it was the last daily paper to leave Fleet Street, in 1987.

The curvaceous exterior curtain wall, made of steel and a type of black glass called Vitrolite, is by Robert Atkinson, designer of the Barber Institute in Birmingham. 'The Sunday Express' is written in period lettering above the reception desk on one side of the oval staircase, 'The Daily Express' on the other, in a lobby that once teemed with messengers and news bringers. 'Britain' and 'Empire' are the titles of the two large gold and silver reliefs by Eric Aumonier on the side walls beneath the beautifully lit aluminium ceiling. The building is generally locked, but there is an excellent view of the lobby through the glass doors.

THE BLACK FRIAR

The brass-rimmed glass doors of the 1930 Daily Telegraph building, a few yards to the west, are also usually locked, and both buildings are listed. The Telegraph building, designed by Elcock & Sutcliffe, has Egyptian columns engaged in theatrical Art Deco style, giving it the air of American newspaper palaces of the time. Twin figures over the entrance depict winged Mercury rushing to all corners of the earth. The balcony that stretches above the entrance was once laid to lawn and the top floor was a penthouse suite.
Telegraph building, 133 Fleet Street, EC4A 2BB. Express building, 120 Fleet Street, EC4A 2BE. Temple, Blackfriars tube. The buildings can be viewed on Open House weekends.

❼ The Black Friar

Great steak pies and sausage and mash are served up in this flat-iron shaped ale house. Over the door stands a jolly, fat friar to welcome visitors to the sole surviving Art Nouveau pub in London. It was built in 1875 on the site of a 13th-century Dominican monastery, and a fine brick, tile and mosaic exterior by the architectural sculptor Henry Poole dates from 1904, but it is the ornate interior that truly dazzles. It is every inch a work of art and whimsy by Poole and the architect H. Fuller Clarke, a fellow member of the Arts and Crafts movement. There are lavish mosaics and marbles. One bas-relief sculpture portrays carolling friars; another, titled 'Saturday Afternoon', shows them harvesting grapes and apples. Low arches lead to a snug bar that would serve very well as a chapel. The Dominican 'black friars' were famed for their intellect, producing many leading theologians and philosophers, and it is perhaps as a witty nod to this that signs admonish drinkers: 'Haste is slow', 'Wisdom is Rare', 'Finery is foolery'.
174 Queen Victoria Street, EC4V 4EG. Blackfriars tube.

❽ St Etheldreda's

Ely Place, a gated cul-de-sac off Holborn Circus, is technically still part of Cambridgeshire, and City police can enter only by permission of the commissionaire. Tucked back from the road, halfway down on the left, is St Etheldreda's, the last remnants of the London Palace of the Bishop of Ely. Dating from 1291, the chapel was dedicated to a 7th-century East Anglian princess. In the 1960s Charles Blakeman carved the life-sized statues in the nave of eight Catholic martyrs put to death in London between 1535 and 1601. The palace's fields of saffron,

orchards, vineyards and the renowned strawberries, mentioned in Shakespeare's *Richard III*, are long gone, but every June they are remembered with a Strawberry Fayre in Ely Place.
14 Ely Place, EC1N 6RY. Chancery Lane tube.

❾ Bleeding Heart Yard

It is no longer possible to get 'drunk for a penny and dead drunk for tuppence' as the keepers of the inn here promised when it was registered as a licensed victuallers in 1746; nor does the Bleeding Heart Tavern feel particularly historic behind the 18th-century façade. But the legend of the yard itself captures the imagination. The name may derive from a Church of the Bleeding Heart that once stood on or near the site and is long lost to memory, but most visitors prefer the story of Lady Elizabeth Hatton, a 17th-century society beauty, a widow whose suitors included a bishop and the Spanish ambassador. At her annual winter ball in January 1662, the doors of the grand ballroom were flung open to admit the ambassador, who had a slight hunch and a clawed hand. He danced her once around the room then led her out into the garden. The next morning she was found torn limb from limb, with her heart still pumping blood. Charles Dickens regarded the tale with some relish, writing in *Little Dorrit* that 'The more practical of the Yard's inmates abided by the tradition of murder.'
Bleeding Heart Tavern, Bleeding Heart Yard, off Greville Street, London EC1N 8SJ. Farringdon tube.

❿ Windows 108

On a darkened street, a lighted window irresistibly draws the eye. The unsuspecting passer-by stops, blinks and ponders. Here might be bold blocks of colour, a fine mosaic, a shadowy figure, conifers in a green mist, rippled muslin, a floral pattern fashioned from rubber gloves and titled 'Marigolds', or cryptic messages ('LOVE HATE', 'WET PAINT', 'NOT NOW'). Since 1993, Maggie Ellenby has used a modest shop window on a busy thoroughfare to display her 'deliberately simple' (one might better say 'deceptively simple') work, so that it may be seen by those on foot, in cars and travelling on the No. 341 bus. The images are by turns haunting, witty, intriguing, beautiful, disturbing. This is, says the artist, one single and continuing artwork, a slow slideshow of indefinite duration.
108 Rosebery Avenue, EC1R 4TL. Angel tube. View free from the street at any time. See First Thursdays website for updates.

CLERKENWELL, SMITHFIELD & BARBICAN

⑪ Marx Memorial Library

Behind a red door lies a hotbed of Communism at the heart of the hedonistic district of the old Clerk's Well. This centre of knowledge and learning on all aspects of Marxism, Socialism and the working-class movement is a delicious anomaly in an area that abounds with hip hotels, trend-setting restaurants and gastropubs. Clerkenwell has come up in the world since the *Illustrated London News* of May 1847 reported on it thus: 'In Clerkenwell broods the darkness of utter ignorance. In its lanes and alleys the lowest debauch, the coarsest enjoyment – the most infuriate passions – the most unrestrained vice – roar and riot.'

There is no darkness of ignorance in the dedicated museum, which occupies a pristine Georgian house, built in 1738 as a Welsh charity school for a princely £332. In 1902–3, in a poky office at this address, the exiled Vladimir Lenin edited and printed the journal *Iskra (Spark)*, and in 1933, on the 50th anniversary of Karl Marx's death, it was decided that here should be a permanent memorial to Marx. A fresco on the wall of the first-floor reading room, painted by Viscount Hastings in 1934 and titled 'The Worker of the Future Clearing Away the Chaos of Capitalism', depicts events and leading thinkers in the history of the British Labour movement. An extensive and constantly updated collection of books, periodicals, artefacts, cartoons and political posters ensures fascinating browsing for all, not just leftwing ideologues
37A Clerkenwell Green, EC1R 0DU. Farringdon tube. Tours Monday–Thursday 1–2pm, or by appointment.

⑫ Museum of the Order of St John

This treasure house of relics occupies a Tudor gateway, which is, in fact, the rightful home of most of the items on display. Armour, chain mail, a breastplate pierced by a musket ball, antique maps, early printed books, illuminated manuscripts, pharmacy jars, a stuffed Maltese falcon – these are clues to the building's long and eventful past. The gatehouse once marked the entrance to the priory of the Knights of St John. Later, the father of the artist and satirical cartoonist William Hogarth ran a coffee house here, and by the 19th century it had become a pub – the Jerusalem Tavern.

The history of the Order of St John spans 900 years, from the founding of the Knights Hospitaller in Jerusalem as military crusaders who also cared for the sick. In 1144, a priory was founded in Clerkenwell, just outside the City wall, from where English knights would set out across London Bridge on the long journey to the Holy Land. The Order was disbanded in 1540, following the Dissolution of the Monasteries by Henry VIII, and revived by Queen Victoria, when, by good fortune, it was able to buy back the Tudor gateway with its stone mullions and exposed roof timbers intact. So the knights recovered their spiritual home. Prudently, their forebears had stashed away many of the treasures on view today.

Wartime bombing damaged the priory church, but the 12th-century crypt, a rare example of Norman architecture, came through the Blitz, preserving the tomb of the last prior, William Weston. He was said to have died of a broken heart when the priory was dissolved. Next to the church a medicinal herb garden recalls the healing work of the original knights – motto: 'Our masters, the poor'.
St John's Gate, St John's Lane, EC1M 4DA. Farringdon tube. Monday–Saturday 10am–5pm; tours Tuesday, Friday and Saturday 11am and 2.30pm. Admission free; donations welcome.

⑬ Charterhouse

One glance at the only surviving monastic building complex in London assures the visitor that this is a special place. The Carthusian Monastery, or Charterhouse, was established here in 1371 with 24 monks, and it soon became a centre of learning. After the Dissolution of the Monasteries, a Tudor mansion was built, the only one remaining in the City. The monastery's church was razed to build the Great Hall and Great Chamber, where James I convened his first council on his arrival in London. In 1611 (the date over the gateway), the buildings were bought by Thomas Sutton, a wealthy Yorkshire merchant, who set up a boys' school and an almshouse to care for 'retired gentlemen', known as brothers. Since then, the almshouse has formally been known as Sutton's Hospital in Charterhouse, and is now home to 40 'brothers', who act as guides for visitors. Sutton is buried in the chapel, which dates from the early 15th century and is open to the public for services.
Sutton Hospital, Charterhouse Square, EC1M 6AN. Farringdon tube.

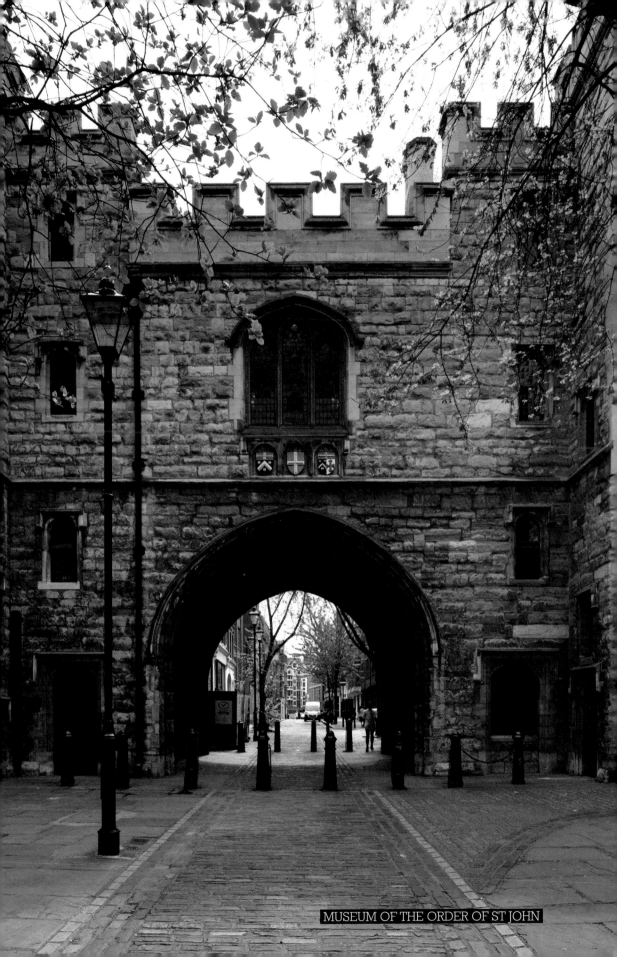

MUSEUM OF THE ORDER OF ST JOHN

⑭ St Bartholomew the Great

Unseen from the street, behind a half-timbered Tudor gatehouse, lies a piece of medieval London. One of the City's oldest churches, St Bartholomew's was begun in 1123 as an Augustinian priory and hospital, in the reign of Henry I, the fourth son of William the Conqueror. The priory was dissolved in 1539 and the nave of the church demolished, but the monastic buildings were left largely untouched, and antiquity hangs in the air like incense. Any sense of *déjà vu* can be explained by the role the church has played in numerous films, including *Four Weddings and a Funeral* and *Shakespeare in Love*.

St Bartholomew's escaped the Great Fire of 1666, and stood firm through the Zeppelin raids of the First World War and the bombing of the Blitz. Restoration by Sir Aston Webb in the 1880s and 1890s endowed it with its porch. Behind this lies Romanesque glory in the shape of a sublime triforium and clerestory. In the sanctuary is the canopied tomb of the church's founder, Rahere, a courtier of Henry I's. While on a pilgrimage to Rome, Rahere was exhorted by Bartholomew in a vision to build a church on a place called Smooth Field (Smithfield).

Rahere's tomb is one of a number of impressive monuments in the church, although the 1652 tribute to philosopher and doctor Edward Cooke, disappointingly, has ceased to 'weep' since central heating was installed. The font – another City oldest – dates from 1405; here the infant William Hogarth, future artist and satirical cartoonist, was baptised in 1697. A rare set of five pre-Reformation bells arrived in 1628 and today hangs in the redbrick Jabobean tower. A small professional choir sings for the Solemn Eucharist, and there is jazz on Fridays in the Cloister Café.
9 Kinghorn Street, EC1A 7HT. Farringdon, Barbican tube. Tourist visits Monday–Friday 8.30am–5pm (4pm winter); Saturday 10.30am–4pm; Sunday 8.30am–8pm. No tourists or guided parties during services. There is a charge for tourist visits to contribute to the maintenance of the building.

⑮ Cloth Fair

This street offers a rare glimpse of a bygone London at the heart of the old drapery district. In the Middle Ages, Cloth Fair, by the churchyard of St Bartholomew the Great, was the scene of the largest textile fair in England. In the 1500s, for a fortnight every August, merchants would do a brisk trade in bolts of cloth for gowns and tunics, cotehardies (flowing dresses), cloaks and kirtles. A great innovation was the handkerchief, reputedly invented by the fashion-conscious Richard II, as royal household accounts include an item: 'little pieces for the lord King to wipe and clean his nose'.

On the corner of Rising Sun Court stands a tall, timbered building with leaded windows, Nos 41–42, dating from the 1600s and preserved from the Great Fire by the sheltering walls of the priory. Neighbouring survivors were demolished in the early 20th century for sanitary reasons. In the Rising Sun pub, pictures of the street as it was before the City fathers ordered its destruction may be seen. Gabled overhangs recall a time when Londoners could lean out of their upper windows to shake hands with people opposite. Poet laureate Sir John Betjeman lived in Cloth Fair until 1971, as a blue plaque records.
Cloth Fair, EC1. Farringdon, Barbican tube.

⑯ St John Bar and Restaurant

'Any part of the piggy is quite all right with me.' Sir Noel Coward would have been in his element in this dining room, where the logo is a flying porker marked out for butchery, and much is made of 'nose-to-tail eating'. Rabbit offal, ox heart, chitterlings, blood cake… 'the whole beast' (or just about) is prepared for the table. Fergus Henderson and Trevor Gulliver opened up here in 1994, in a former smokehouse appropriately located on a corner of Smithfield Market. The Georgian building is unspoilt. The food had rave reviews from the start – though it is not for the squeamish.
26 St John Street, London EC1M 4AY. Farringdon tube. Open Monday–Friday noon–3pm; Sunday 1–3.30pm; Monday–Saturday 6–11pm.

⑰ Smithfield Market

Most wholesale food markets have been moved out of the city centre, but not this venerable survivor. Housed in a triumph of Victorian architecture, the market opens early every weekday morning, when the business of buying and selling meat begins. It stands on a 4ha (10 acre) site, and the building is of Kentish brick, Portland stone and intricate wrought iron, designed in a style that the architect Sir Horace Jones described as 'Italian' and 'more nearly Renaissance' than 'more severe Palladian'.

The market began as a place of trade on a 'smooth field' more than 800 years ago. In 1174, William Fitzstephen, a clerk to Thomas Becket, described 'a celebrated rendezvous of fine horses to be sold, and in another quarter are placed vendibles of the peasant, swine with their deep flanks, and cows and oxen of immense bulk.'

In 1305, this was the scene of butchery of another kind, when the Scottish 'Braveheart' hero William Wallace was hanged, drawn and quartered. Here, too, in 1381, Wat Tyler, leader of the Peasants' Revolt, met his bloody end.

More happily, it was a recreational space for London, a place of tournaments and jousting. Today, the area is again a place of recreation, with surrounding fashionable restaurants and bars. The best time to visit is at 7am, when trade is in full swing, and pubs and cafés – open since the small hours – serve some meaty breakfasts.
Charterhouse Street, off Farringdon Road. Farringdon tube. Monday–Friday 4am–noon, except bank holidays.

⑱ The Golden Boy of Pye Corner

This is where the Great Fire of London, ignited by 'the sin of gluttony', fizzled out three days after it began. A plump and gilded cherub set high into a wall marks the western extent of the flames that consumed the city in 1666. The wooden statue, thought to have been plundered from the ruins, was at first placed here in the wall of a pub, The Fortune of War, where body snatchers would leave their cadavers for the surgeons of St Bartholomew's Hospital.

Pye Corner was celebrated for its pig roasts during the annual Bartholomew Fair, and the fact that the fire had blazed from Pudding Lane a mile away (see Monument page 30) encouraged one puritan preacher to declare that the conflagration was divine retribution for Londoners' greed. An inscription reads: 'This Boy is in Memory Put up for the late Fire of London, Ocassion'd by the Sin of Gluttony, 1666'. The preacher held that if licentiousness had been the cause, the fire would have started in Drury Lane; if blasphemy had been responsible, it would have broken out in Billingsgate, where fishmongers were notorious for their foul language; and if lying had sparked the flames, it would have begun at Westminster.
On the corner of Giltspur Street and Cock Lane, EC1A. St Paul's tube.

⑲ Christ Church, Greyfriars Garden

Nature's church has pergolas for columns, hedges for pews and rose beds tracing Wren's floorplan. It was one of six City churches destroyed in a single night of the Blitz, and the only stones left standing are the nave walls and tower. Wren's building covered just the chancel of what had been the second-largest church in the City after St Paul's, and was the burial place for several royals, starting in 1291 with the heart of Eleanor of Provence, wife of Henry III. The only item rescued from the Blitz, by two postmen, was the carved font cover, which can now be seen at nearby St Sepulchre's, Newgate, where the bell that was tolled before an execution at Newgate Prison may also be seen.
Newgate, EC1A. St Paul's tube.

⑳ The Viaduct Tavern

'Ask to see the cells' instructs a notice on a board at this beautiful Victorian public house. In the basement is a cell that was once part of Giltspur Street Compter, a debtor's jail demolished in 1854 and connected to Newgate Prison. The dank room, little bigger than a bathroom, has 16 metal cages each of which was, apparently, the allotted space for a miscreant. Much cheerier is the tavern itself, a beautiful Victorian public house, with wrought-iron pillars rising to a bright ceiling of beaten copper. Etched mirrors are set off by elegant paintings on glass, depicting three of the four statues on adjacent Holborn Viaduct, 'the world's first flyover'. The figures represent Commerce, Agriculture, Science and Fine Arts.
126 Newgate Street, EC1A 7AA. Closed at weekends.

㉑ Great Hall, Bart's Hospital

William Hogarth had a lifetime's association with Bart's Hospital. He was born in Bartholomew Close in 1697, and baptised in St Bartholomew the Great (see page 16). Among his early memories would have been the erecting of the Henry VIII Gate in 1705, which has London's only surviving public statue of the Tudor king. Henry had re-founded the hospital after the suppression of monasteries, granting the remaining chapel of St Bartholomew the Less, just inside the gate, its unique parish of the hospital.

Hogarth must have watched the handsome square take shape under architect James Gibbs. The Great Hall, just past the church, was completed in 1732. When the artist Hogarth heard that a commission for paintings to decorate the building was to go to an Italian, he volunteered two pictures, free of charge. The result is 'The Pool of Bethesda' (1736) and 'The Good Samaritan' (1739), which hang on the staircase of the Great Hall and show that Hogarth was a serious Academy painter, not merely a streetwise satirist.
23 West Smithfield, EC1A 7BE. Farringdon tube. Guided tours every Friday at 2pm.

22 Postman's Park

Otherwise unsung heroes are remembered in this city park in a remarkable way. In a cloister-like loggia, coloured ceramic tiles are displayed, with inscriptions about people who have died trying to save others. The Heroic Self Sacrifice Memorial was the idea of George Frederick Watts (1817–1904), an artist who chronicled the plight of the populace in such paintings as 'Found Drowned', 'Under the Dry Arch', 'The Seamstress or Song of the Shirt' and 'The Irish Famine'. The tiles were made in Arts and Crafts style by William de Morgan and the Royal Doulton manufactory, and the inscriptions tell of great personal tragedies: 'Soloman Galaman, aged 11, died of injuries after saving his little brother from being run over in Commercial Street: "Mother I saved him but I could not save myself" '; 'Sarah Smith, pantomime artist, at Prince's Theatre, died of terrible injuries received when attempting in her inflammable dress to extinguish the flames which had enveloped her companion'; 'Thomas Simpson died of exhaustion after saving many lives from the breaking ice at Highgate ponds'; 'Frederick Albert Croft, inspector, aged 31, saved a lunatic woman from suicide at Woolwich Arsenal Station but was himself run over by a train'. They could be taken from the headlines of Victorian 'penny dreadful' newspapers, but in this setting they are poignant. Without public support, and with the help of his wife, Mary, Watts set up the memorial in the former burial ground of St Botolph's, Aldersgate. He had initially been inspired by the story of Alice Ayres, 'who saved 3 children from a burning house in Union Street, Borough, at the cost of her own young life'.

Between King Edward Street and Aldersgate Street, EC4M 7DQ. St Paul's tube.

23 Goldsmiths' Hall

The building that gives its name to hallmarks on silver and gold belongs to the Worshipful Company of Goldsmiths. Theirs is one of the grandest of the 40 remaining City Livery Company Halls. A dedicated hall has stood on this site since 1366, although the present Renaissance-style building dates from 1835. The main room, the glittering Livery Hall, can accommodate around 230 at a banquet. Its ceiling is decorated in gold leaf, which dazzles above chandeliers that are now lit with electricity. At the end of the room a display embrasure is reserved for the company's plate, which is used only on special occasions. An Exhibition Room with walnut display cases, and a Drawing Room hung with tapestries and decorated in the 1950s, act as reception rooms prior to banquets.

The Goldsmiths' Company keeps around 8,000 items dating from the 15th century until the present day, and it still acts as an assay office. It is highly active in supporting and promoting work in silver and gold, particularly at the two-week Goldsmiths' Fayre, which is held in the Hall in autumn.

Today, there are more than 100 livery companies. Some have been founded recently, such as the Information Technologists and Security Professionals, but most date from before the 16th century. The Worshipful Company of Weavers is the earliest known guild, first mentioned in 1130; the oldest surviving Livery Hall, from 1670, belongs to the Apothecaries, who share a former friary complex with the Worshipful Company of Spectacle Makers. Each livery company has to be contacted separately for visiting arrangements.

13 Foster Lane, EC2V 6BN. St Paul's tube. Hour-long tours are arranged throughout the year.

㉔ Museum of London

'London pride has been handed down to us, London pride is a flower that's free.' Noel Coward's lyrics very well describe the world's largest urban museum, opened in 1976 as part of the Barbican estate (see next column). There is no entry charge for this walk through prehistory, Roman London, war, plague, conflagration, more war and austerity, to the present day and beyond.

Roman invaders founded the city of Londinium as a trading port and northernmost province of the Roman Empire in around AD 50. They bridged the river and built a road network to connect it with the rest of Britannia. Little knowing that they would one day endow a museum, when they decamped they left behind them such treasures as a fine marble sculpture from the Temple of Mithras, craft tools, pottery, glass, mosaics. Today remnants of their occupation are still coming to light – before No. 1 Poultry rose up on its corner site (see page 26), the museum's archaeologists unearthed a wooden drain alongside the old Roman road.

The eclecticism of the collection here is part of the delight. From Neolithic axes to the Olympic legacy, London in all its aspects is explored. Oral history, street photography, fashion, a debtor's cell, a Victorian street, the Lord Mayor's ceremonial coach, Andy Pandy the puppet, the death mask of Oliver Cromwell … the visitor may be reminded of Dr Samuel Johnson's remark to his friend and biographer James Boswell: 'No, Sir, when a man is tired of London, he is tired of life; for there is in London all that life can afford.'

150 London Wall, EC2Y 5HN. Barbican, St Paul's, Moorgate tube. Open daily 10am–6pm (except December 24–26).

㉕ Barbican Arts Centre

'One of the wonders of the modern world' or 'London's ugliest building', Europe's biggest multi-arts centre brooks no compromise. It was the Queen, at the official opening in 1982, who declared this a wonder, and those who have set their faces against brutalism, and will not be reconciled to Chamberlin, Powell and Bon's concrete ziggurat, are missing a great deal. Situated just within the City, and set apart from London nightlife, the Barbican is a destination in its own right, a place where visitors can spend a day or make a night of it. A concert hall, two theatres, three cinemas, two art galleries, a lakeside terrace, tropical rooftop conservatory, exhibition halls, three restaurants, cafés and a food hall all occupy the one site. Programming is vibrant and imaginative; the whole enterprise is buoyant. The Barbican is home to the London Symphony Orchestra, and thanks to improvements in the acoustics, the 1,943 seater Barbican Hall is a resounding success.

Silk Street, EC2Y 8DS. Barbican, Moorgate tube. Open Monday–Saturday 9am–11pm; Sunday and public holidays noon–11pm. Call the box office to see the Conservatory.

㉖ The Old Bailey

Not all the court rooms in the Central Criminal Court look as if they are sets for 'Rumpole of the Bailey', but courts Nos 1–3 would be familiar to anybody who saw the TV series. Such notorious criminals as Dr Crippen, the Kray Twins and the Yorkshire Ripper have stood in the docks of these oak-panelled chambers, watched by the public in the galleries. The imposing Edwardian building, which has a dome that echoes that of St Paul's, stands on the site of Newgate Prison. A statue of Elizabeth Fry, who worked to improve conditions for women in that infamous jail, stands among others in the handsome marble Grand Hall. Murals in the hall include, above Court No. 1, a figure of Justice on the steps of St Paul's. Outside, Lady Justice, the 3.5m (12ft) tall golden figure on top of the dome, holds a balance and sword, but she isn't wearing a blindfold – sculpted by F.W. Pomeroy, she is intended to look pure enough not to need one.

Old Bailey, EC4M 7EH. St Paul's tube. Courts are in session Monday–Friday 9.30am–1pm and 2–5pm. Entrance to the public galleries is in Warwick Passage at the east end of the modern extension. Note that cameras and phones are not allowed into the building and there is no place there to keep them. Bailey's, a café opposite, will take care of them for a small fee.

Tales of the city

What could be more enthralling than to explore the history of this great city through the eyes of those who lived in momentous times and who bring events so vividly to life?

That most famous diarist of all, Samuel Pepys (1633–1703), kept a journal for ten years from January 1, 1660, not for the enlightenment of others, but for his private gratification, dashing off shorthand and encoded mixtures of French, Spanish and Latin, spicing the historic narrative with accounts of his numerous infidelities. The reader finds Pepys eating, drinking, attending the theatre, learning the recorder, and mixing in high circles in his role as an administrator in the Admiralty. He had lived through the Civil War, and in the decade that he kept his diary, scratching out a million words, bore witness to the Restoration, war with Holland, the Great Plague of 1665 and the Great Fire of 1666. Pepys gave up his diaries in fear for his eyesight, although he did not go blind. He and his wife Elizabeth are buried in St Olave Hart Street in the City.

The memoirs of Pepys' friend John Evelyn (1620–1706) recall the same turbulent episodes, but go on to span most of his life. Having no sexual indiscretions to conceal (or else concealing them completely), he had no need for encryption, although his *Fumifugium or The Inconvenience of the Aer and Smoak of London Dissipated*, a treatise on the problem of pollution, might read like code today.

Men such as Samuel Johnson (1709–84), a playwright, essayist, lexicographer and gifted hack, illuminate the view of 18th-century London. Generous, humane, religious, melancholic, larger than life, Johnson is one of the most quoted authors of his day, thanks in no small way to his biographer, James Boswell (1740–95), who set down his friend's brilliant aphorisms.

Wealth and poverty

The 18th century was a golden Age of Enlightenment, and fashionable London was a playground for the wealthy intellectual élite, but it was also a time of appalling poverty, evoked by the satirical anecdotal pictures of the artist William Hogarth (1697–1764). In the stews of the city he found his artistic milieu, a world of harlots and brothel-keepers, drunken debauchery, collapsing houses, pawnbrokers, din and gin, chaos and depravity, squalling infants, street musicians and emptying piss-pots. Hogarth knew Samuel Johnson and evidently shared his view that society should be judged by how it treats its poor. He was a governor of Captain Thomas Coram's Foundling Hospital, where some of his paintings can be seen.

Samuel Johnson memorably said that when a man is tired of London he is tired of life, and a century later Charles Dickens (1812–70) said something similar in his *Sketches by Boz*, which range around pawnbrokers, gin shops, Vauxhall Pleasure Gardens, the river, the Courts of Justice, horse-drawn omnibuses and shabby gentility. 'We have not the slightest commiseration for the man who can take up his hat and stick, and walk from Covent-garden to St Paul's Churchyard, and back into the bargain, without deriving some amusement – we had almost said instruction – from his perambulation.' His own perambulations so enrich his novels, the reader is inspired to take up the proverbial hat and stick and to make that walk.

> 'What inexhaustible food for speculation do the streets of London afford!'
>
> CHARLES DICKENS

The seeker after Dickens will not find the blacking factory where he worked as a 'poor little drudge'. Of the Marshalsea debtors' prison where his father served time and in which the author set *Little Dorrit*, only a grim remnant of wall remains by Borough High Street. Yet visitors can picture Dickens, a young man, newly married to Catherine, in Doughty Street, feverishly scratching away at *The Pickwick Papers*, *Oliver Twist*, *Nicholas Nickleby* ... They can imagine him drinking ale in the Olde Cheshire Cheese or Prospect of Whitby; enjoying a whitebait supper at the Trafalgar Tavern in Greenwich; engaged in lively discourse with Thomas and Jane Carlyle in their parlour. His shade is still abroad in Lincoln's Inn, Covent Garden and breezy Greenwich Park.

No writer today could have so intimate a relationship with this city. There cannot be a Dickens for our times. But in his mighty and compendious *London: the Biography*, Peter Ackroyd, a native Londoner, confronts a city 'half of stone, half of flesh', the 'capital of capitals', deeply rooted in history, too vast to be perceived in its entirety, still best explored on foot.

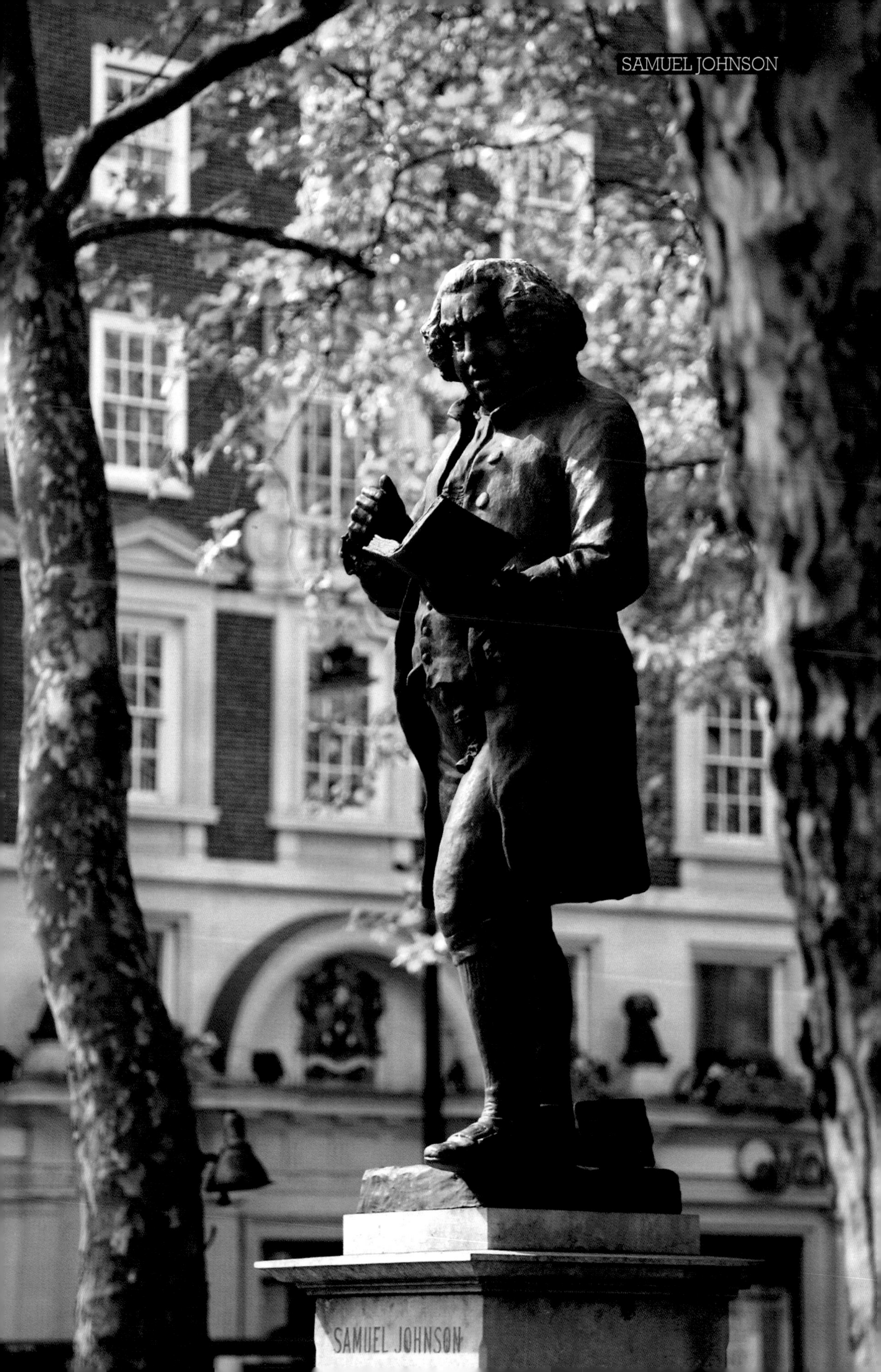

SAMUEL JOHNSON

ST PAUL'S TO BLACKFRIARS

㉗ YHA

A fancy terracotta-coloured façade looks too grand for a youth hostel, and clues to the building's past are provided by the music notes and Latin inscription. It was built in 1874 for 40 boys and 18 men of St Paul's Choir School, and was used by the school until a new one was opened in 1965 in New Change. The pupils continue a long tradition, since choristers of St Paul's School have served St Paul's Cathedral since the 7th century.

The interior of the Carter Lane building today is utilitarian, with 190 beds, a canteen and TV lounge. Just around the corner from the cathedral, it offers among the most reasonably priced accommodation in London.
36 Carter Lane, EC4V 5AB. St Paul's tube.

㉘ St Paul's Cathedral

City skyscrapers cannot detract from the magnificence of St Paul's Cathedral. Indeed, they seem only to confirm it. Sir Christopher Wren's immense 17th-century church at the top of Ludgate Hill, the highest point in the City, is at least the fourth to stand on the site. Its stupendous dome, topped by a cross 111m (365ft) above the ground, is comparable to that of St Peter's in Rome. Its ceiling, decorated with scenes from the life of St Paul by John Thornball, is false, a matter of architectural aesthetics best appreciated from the perspective of the Whispering Gallery. Such are the acoustics here that a *sotto voce* murmur on one side can be heard by someone putting an ear to the wall 30m (100ft) away on the far side of the dome.

Any visitor fit enough to climb the 530 steps to the Golden Gallery is rewarded with magnificent views across London, but must bear in mind that, just a short distance away, the northwest tower houses one of the largest peals of bells in the world. In the southwest tower Great Paul, Britain's largest bell at 16½ tons, is rung for five minutes every day at 1pm, and Great Tom is rung on the hour.

Choir stalls and iron gates, fashioned by Grinling Gibbons and the French master metal worker Jean Tissot, provide decoration for Wren's church. The ceiling mosaics and the single painting, William Holman Hunt's 'The Light of the World', arrived in the late 19th century, and the image of a rocket in a wood panel in the American Memorial Chapel commemorates US journeys into space.
St Paul's Churchyard, EC4M 8AD. St Paul's tube. Monday–Saturday 8.30am–4pm.

㉙ St Paul's Cathedral Triforium

The traditional way up to the triforium is via the beautiful geometric staircase, or Dean's Stairs, a spiral vortex of exceptional audacity and perfection in the north aisle. Today, however, visitors arrive via the staircase to the Whispering Gallery.

The triforium is the cathedral's storehouse, and contains stones from the former church, old pulpits, sculptures, paintings and prints. Here, too, is the wood-panelled, dimly lit Library of the Dean and Chapter, with some 30,000 books, sermons, pamphlets and music scores, looking much as it did when it was completed in 1709. The collection is not a major one, since St Paul's was never a monastery, so had no tradition of teaching or copying manuscripts, but a number of books kept here were saved from the Great Fire of London in 1666, and date back several centuries. The library is generally open to researchers by prior appointment.

LIBRARY OF THE DEAN AND CHAPTER

The gallery above the great west door provides a wonderful, angel's-eye view over the nave. A fanfare from the royal trumpets installed here for the Queen's Jubilee gave her such a start that they have remained silent in her company ever since. The gallery leads to the Trophy Room, so named after Nelson's trophies were put on show here following his death. Today, the room contains architectural plans and is centred on Wren's Great Model, a version of his cathedral based on a Greek cross and large enough for a person to enter.
St Paul's Churchyard, EC4M 8AD. St Paul's tube. Monday–Saturday 8.30am–4pm.

㉚ St Paul's Crypt

Britain's heroes of the Napoleonic Wars, Admiral Nelson and the Duke of Wellington, lie in the spacious crypt, although more elaborate monuments to them are to be found on the ground floor. Nelson's body lies in a lead-lined casket filled with brandy, camphor and myrrh.

The flags that hang over Wellington's casket are from his funeral procession of 1852. The Prussian one is missing, taken down in the First World War and lost. Memorials to subsequent military heroes dot the crypt. At the east end, a chapel is devoted to holders of the Order of the British Empire, the first decoration to include women, which was introduced in 1917. Memorials to OBE recipients in the sciences and the arts are presented in Art Deco style, and are lively and engaging. The artist J.M.W. Turner is buried here, at his own request beside his mentor, Sir Joshua Reynolds. The most relevant tomb is the modest slab of Sir Christopher Wren. Above it, an epitaph by his son, in Latin, translates as 'Reader, if you seek his monument, look around you'.

The western end of the crypt has a restaurant, spacious café and shop, which do not require an entry ticket and have a separate entrance on the north side of the cathedral.
St Paul's Churchyard, EC4M 8AD. St Paul's tube. Monday–Saturday 8.30am–4pm.

31 Paternoster Square

The only surviving City gate, Christopher Wren's Temple Bar, is a triumphal arch leading to ultramodern Paternoster Square, beside St Paul's Cathedral. Through the archway, the square's modern buildings provide 93,000 sq m (1 million sq ft) of office and retail space for shops, top finance houses and the London Stock Exchange, Europe's largest, which moved here in 2004. The Noon Mark, high on the Stock Exchange building, shows the date at midday. Erected in 2000, the Paternoster Square column – Wren's Monument in miniature – is designed to commemorate the millions of books destroyed in the Blitz. Before then, this area had been a warren of book publishers, which is hard to imagine today.

Paternoster Square, EC4M 7LS. St Paul's tube.

32 St-Mary-le-Bow

Nothing if not resilient, St-Mary-le-Bow is an enduring part of the rich tapestry of London history. 'Le Bow' is a reference to the bowed arches in the 11th-century crypt, where Norman columns can still be seen. The tower and spire, soaring heavenward to 66m (217ft), are topped with a gilded flying-dragon weathervane. After the Great Fire of 1666, Wren modelled the new St Mary's on the basilica of Maxentius in Rome. He included a memorial balcony, recalling the day in 1331 when a wooden balcony collapsed during a joust being held to celebrate the birth of a son, Edward, to Edward III and Philippa of Hainault. The Queen and her ladies were sent crashing to the ground. From 1818–20, the upper spire was rebuilt by George Gwilt, and after wartime bomb damage, the steeple was taken down and kept in store for almost 20 years.

But it is less the beautiful church than the bells – especially the great tenor bell named Bow – that resonate with Londoners. The story has it that the orphaned Dick Whittington, resting at Highgate on his flight from London, was summoned back by the sound of Bow bell bidding him, 'Turn again, Whittington, Lord Mayor of London.' If the bells did not literally speak to Whittington, they must have struck at his heart, for he turned again, and was indeed three times Lord Mayor – in 1397, 1406 and 1409. He endowed the city with a refuge for unmarried mothers and a public lavatory. He and his cat have been celebrated in Christmas pantomimes ever since.

At the waist of the Bow bell an inscription reads: 'The bell of the parish of St-Mary-le-Bow. Rung for curfew 1334. Destroyed by fire 1666.

Recast 1669. Recast 1738. Destroyed by enemy action 1941. Recast 1956.' The bell is mentioned in a law of 1469 decreeing that it should toll at 9pm – a signal that the City gates must close. Hence, perhaps, the saying that to be a true 'cockney', a dyed-in-the-wool East Ender, you must be born within the sound of Bow bell. *Cheapside, EC2V 6AU. Bank, St Paul's tube.*

㉝ Guildhall Clockmakers' Museum

One of the finest collections of clocks, watches, marine timekeepers and sundials in the world is to be found here. On any day, some 600 exhibits are displayed, most produced between 1600 and 1850. Among them are such oddities as Mary, Queen of Scots' macabre skull pocket watch, animated by the mechanism where the brain would be, and a decimal watch from 1862, made to run anticlockwise and dividing the day into 10 hours of 100 minutes, each minute comprising 100 seconds. The collection was begun in 1814 and tells the story of the clockmakers of London. The Worshipful Company of Clockmakers, established by Royal Charter granted by Charles I in 1631, ranks 61st on the list of City of London Livery Companies. The magnificent clocks should not be taken just at face value. Their true beauty lies in the exquisite craftsmanship of the internal workings. *Guildhall Library building, 5 Aldermanbury, EC2V 7HH. Bank, St Paul's tube. Monday–Saturday (except public holidays) 9.30am–4.45pm.*

㉞ Guildhall Art Gallery

The story of the Guildhall Gallery might have ended when it burnt down during an air raid in May 1941 were it not for an amazing discovery made 47 years later. Archaeologists from the Museum of London uncovered the capital's only Roman amphitheatre, where 6,000 spectators would once have bayed for blood. The site became a protected monument, and it was decided by the City of London that it should be integrated into a proposed new art gallery. Building began in 1992, and the extent of the amphitheatre is marked in the paving stones that can be seen in Guildhall Yard. The gallery opened in 1999. There is not much left of the amphitheatre below the gallery, but low lighting with shadowy figures and sounds of the Roman crowd conjure an atmosphere. *Guildhall Yard (off Gresham Street), EC2V 5AE. Bank, St Paul's tube. Monday–Saturday 10am–5pm; Sunday noon–4pm.*

BANK & MANSION HOUSE

35 Mansion House

For his elected year in office, the Lord Mayor of London and his family live in Mansion House, the City's only surviving town palace. Completed in 1752, Mansion House was designed by George Dance, Clerk of the City Works, specifically for the purpose of allowing the Lord Mayor to represent the City with appropriate style. One of the world's largest gold and silver-plate collections is to be found here, some of which is brought out for banquets.

The Lord Mayor is also the chief magistrate of the City of London, and the court used to sit at Mansion House. Eleven holding cells, including 'the birdcage' for women, in which the suffragette Emmeline Pankhurst was locked, are now used as office and storage space. One surprising highlight of a tour is to be shown into the gents' lavatory. Formerly part of the servants' quarters, it has an iron kitchen range with various inscriptions, including one that reads: 'Swear not, lie not, neither repeat old grievances. Whosoever eats or drinks in this hall with his hat on shall forfeit sixpence or ride the wooden horse.' The wooden horse was a military punishment; suffice it to say sixpence would be money well spent.
Mansion House Street, EC4N 8BH. Hour-long tours start at 2pm every Tuesday.

36 St James's Garlickhythe

The interior of St James's is flooded with natural light, and became known as 'Wren's lantern', but no light has been cast upon the church's greatest mystery – who was Jimmy Garlick? In the mid 1800s, under the chancel floor, workmen found the desiccated corpse that acquired the nickname Jimmy Garlick. Nobody could say why his remains were so perfectly preserved. He was ignominiously stashed in a cupboard, then put on show at a few pennies a peep. The visitor can no longer view Jimmy, but can admire the ascending tiers of the baroque spire, and see a mayoral sword rest with lions and unicorns, a magnificent organ by the master organ builder Bernhard Schmidt, installed in 1717, and a wig stand on the pulpit.
Garlick Hill, EC4V 2AL. Mansion House tube.

37 Sweetings

In his *Forsyte Saga*, John Galsworthy described Sweetings as the 'celebrated eating house' where Soames Forsyte ordered smoked salmon and a glass of Chablis, which he consumed standing up, 'finding the position beneficial to his liver'. Would-be lunchers today must expect to stand and wait, as white-coated retainers serve the packed tables. Sweetings has occupied this site since 1889. The food is fish and shellfish, plain, simple and perfect, and Guinness comes in pewter tankards. Such is the demand at peak time, coffee is not served, so that customers will not linger.
39 Queen Victoria Street, EC4N 4SF. Mansion House tube. Weekdays, lunch only.

38 St Stephen Walbrook

'The pride of English architecture and one of the few churches in which the genius of Wren shines in full splendour.' So said the architectural historian Sir John Summerson of St Stephen's. The great Italian neoclassical sculptor Canova declared in the 18th century that he would gladly return to London to see again St Paul's Cathedral, Somerset House and, above all, St Stephen Walbrook, for Rome had nothing to touch it. In the eyes of architectural historian Nikolaus Pevsner, it was one of the ten most important buildings in England. The vast white stone altar is by Henry Moore. The Thursday sung Eucharist brings tears to the eyes.
39 Walbrook, EC4N 8BN. Bank, Cannon Street tube. Open weekdays 10am–4pm.

39 Number One Poultry

Bold of form and colour, this postmodern building stands on the spot where Roman Londinium began – and conceals a surprise. Faced in sandstone and granite with bronze finish, and set at the junction with Queen Victoria Street, it exploits its triangular position to great effect, with a tall 'prow' that makes play with cylindrical and angular shapes. From street level, this development, designed by the late James Stirling with Michael Wilford, is something to be seen, but it tucks away from the eyes of the pedestrian its ultimate caprice. Above the shops and offices, there is a surreal 0.2ha (half-acre) roof garden with verdant lawns, clipped box hedges and eerie stone globes, by the award-winning landscape artist Arabella Lennox-Boyd. Such familiar landmarks as the Gherkin and the dome of St Paul's appear all the more extraordinary viewed from this peculiar vantage. A glass lift whisks visitors to the garden and the expensive Coq d'Argent restaurant. Bar snacks are also on offer, with the promise of 'soothing cocktails'. Lovers can order aphrodisiac oysters – but they might find themselves sharing a table.
1 Poultry, EC2R. Bank tube.

NUMBER ONE POULTRY

❹⓿ The Tent, St Ethelburga's

A Bedouin-style tent is not the first shelter that comes to mind when thinking of the City, so it is a surprise to encounter one at the back of St Ethelburga's. The City's smallest church is often overlooked in busy Bishopsgate, and it is something of a miracle that it is there at all. One Saturday in April 1993, a lorry packed with a tonne of explosives was parked outside by the IRA, and when detonated, it caused £1 billion worth of damage, injured 50 people and killed a 34-year-old photographer. Some 60 per cent of the church disappeared, and when it was discovered that its insurance had just run out, demolition seemed the only answer.

The Bishop of London had different ideas, and today his campaign to maintain what was left of the church has resulted in the Centre for Reconciliation and Peace, a space for meeting, music and theatre. The tent, pitched in its small garden, is made of goat's hair, furnished with carpets and sofas, and hung with lamps. The aim is to create an atmosphere conducive to fostering relationships across religious divides.

78 Bishopsgate, EC2N 4AG. Liverpool Street, Bank tube.

❹❶ London Wall

The Romans came, they saw, they conquered, and they left their footprints all over the city. Everywhere relics of their trading port are to be seen, including the remains of a three-mile defensive wall built in AD 200 and defining what has become the City of London. If it stood seamlessly today, it would run from Blackfriars north to the Barbican (site of the Roman fort) then east to Bishopsgate, Aldgate and the Tower of London.

Substantial weathered fragments still crouch against a shiny 21st-century backdrop. A stout bastion can be seen in the Barbican estate, and there are stretches in Cooper's Row, close to the Tower of London; in St Alphage Garden on the site of a church destroyed by the Great Fire, there is a remnant, just off the eminently unhistoric road named London Wall; and another is to be found right outside Tower Hill tube, by a statue of the emperor Trajan. Such was Londoners' faith in the protective qualities of the wall that Daniel Defoe, the creator of Robinson Crusoe and Moll Flanders, declared in *A Journal of the Plague Year*, 60 years later, that the Black Death could not get through it. Defoe lies buried in Bunhill Fields (see page 29) a place reserved for Dissenters.

Barbican, Moorgate, Tower Hill tube.

❹❷ Exchange Square

In the busy heart of the business district, Exchange Square presents welcome, if unexpected, recreational opportunities for City workers. On the manicured lawn in summer, teams in the Corney & Barrow Croquet League play their matches in earnest. Despite its image as a quintessentially genteel game, croquet is no mere exercise in pat-ball, although the American critic Alexander Woollcott perhaps went too far when he commented that it was 'no game for the soft of sinew and the gentle of spirit'. In winter the square is transformed into an ice rink, and skaters zip around, watched from on high by investment bankers.

One of the surrounding buildings, Exchange House, is built directly over the railway tracks into Liverpool Street station and is a unique piece of engineering – with no scope for traditional foundations, the entrance lobby is suspended from the structure above.

By Liverpool Street station, EC2A 2EH. Liverpool Street rail and tube.

❹❸ Armoury House

A second look is sometimes necessary to make sure that the battlemented Armoury House on the north side of the City is genuine. Is this really a giant castle in the middle of town? In fact, it is the home of the Honourable Artillery Company. The building dates from 1735 and has been much added to since then. The large drill hall is named the Prince Consort Room after Prince Albert, who was Captain General of the Company. The present Captain General is HM The Queen and her portrait hangs with those of her predecessors in the dining room, known as the Long Room. Iron gates in the main block give on to the great stairway, at the top of which are two brass cannons, given to the Company by a grateful Lord Mayor for quelling the 1780 Gordon Riots. The Court Room is the governing body's meeting room and one of the most attractive in the complex. It has friezes by Francis Holman and a suit of Elizabethan tilting armour.

Artillery Garden is an adjoining 2.5ha (6 acres) of playing fields, which are sometimes open to the public. The first balloon flight in England took off from here in 1784. Thousands turned up to watch Vicenzo Lunardi take to the air, accompanied by a dog, a cat, a caged pigeon and a bottle of wine.

City Road, EC1Y 2BQ. Old Street, Moorgate tube. Tours by appointment.

㊹ Bunhill Fields

Artist and poet William Blake is among the literary giants commemorated in this shaded spot just off the City Road. The cosy-sounding 'Bunhill' is a derivation of 'Bone Hill', and this is a burial ground for nonconformists – some 12,000 of them lie in mostly unmarked graves. On the modest stone that marks the passing of Blake and his wife, Catherine Sophia, admirers often leave small gifts and coins. There are fine monuments to John Bunyan, the author of *A Pilgrim's Progress*, and to Daniel Defoe, whose most famous novel is *Robinson Crusoe*.

Bunhill Fields is a peaceful place to sit, on the edge of the flourishing City, under a canopy of London planes, oaks, ash and limes, and listen to the fluting, cooing birdlife above. In spring, crocuses carpet the north lawn, while the grass around the graves on the south side is bejewelled with snowdrops, and bright with daffodils and hyacinths. To the west, on Banner Street, is another nonconformist site, the Quaker burial ground and Bunhill Fields Meeting House. Quaker pilgrims arrive there from around the world.
City Road, EC1Y 1AU. Old Street tube.

㊺ John Wesley's House

The house and its museum provide an intimate glimpse of the last years of a man who inspired a religious movement. John Wesley was a man on fire, who famously gave sermons in open spaces – so-called 'field preaching'. People would come in their thousands to 'watch him burn'. In the last dozen years of his life, he wintered at this Georgian townhouse, built for him in 1779 beside a Methodist chapel, which now houses a museum of Methodism in its crypt. Wesley's fascination with 'primitive physick' is apparent in his Chamber Horse, a springy wooden chair that simulated horse riding, on the theory that being bounced around would stimulate the liver. He held that cleanliness was next to godliness, and condemned black slavery as 'execrable villainy'. Among his worldly goods is a pair of buckled shoes called 'straights', each to be worn on either foot. A prayer room is regarded by followers worldwide to be the power house of Methodism – that is, living by the 'methods' of the Bible.
49 City Road, EC1Y 1AU. Old Street, Moorgate tube.

LONDON WALL

BISHOPSGATE TO ALDGATE

46 No 30 St Mary Axe

Norman Foster's radical design for No 30 St Mary Axe, better known as the Gherkin, used green principles to create London's first ecological building. The external aerodynamic form of the 180m (590ft) tall office block, which opened in 2004, has made as much impact on the public as it has on the skyline. But the shape is not a whim – it allows wind-pressure differentials to form natural ventilation within the building, reducing energy consumption. The use of glass for much of the exterior ensures maximum daylight penetration, reducing the need for artificial lighting. Even the building's bulging middle and the tapering top and bottom have a benefit – on street level the huge size of the structure is not obvious. It really is a building of the future. The Gherkin is not open to the public, but a café on the ground floor is accessible.
30 St Mary Axe, EC3A 8EP. Liverpool Street, Bank tube.

47 Bevis Marks Synagogue

The country's oldest synagogue, which still contains original furnishings, remains almost exactly as it was when it was built in 1701, less than half a century after Jews were allowed to return to Britain following 366 years of banishment. The master builder Joseph Avis, a Quaker, was influenced by the English baroque style of Christopher Wren, even to the extent of making the Ark (Echal) an echo of Protestant altarpieces. The synagogue was built for Sephardim, descendants of Spanish and Portuguese Jews, and the family of Benjamin Disraeli, Britain's prime minister in the 1860s and 1870s, was among its congregation. The whole of Anglo-Jewry has now been invited to use Bevis Marks as a cathedral synagogue, and since the financial boom of the 1980s the congregation has increased. The synagogue is open for services on weekdays.
40 Hineage Lane, EC3A 5DQ. Aldgate tube. Open to visitors Monday, Wednesday, Thursday 10.30am–2pm; Tuesday, Friday 10.30am–1pm; Sunday 10.30am–12.30pm.

48 Leadenhall Market

Stumbling upon Leadenhall Market in the grey labyrinth of the City is like suddenly being blessed with the gift of sight. It is the most colourful market in London. Painted a uniform cream, maroon and cedar green, the cross-shaped building is a harmonious whole. Shops have large plate-glass windows with wrought-iron patterned grilles above and below, and their names or products are written above them in the same typographic style. The visitor, looking higher still, sees floral ceramic panels, griffins and friezes of the City's coats of arms and Ancient Greek palmettes. Rows of vicious-looking spikes remain in the western avenue, a reminder that this was once the domain of poulterers. The Victorian makeover, completed in 1881, was by the City architect Sir Horace Jones, who rebuilt Smithfield and Billingsgate markets and designed Tower Bridge. Beneath the central dome, in the Lamb Tavern (Nos 10–12), pints have been pulled since 1780. In the ground floor bar, ceramic tiles depict Sir Christopher Wren showing the plans for the Monument (see below).
Between Gracechurch Street and Lime Street, EC3V 1LR. Bank tube.

49 Lloyd's of London

The insurance company's image switched from 17th-century coffee house to radical chic with Richard Rogers' 1980s space-age, inside-out look, which he had practised on the Pompidou Centre in Paris. The design marked a turning point in the landscape; from now on, the City would be a place for modern architects to cut a dash. Cranes above the three service towers have been left in place, and the building wears its heart on its sleeve, with lifts and air-conditioning ducts on the outside, adding a sculptural edge. This has created a vast uncluttered interior, with an atrium rising to 60m (197ft), making a large central trading space. At the centre of the ground floor, the Lutine Bell still hangs on its ornate wooden rostrum. It used to be rung once when any ship was reported overdue, and twice for a safe return. Now it is used for major terrorist attacks and natural disasters, royal deaths and the annual armistice 2 minutes' silence. Even more out of place among the gleaming glass and steel is the Committee Room on the 11th floor. Designed by Robert Adam in 1763 as a dining room for the Earl of Shelborne, it was bought by Lloyd's and transferred here from the previous building at 51 Lime Street.
1 Lime Street, EC3 M7. Bank, Monument tube. Visits by appointment.

50 The Monument

Among the City's high-rise blocks, it is easy to overlook the tallest freestanding stone column in the world. London's first public viewing platform is reached via a spiral staircase of 311 steps, and it is still such a memorable experience that visitors are given certificates to prove they have made it to the top. Erected to commemorate the Great Fire of London, it is 62m (202ft) tall and stands exactly that distance from Thomas Farriner's bakery in Pudding Lane, where the fire is thought to have started just before 2am on September 2, 1666. It was designed jointly by the scientist-architect Robert Hook and Sir Christopher Wren, who masterminded the rebuilding of the City. Completed in 1677, it had been intended for use for scientific and astronomical research, but the thunderous city traffic caused so much vibration that it was abandoned entirely to pleasure.

The fluted Doric column is made of Portland stone, and sits on a square pedestal with four Latin inscriptions in panels on three sides relating the extent of the blaze that destroyed 400 streets, 13,200 houses, 87 churches, four City gates, the Guildhall, schools, hospitals and 'many magnificent mansions' across 176ha (436 acres). The iron grille enclosing the viewing platform was installed in 1842 after Jane Cooper, a serving girl, became the sixth suicide to use it. Despite the high-rise buildings, there is still a fine view of London and the river from the top, and for those disinclined to tackle the eternity of the stairs, a live webcam is positioned by the entrance.
Monument Square, EC3R. Bank, Monument, London Bridge tube. Open daily, last admission 5pm.

51 All Hallows by the Tower

A barrel used as a crow's nest for Ernest Shackleton's last Antarctic voyage is just one piece of historic flotsam washed up in All Hallows by the Tower. The story of the City's oldest church begins with the bedrock of the Roman settlement; domestic items, a tessellated 1st-century pavement and a model of the Roman city are highlights of the Crypt Museum in the undercroft. But it is the Saxon arch with a fan of re-used Roman tiles in the west end of the nave that dates the church's foundation to the late 7th century. It is the only standing Saxon structure in London, founded as part of Barking Abbey nearly 10 miles to the east.
Byward Street, EC3R 5BJ. Tower Hill tube. Brass rubbing Monday–Friday 2pm–4pm.

52 The Tower of London

The Chapel Royal of St John the Evangelist and Sir Walter Raleigh's room are two defining elements of the Tower of London. The chapel, on the second floor of the White Tower, is a perfect Norman construction on two storeys, the

upper being a clerestory and triforium, or gallery, where ladies of the court sat. Below, the men stood or knelt on the rush-covered stone floor, while the royal family were seated with their backs to the west wall. The barrel-vault and rounded arches are of such solid purity that the chapel immediately expresses the unyielding strength of Norman faith. Built by Gandulph, William the Conqueror's Bishop of Rochester, a dozen years after the invasion in 1066, it is constructed of the Caen limestone they favoured, although its coloured decoration has long since worn away. The chapel was also used by Knights of the Order of the Bath, who, having bathed, would spend a night of vigil here before their investiture.

The highlights of the Tower leap forward from medieval to Tudor and Elizabethan times, best imagined not for the executioner's gore, but in the room where Sir Walter Raleigh was incarcerated in 1603. Poet, scientist, buccaneer, he spent 13 years locked up here before being given one last chance to find El Dorado in South America, after which he was executed to appease the Spanish, whose treasure ship he had dared to attack. In this single room, with leaded window and heavy, carved oak furniture, it's easy to imagine the restless sound of his boots echoing on the cold brick floor, and the smell of his pipe tobacco, and to sense his pen scratching on parchments, wringing out poetry that attempted to define the human condition.
Tower of London, EC3 N4. Tower Hill tube. Open daily.

53 Tower Bridge

This bridge is impressive from a distance, and from the high-level walkway that spans the towers 42m (138ft) above the River Thames, it is even more so. A lift whisks visitors up the northern tower to the walkway, a long corridor that feels firm beneath the feet and makes it easy to appreciate and photograph the riparian city stretching out in both directions. A walk down the south stairs reveals dummy labourers perched high in the rafters, as the workers who completed the bridge in 1894 might have been. The tour continues to the south bank and the Victorian Engine Rooms. The bascules, the two bridge arms that swing upwards to allow ships to pass, were until 1976 powered by steam, and the huge wheels, pistons and cylinders of the redundant pumping engines and accumulators, in gleaming brass and moss green, show the perfect beauty of industrial engineering.
Tower Bridge Exhibition, SE1 2UP. Tower Hill tube. Open daily.

Central

Theatres and museums abound in this vibrant neighbourhood. The Royal Opera House and British Museum pave the way to the Foundling Hospital, the houses where Charles Dickens and Sir John Soane once lived and an old coffee shop now devoted to tea.

KING'S
CROSS

ST PANCRAS

43

Road

Judd Street

EUSTON

36

Euston

34

EUSTON
SQUARE

Tavistock
Square

37

Hunter Street

38

40

WARREN
STREET

Woburn
Place

Guilford Street

41

Gray's Inn Road

35

Gower Street

39

RUSSELL
SQUARE

Tottenham

Southampton Row

GOODGE
STREET

Theobald's Road

42

Court

30

Bloomsbury Street

33

29

Road

32

Bloomsbury Way

High Holborn

31

22

High Holborn

24

HOLBORN

23

25

CHANCERY
LANE

Ave

Chancery Lane

Fetter Lane

TOTTENHAM
COURT RD

Shaftesbury

19

20

Kingsway

26

Charing

Monmouth

Long Acre

28

27

Street

Bow Street

Aldwych

11

16

10

Cross

18

13

17

9

COVENT
GARDEN

12

14

15

8

LEICESTER
SQUARE

21

Strand

7

TEMPLE

Road

4

6

Victoria Embankment

5

Waterloo Bridge

Thames

CHARING CROSS

1

3

2

EMBANKMENT

KEY

Charing Cross &
The Strand

Covent Garden

Holborn

Bloomsbury

CHARING CROSS & THE STRAND

❶ British Optical Association Museum

More than 2,600 pairs of glasses, from early 17th-century models to the latest designer eyewear, form this extraordinary collection. Founded by J.H. Sutcliffe in 1901, it covers the history of optometry, the human eye and visual aids, as well as the representation in art of the windows of the soul. The Association was disbanded in 1980, but the museum lives on as one of the oldest and finest optical museums in the world. Pince-nez, lorgnettes, folding eyeglasses, scissor spectacles, magnifiers, quizzing glasses, monocles, trifocals and binocular spectacles are on show. Glasses worn by the famous and infamous are here, from Samuel Johnson (round tortoiseshell frames with a red leather case lined with purple silk and blue velvet) and Dr Crippen (just the cable-curl sides) to C.P. Snow (small, round, close-inspection loupe glasses) and Ronnie Corbett. There are porcelain eyebaths, prosthetic eyes and 160 glass eyes designed to illustrate eye disease, injury and malformation. They even have a pair of Leonardo di Caprio's contact lenses.
College of Optometrists, 42 Craven Street, WC2N 5NG. Charing Cross tube. Visits by appointment.

❷ Benjamin Franklin's House

'A house is not a home unless it contains food and fire for the mind as well as the body,' said Benjamin Franklin, a key founder of the United States, kite-flier and 'father of electricity', who lodged here from 1757 to 1775. Throughout his tenure, he pursued his love of science, researching inoculation and a cure for the common cold, writing his witty *Craven Street Gazette,* inventing bifocals and a glass armonica for which Mozart, Bach and Beethoven composed, mediating relationships between Britain and America in his role as a diplomat, and developing an alternative alphabet. A superior lightning rod that he made was installed on the dome of St Paul's cathedral.

Since he left only a 'footprint' at this Grade I listed house, it is not so much a shrine to him as a theatre, with live performances, sound, lighting and visual projection. The serious Franklin student can view the only comprehensive record of his writings in the upstairs Scholarship Centre, catalogued by academics at Yale University.
36 Craven Street, WC2N 5NF. Charing Cross, Embankment tube.

❸ York House Watergate

An Italianate baroque archway with no apparent purpose stands in Embankment Gardens by Charing Cross station. It is not a folly, but was created by Inigo Jones in 1626 for George Villiers, the first Duke of Buckingham, at which time it was indeed a water gate, giving on to the river – now 150m (164yd) away. York House was one of a row of noblemen's mansions that once lined the Strand, on the route from the City to the royal court at Westminster. Daniel Turner's 'The Adelphi Terrace and York Watergate' shows it lapped by the Thames. The construction of the Thames Embankment in 1864–70 by Sir Joseph Bazalgette meant these grand houses were cut off from the river, and left the Strand high and dry.
Embankment Gardens, WC2N. Charing Cross, Embankment tube.

❹ Simpson's-in-the-Strand

Since 1984, women have been permitted to use Simpson's panelled street-level dining-room at lunchtime, but the establishment remains uncompromisingly masculine. It began life in 1828 as the Grand Cigar Divan coffee house and 'the home of chess'. Famous people to pass through its doors include Charles Dickens, prime ministers Gladstone and Disraeli, and George Bernard Shaw. To avoid disturbing the players' concentration, the practice was introduced of trundling silver-domed trolleys to guests' tables. Today the trolleys are still plying up and down, and tableside carving is very much a part of the show. Roast beef is the thing at Simpson's, although they serve a hearty English breakfast, and cocktails in the bar. You can even take a 90 minute masterclass in 'the forgotten art of carving' – the price includes a certificate of competence, a presentation carving knife and fork, and lunch.
100 Strand, WC2R 0EW. Charing Cross, Embankment tube.

❺ Savoy Hotel

One of London's landmarks, the Savoy has undergone restoration and refurbishment at a cost of £100 million, yet still wears its history well. The vast riverside Savoy Palace was built in the 13th century and episodes from its history are told in plaques on the left of the main entrance. The hotel as we know it today was designed in

SAVOY HOTEL

1889 by Arthur Mackmurdo for the impresario Richard d'Oyly Carte, who had commissioned the Savoy Theatre on the site of the palace of Count Peter of Savoy, to stage the works of Gilbert and Sullivan. The 'Savoy Operas' were so popular that d'Oyly Carte decided to build a hotel as well, to emulate those he had visited in America. The luxurious new hotel was furnished with electric lights, electric lifts and cascading showers. The great chef Auguste Escoffier was installed in the kitchen, where he created Melba toast and *pêches* Melba for the soprano Dame Nellie of that ilk.

Such was the success of the enterprise that, in 1904, d'Oyly Carte commissioned a second block, this time by Thomas Collcutt, designer of the Wigmore Hall. In 1929, the entrance court was restyled, introducing a steel Art Deco look. The private road that leads up to the main doors and serves the theatre is the only one in Britain where Britain drives on the right.

Noel Coward, George Gershwin, George Bernard Shaw and H.G. Wells all ate in the Savoy's restaurants and drank in the celebrated American Bar. In the front hall, Laurence Olivier met the 'fatefully irresistible' Vivien Leigh and embarked with her on an affair of 'rapturous torment'. Photographs of Marilyn Monroe are on show in the hotel museum, together with a note from Princess Margaret to the general manager, dated 1951.

The longest-serving member of the Savoy team is Kaspar, a cat crafted by Basil Ionides in the 1920s. He makes up the numbers for parties of 13, sitting with them at table. He was once kidnapped by RAF pranksters, and owed his safe return to regular diner Sir Winston Churchill. *Strand, WC2R 0EU. Charing Cross tube.*

❻ Savoy Chapel

A Saudi prince may now own the Savoy, but the Savoy Estate still belongs to the Queen in her role as head of the Duchy of Lancaster. The Queen's Chapel of the Savoy is the last remnant of a hospital for homeless people founded by Henry VII in 1512. Mentioned by Evelyn Waugh in *Brideshead Revisited* as 'the place where divorced couples got married in those days – a poky little place', it has a fine filigree altar and a stained-glass window commemorating Richard d'Oyly Carte. This was the first place of worship in Britain to have electricity. The ceiling was restored in 1999, and the garden landscaped in honour of the Queen's Golden Jubilee. *Savoy Street, WC2R 0DA. Charing Cross tube.*

⑦ Somerset House

Visitors stepping through the gateway of Somerset House from the Strand on a cold December evening enter a winter wonderland where skaters glide around a temporary rink in the light of flaming torches. In summer, in this grandly conceived classical urban space, fountains play and so, sometimes, do musicians and films.

Until 1775 a Tudor palace stood on this site, but it fell into ruin and was demolished. Sir William Chambers, George III's favourite architect, was eventually commissioned to design 'a great public building', 'an object of national splendour' to accommodate not just the Royal Academy of Arts, the Royal Society and the Society of Antiquaries, but government departments, the Navy Board and the King's Bargemaster. It would require direct access to the Thames, and, indeed it stood right on the river, until the construction of the Embankment. The driving through of a new road under the modernising Victorians meant that its water gates looked upon a carriageway. The Victorians extended the building, adding the wings, and Charles Dickens' father worked there, employed as a clerk in the navy pay-office, when he was not confined in the Marshalsea, the debtors' prison.

The Inland Revenue made itself nicely at home in Somerset House from 1849 until it was evacuated in the Second World War and the Ministry of Supply moved in. Hidden from view, the courtyard provided hard standing for Lanchesters and Daimlers, Sunbeams, Talbots, Wolseleys and Crossleys. In the post-war years, the General Register Office occupied Somerset House, keeping records of every birth, death and marriage in the kingdom and issuing certificates.

Chambers did not live to see the completion of his building. He resigned in March 1795, pleading 'infirmities incident to old age', died of the same within the year, and would not have been pleased to see his great creation turned over to bureaucracy. Today, it is at the very heart of the capital's cultural life – and home to pen-pushers of a different kind, the Royal Society of Literature. It is, at last and as Chambers intended, devoted to 'the reception of useful learning and polite arts'.

Strand, WC2R 1LA. Temple, Covent Garden, Charing Cross, Embankment tube.

IN THIS CLASSICAL URBAN SPACE, FOUNTAINS PLAY
SOMERSET HOUSE

8 Courtauld Gallery

It is astonishing to see how many well known paintings are gathered in such a small gallery, part of the highly respected Courtauld Institute used in teaching the history of art. The North Wing of Somerset House was home to the Royal Academy until, under pressure from government, it moved to Burlington House in the 1870s, and bureaucracy moved in. After the Registrar General vacated it in 1970, the splendid space stood empty for 20 years before providing a very fine, accessible new home for the Courtauld Institute.

The Institute was founded by textile industrialist Samuel Courtauld, who presented it with a collection of mainly French Impressionist and Post-Impressionist paintings in 1932, since when it has built up a treasure store of art. The collection covers a broad sweep from the Gothic and medieval to the 20th century, from Fra Angelico to the Fauve artists, via the Renaissance, Rubens and the baroque and the 18th century. What is especially wonderful is the wealth of contrast hung in what feels like the private rooms of a great mansion.
Strand, WC2R 0RN. Charing Cross, Temple tube.

9 Aldwych Station

Also known as Strand, this is one of many ghost stations on the underground system. Passengers rattling around under London's streets might now and then catch glimpses in the darkness of disused tracks, empty platforms, the stations that time forgot. Of 40 stations abandoned or relocated, some have left no trace, but a few, by their street presence, remind the passer-by that they are down there. Deep-level Aldwych Station served as a shelter during the Blitz. It closed in 1994, but is used for filming and occasional performances, and tours are sometimes arranged by the London Transport Museum (see page 38). The original ticket office is in fine condition, having been restored for a period drama. '3d Single, 6d Return – Any Station' reads an anachronistic sign.
Surrey Street, WC2. Covent Garden, Temple, Holborn tube.

10 Twining's

Tea has been served in this long, narrow shop – and now small museum – since Thomas Twining opened Tom's Coffee House in 1706. Samuel Johnson must have known it; his house is a short stroll away. Today, as in his time, there are conflicting views about the benefits and ills of tea drinking, but in the 18th century the debate did not so much simmer as boil. In 1757, the philanthropist Jonas Hanway published an essay on tea, 'considered as pernicious to health, obstructing industry and impoverishing the nation'. Johnson, confessing himself a 'hardened and shameless tea drinker … whose kettle scarcely has time to cool', brought his great satirical wit to bear in pouring scorn on Hanway by means of a review in the *Literary Magazine*. On one thing Johnson and Hanway could agree – tea brought people together, serving, as Johnson put it, as 'a pretence for assembling to prattle, for interrupting business', in which Hanway saw great harm where Johnson saw great charm.

Visitors to Twinings, across the street from the Royal Courts of Justice, may be charmed by the shop itself, by the Loose Tea Bar with sampling dishes, and by the exhibits – old photographs, packaging, vintage tins and caddies, a picture of the *Gauntlet* tea clipper. A 90 minute tasting session is on offer, including sampling varieties of the drink that 'amuses in the evening, solaces the midnights, and welcomes in the morning' as Johnson, great wit and lexicographer, extolled it.
216 Strand, WC2R 1AP. Temple tube.

11 Royal Courts of Justice

On the Strand, by Fleet Street, at the border of the City, stands a Gothic grey-stone edifice designed by George Edmond Street, which harks back in style to the 13th century. Commonly known as the Law Courts, these are Britain's main civil courts, and were opened by Queen Victoria in 1882. Here are the Court of Appeal and the High Courts of Justice. Passing through the iron gates and elaborately carved porches of 'London's last great secular building of the Gothic revival', the visitor might be entering a cathedral.

Within, the atmosphere is solemn, majestic, overawing. The Great Hall is 24m (80ft) high, with Italian marble mosaic flooring, and heraldic devices in the tall windows. Litigants – the injured, the divorced, the aggrieved, the disinherited, the traduced, the libelled, the wronged and wrongdoer – must feel that the law is mighty. Those with less of an investment can simply appreciate the glorious scale, the fine detail, the craftsmanship – then observe some real-life human drama. All courtrooms, which are individually designed, are open to the public over the age of 14, except where cases are being held 'in camera'. Entrance is free but there is a charge for guided tours.
Strand, WC2A 2LL. Temple tube.

COVENT GARDEN

⑫ St Paul's Church

St Paul's Covent Garden has been beloved by thespians since the 17th century. George Bernard Shaw based the first scene of his play *Pygmalian* – brought to the stage as the musical *My Fair Lady* – under Inigo Jones's monumental portico to this church. Part of a commission by Francis Russell, the Earl of Bedford, to create in Covent Garden 'houses and buildings fit for the habitations of Gentlemen and men of ability', it was built in 1631 at a cost of £4,000. Known as 'the actors' church', it has a long association with the theatre community, from the time when the Theatre Royal was established in Drury Lane in 1663, and it even has its own in-house theatre group.

On the second Sunday in May, the garden hosts the annual meeting of Punch and Judy men – or 'professors' – preceded by a brass-band parade, with performances and puppetry all afternoon. At other times, the garden is a tranquil open space. Margaret Ponteous, the first known victim of the 17th-century plague epidemic, was buried here in 1665, and Thomas Arne, the composer of 'Rule Britannia', in 1778. The artist J.M.W. Turner was baptised here, and in the church are memorials to Charlie Chaplin, Noel Coward, Ivor Novello, Gracie Fields and Vivien Leigh. *Bedford Street, WC2E 9ED. Charing Cross, Leicester Square, Covent Garden tube.*

⑬ The Apple Store and Piazza

Alfred Hitchcock filmed *Frenzy* around the Covent Garden Piazza, and 'frenzy' would describe the mood as visitors flooded through the doors of the world's largest Apple store when it opened here in August 2010. Some had camped outside all night to get their hands on the latest techno-wizardry on offer from the innovative global computer company.

The location of the store within these cavernous historic premises artfully contrasts the illustrious past with the brave new and ever-changing present. The name is appropriate since this was the home of the old wholesale fruit and vegetables market, which moved south to Nine Elms in 1973, when the Apple Market was given over to antiques and craft stalls. The Italianate building was designed by Inigo Jones as part of an ambitious commission by the Earl of Bedford (see St Paul's Church above).

The store is set over three floors and blends original exposed brickwork with a metric tonne of glass. The thirsty should give the Genius Bar a miss – this is not a watering-hole but a source of technical support. The first Punch and Judy show in Britain was said by the diarist Samuel Pepys to have been performed in the Piazza in May 1662. *1-7 The Piazza, WC2E 8HA. Covent Garden, Charing Cross tube.*

⑭ The Market Central Court

Boutique shops now occupy the floor space under a glass-and-iron roof that once rang with the cries of costermongers. By 1678, there were more than 20 shops with cellars in Inigo Jones's central market building, but residential buildings – habitations not to the liking, perhaps, of the 'gentlemen and men of ability' for whom they were designed – were unsuccessful. Although the daily fruit and vegetable market continued, in 1830 a new building, by Charles Fowler, was raised upon the site at a cost of £70,000. It was this that Charles Dickens recalled in *Martin Chuzzlewit* – the scene of 'many a pleasant stroll', where could be seen 'the magnificence of the pineapples and melons', 'rows and rows of old women, seated on inverted baskets, shelling peas', and such 'unutterable things as fat bundles of asparagus with which the dainty shops were fortified as with breastwork'. Today the dainty shops are fortified with high-street fashion clothes and shoes, trinkets, Belgian chocolates, old-fashioned toys, English teas and marmalades, cigars and snuff. On the cobbled square at the west end, street performers – jugglers, musicians, magicians – continue the tradition begun by Mr Punch in the 17th century. That's the way to do it! *Covent Garden, WC2. Covent Garden, Charing Cross tube.*

⑮ London Transport Museum

In the West End, red buses travel bumper to bumper, black cabs appear to be marooned in traffic, while passengers watch their meters tick over inexorably, and intrepid cyclists weave their way along busy roads. But away from the hubbub and exhaust fumes, in what was once Covent Garden's dedicated flower-market building, the visitor can explore how Londoners got about – for better or worse – in centuries gone by, using the sedan chair, the cabriolet, the horse-drawn omnibus, river taxis ('wherries'), steam train, tram and trolley bus.

The London underground system, the world's oldest, was begun in 1860 – to be steam-driven, of course – and here is steam locomotive number 23, the handsome sole survivor from that time. By 1900, the capital's public transport relied on

50,000 horses plying the streets. Models, photographs, engravings and artefacts tell the tale of London on the move, and fine veteran vehicles challenge ideas of progress.

The Piazza, WC2E 7BB. Covent Garden, Charing Cross tube.

⑯ Royal Opera House

Sir Edward Middleton Barry's 19th-century colonnaded building is home to both the Royal Opera and the Royal Ballet, and is open to all, not just to theatre goers. This is the third grand theatre to stand on the site. The first, the Theatre Royal, was built with funds raised by the actor/manager John Rich. He was carried there in triumph for the first night, to see William Congreve's *The Way of the World*. A performance of Handel's *The Messiah* in front of George II began the tradition of holding oratorio performances at Lent. Handel bequeathed his organ to Rich, but it was lost in a fire that destroyed the building in 1808. The second theatre, one of the largest in Europe, opened with *Macbeth*, and also fell victim to fire but not before a rise in ticket prices from six to seven shillings (30–35p) caused riots, and a live elephant was brought on stage for the spectacular pantomime *Bluebeard*.

The present building dates from 1858. During the First World War, it was used as a furniture repository by the Ministry of Works, and in the Second World War it became a dance hall. It reopened as a theatre in 1946 with a performance of *The Sleeping Beauty* by Sadler's Wells Ballet. In the 1990s, £216 million was lavished on it, transforming it into one of the most exciting public spaces in the capital, with restaurants and bars. The Amphitheatre Bar looks down on the Floral Hall (page 40) and its terrace has a great view over Covent Garden.

The delicate statue, 'Young Dancer', on Broad Court opposite, is one of a number on London streets by the late Enzo Plazzota. Admirers should see also 'Jeté' on the Thames Embankment between Tate Britain and Vauxhall Bridge.

Bow Street, WC2E 9DD. Covent Garden, Charing Cross tube. 'Velvet, Gilt and Glamour' tours by pre-arrangement.

LONDON TRANSPORT MUSEUM

🟦 Floral Hall

The beautiful old flower market is now a stately pleasure dome. Next door to the Opera House, the former Floral Hall has been rebuilt in all its light-filled glory. This is a third incarnation. The original glass-and-iron structure by E.M. Barry, with its high, arched roof, burnt down in 1956. Today, it is officially called Paul Hamlyn Hall, after the publisher whose estate stepped in with a donation of £10 million for redevelopment. For Londoners, however, it remains Floral Hall, and is now used to cater for the Opera House audience. Charmingly, wartime tea dances have been revived. They are held on one Friday a month, and American veteran GIs have been known to come along to swing once more to the resident band.
Bow Street, WC2E 9DD. Covent Garden, Charing Cross tube.

🟦 St Martin's Theatre

Handsome St Martin's, designed by theatre architect W.G.R. Sprague, opened on November 23, 1916 with a musical comedy entitled *Houpla*. In 1973 it was granted Grade II listed status by English Heritage, and in 1974 the show with which it is for ever associated – *The Mousetrap* – seamlessly transferred from the Ambassadors next door and has been playing there ever since. *The Mousetrap* has held theatre-goers in its thrall since it first opened in November 1952, in an era of post-war austerity. Agatha Christie's ingenious plot, her ear for dialogue and her brilliance in sustaining suspense still have audiences on the edge of their seats. 'It's not really frightening. It's not really horrible. It's not really a farce. But it has a little of all these things and perhaps that satisfies a lot of people,' the playwright herself once said of it. When it was suggested that the play might close, people rushed to catch the last performance – in 1955. In St Martin's, restored woodwork, silk wallpaper and new upholstery make visitors feel welcome, adding to the pleasure of a good night out.
West Street, WC2H 9NZ. Leicester Square, Covent Garden tube.

🟦 Poetry Café

This lively vegetarian café, tucked away in a back street, is Covent Garden's own Poets' Corner, the public face of the Poetry Society. In the daytime, customers sit over lunch, or coffee and a muffin, or a glass of wine, while penning the odd epic, clerihew or haiku. In the evenings there are poetry readings. 'Poetry unplugged' is an open-mic session for anyone from established poets to first-timers. The modest snacks on offer in the evening may not have guests waxing lyrical, but the creative atmosphere at any rate inspires.

22 Betterton Street, WC2H 9BX. Covent Garden tube. Closed Sundays.

⑳ Freemasons' Hall

There is nothing clandestine about the presence on Great Queen Street of the headquarters of the English Freemasons. It looms large, and has a splendid tower. The United Grand Lodge occupies the only Art Deco building in London that remains unaltered and is still used for its original purpose. The date 1717 is inscribed near the top but this refers to the origins of English Freemasonry. This building, the third Freemasons' Hall to stand on the site, dates from 1933, and is a memorial to the 3,224 Freemasons killed on active service in the First World War.

There are up to five conducted tours a day, when the Grand Temple is not going about its arcane business. Tours start in the Library and Museum of Freemasonry, and much is made of the hall's accessibility for film and television shoots. It has appeared in every episode of the BBC series *Spooks*, in feature films such as *Wings of a Dove*, *The Hitchhiker's Guide to the Galaxy* and *Penelope*, in an Aquascutum advertising campaign and in Westlife's pop video for their song 'Mandy'. Masons are forbidden to write, print, stamp, stain, cut, carve, hew, mark or engrave any of their deepest secrets, but Masonic aprons and other fine regalia are for sale.

60 Great Queen Street, WC2B 5AZ. Holborn tube.

㉑ Rules

'Unique, irreplaceable, and part of literary and theatrical London,' said poet laureate John Betjeman of London's oldest restaurant. In more than 200 years, Rules has been owned by just three families. It is changeless, comfortable and comforting. The present building was designed for Benjamin Rule, fishmonger and oyster-bar proprietor, by Alfred Cross in 1873, but as long ago as 1798 one Thomas Rule had an oyster or fish stall on Maiden Lane. In 1971, Betjeman was an advocate for this London institution before the Greater London Council, who would have seen it bulldozed. He spoke lovingly of its paintings and prints, busts and bronzes, red plush seats, stained

glass and theatrical relics. 'A place that has been constantly used by actors, managers and famous people, as Rules has,' he said, 'acquires an invisible atmosphere, just as a church frequented by praying people acquires an atmosphere … When the atmosphere is pleasant and welcoming, as it is at Rules, it is something to be treasured and protected so that posterity may enjoy it too.' Posterity duly flocks here to fill up on hearty John Bull fare – including game from Rules' Pennines estate – surrounded by gilt-framed mirrors, old cartoons, ormolu and alabaster. Every surface is crammed, and the whole agglomeration has been compared, affectionately, to 'a DIY version of the Soane Museum'.

Intimate private dining rooms recall past famous patrons. The Greene room is a shrine to Graham Greene, who chose to celebrate his birthday here when in London. Rules appears in some of his novels, including *The End of the Affair*, and letters written by him are framed on walls that are hung head to foot with memorabilia. Fittingly, there is a Sir John Betjeman Room.

Edward VII, when Prince of Wales, wined and dined his mistress, the actress Lillie Langtry, at Rules. Other famous diners have included actors Henry Irving, Laurence Olivier, Buster Keaton, Charles Laughton, Clark Gable and Charlie Chaplin, and writers John Galsworthy and H.G. Wells. But any claims that Charles Dickens knew the restaurant as it is should be taken with a large pinch of Maldon salt, since he died in 1870.

For visitors not tempted by steamed syrup sponge, an upstairs bar, with latticed windows, serves cocktails.

35 Maiden Lane, WC2E 7LB. Charing Cross, Covent Garden, Leicester Square tube.

㉒ James Smith & Sons, Umbrellas

The Smiths have been keeping Londoners dry since 1830 when the family business first set up in the West End. Behind a perfect Victorian shop front, arrays of seating sticks, walking sticks, silver-topped canes and rustic staffs are offered for sale alongside the full panoply of umbrellas, from the classic City gent's rolled black brolly, to ladies walking-length strollers and frilly parasols. Bespoke mahogany fittings, mirrors, racks, stands and glass cases create a dazzling interior. 'Established over half a century' proclaims a 19th-century sign. Thanks to the British climate, London is 'the home of the best umbrellas'. The workshops are still in the basement.

53 New Oxford Street, WC1A 1BL. Tottenham Court Road tube.

Gilding the lily

The artful adornment of London, whether with Victorian folderols or modern sculpture, decorative or practical, adds enormously to the atmosphere of this distinctive city.

'Look up! Look up!' teachers of architecture always tell their students. It's good advice. Revelling high above the pavements of London are damsels and cherubs, wild animals and strongmen, ancient gods and figures of every allegory under heaven. Golden divers hurl themselves from the rooftops in Coventry Street, mice nibble cheese above Philpot Street in the City, and a sinister, cowled figure of Justice by Herbert Binney looms large over Piccadilly on a former insurance company building, although few Londoners notice it. Window shoppers must raise their eyes to see the wonderful ceramic panels on the façade of Heal's in Tottenham Court Road, or the glittering gold and blue bronze *Queen of Time* by Gilbert Bayes on the front of Selfridge's in Oxford Street. In Widegate Street, Spitalfields, ceramic figures go about the business of baking.

Modern developers chasing cool, minimalist lines seldom allow for such embellishments, and make amends by placing statues nearby: William Blake at the London Library, Fernando Botero's plumptious Venus in Broadgate, the tangled steel of *Eye-I* just beyond on the edge of the City. Antony Gormley, designer of street bollards, placed his figures on the top of buildings around town. These are all a far cry from the 19th- and 20th-century statues that immortalised men of state and war.

Flowing water

With statues come fountains. The latest are as simple as possible, such as the playful pavement eruptions outside the Royal Academy and in the courtyard of Somerset House. Others are plain water features – the Canadian Memorial in Green Park and the Princess Diana fountain in Hyde Park. A programme of restoration of park fountains began in 2010 shortly after a 1m (3ft) wide stainless steel ball by sculptor David Harber was installed in Hyde Park, the first new drinking fountain in London for 30 years. At the same time, a grey pillar with a spout was erected in St Paul's Churchyard, and plans were announced to install 50 more across the City.

Red phone boxes, blue police boxes and green cabbies' shelters once coloured the city streets, but most have disappeared. The original wood template for the K2 red phone box, designed by Sir Giles Gilbert Scott in 1926, stands just inside the entrance to the Royal Academy. Dr Who-type police boxes, which kept constables warm and in touch with their stations, were reinvented in 1996 when a slightly larger-sized Tardis appeared outside Earl's Court station, designed for the public to get in touch with the police. As for cabbies' shelters, the 13 that remain are protected by law. Looking like fancy garden sheds, they are little changed since they were introduced to give shelter to Hansom cab drivers in 1875.

Clock watching

Street timepieces are also a feature of the past. The largest clock face on display is not on the clock tower of the Houses of Parliament, but above the Shell Mex building a few hundred metres away, fronting the Thames. Clocks that have automatons – figures that move as the clock strikes the quarter hours – are to be seen outside Fortnum & Mason, Liberty and St Dunstan's in the West in Fleet Street. This was the first public clock in London to have a minute hand. In 2007, the Newgate Street clock was installed near St Paul's to celebrate the 375th anniversary of the Worshipful Company of Clockmakers. This is known as the 'wandering hour' clock and is based on 17th-century designs, in which the hours travel in an arc over a dial, as if moving across the sky.

Street lighting arrived in 1807, and almost 2,000 lamps in the city are still powered by gas. Their warm glow adds to the Dickensian atmosphere of Middle Temple, Green Park, Gough Square and the cobblestones outside Covent Garden's Lamb and Flag pub. Half a dozen lamplighters ensure the mantles are in order, and each week wind up the clockwork time switches that ignite the lamps at dusk and turn them off at dawn. Electric lamps can be attractive, too. The sturgeon or dolphin lamp standards on Embankment were designed by George Vulliamy in 1865, and copied a century later by the London County Council for the South Bank. Vulliamy also designed the sphinxes beneath Cleopatra's needle, which are complemented by the mythical Egyptian creatures that uphold the Embankment's street benches.

When it comes to sitting down, most Londoners head for squares and parks, but street seating is becoming increasingly sociable. And none appears more sociable than 'Allies' by Lawrence Holofcener in Bond Street, a sculpture of Winston Churchill and Franklin D. Roosevelt enjoying a discussion while sitting on a park bench. They are far enough apart for people to slip in between them to join in the chat and be photographed.

DOLPHIN LAMP STANDARD

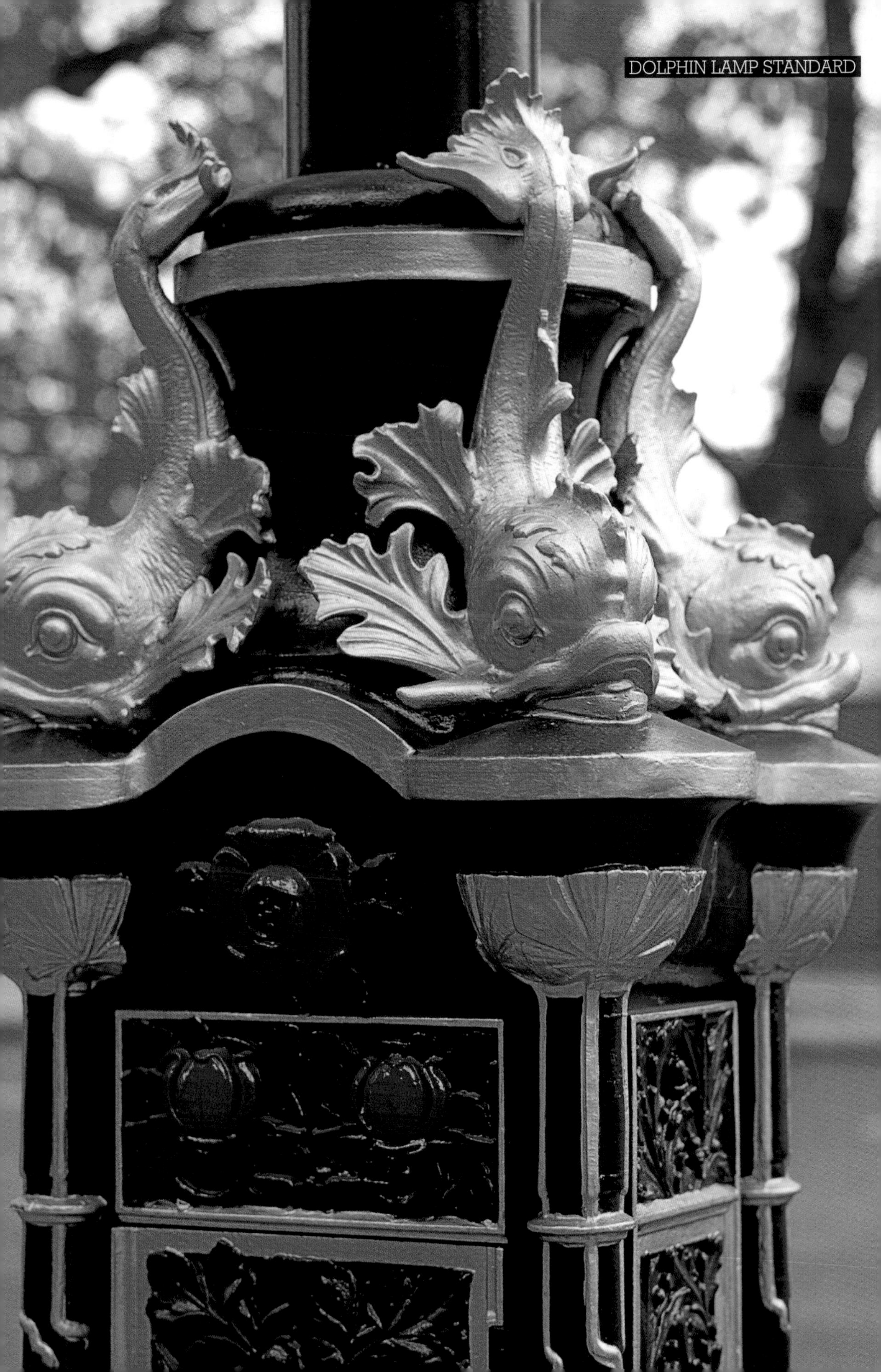

HOLBORN

㉓ Sir John Soane's Museum

A vast collection of books, casts, paintings and antiquities in the smallest possible space in this imaginative little museum.
Sir John Soane was architect of the Bank of England and Dulwich Picture Gallery, and Professor of Architecture at the Royal Academy, and he used his collection as a resource for his students. His home, unchanged since his death in 1837, comprised three adjoining houses that he knocked together to make an extraordinary series of rooms and passages to accommodate these myriad objects.

Mainly assembled after the death of his wife in 1815 – some say as a means of dealing with his grief – the Aladdin's cave of treasures contains a shrine to Shakespeare, Apulian vases, architectural models and the sarcophagus of the pharaoh Seti I. Paintings by Canaletto, Reynolds and Turner are on show, and the ingeniously designed, top-lit Picture Room has Hogarth's original satirical series 'The Rake's Progress' and 'The Election'. Hinged screens reveal another 100 pictures. There are timepieces, Napoleonic medals, 325 items of furniture, many designed by Soane, a model of his wife's tomb and the grave of Fanny, her lapdog.

The museum of this remarkable man, the son of a country bricklayer, is highly eclectic and crowded, but it delivers what Soane wanted – an emotional punch – and it is especially atmospheric by candlelight.
13 Lincoln's Inn Fields, off Kingsway, WC2A 3BP. Holborn tube. Open Tuesday–Saturday. Visitors are limited to 40 at a time. Candlelit tours on the first Tuesday of each month, no booking.

㉔ Princess Louise, High Holborn

The jewel of Victorian pubs, Princess Louise simply sparkles. Its cut glass and gilt mirrors, coloured tiles depicting bowls brimming with fruit, ornate ceiling plasterwork, gleaming brass, painted pillars and buffed mahogany are all authentic. Owned and refurbished by Yorkshire brewers Samuel Smith, who ban music from their pubs, it is laid out around an island bar with a handsome clock. Partitions at the bar create separate booths with stools, each with its own entrance, leaving a tiled corridor down each side. Upstairs is a club-like room and downstairs there are more small booths. The gents' lavatories are Grade II listed, along with the rest of the building, and are particularly spacious. Princess Louise was built in 1872 with tilework by William Butler Simpson (the family firm is still in business) and mirrors by R. Morris

& Son of Kennington. A year earlier, Princess Louise, the artistic and popular sixth child of Queen Victoria, had married the Marquess of Lorne. It was the first time a member of the royal family had married a 'commoner' since 1551, and the occasion was particularly ostentatious.
208–9 High Holborn, WC1V 7BW. Holborn tube.

㉕ Lincoln's Inn

The huge dark entrance of Lincoln's Inn on Chancery Lane, dating from 1564, seem more fit for a prison than for the home of lawyers. The coat of arms of the Inn's founder, Henry de Lacey, Duke of Lincoln, are above the doors on the left. An array of Tudor-looking redbrick buildings lie between the doors and the 16th-century Gatehouse facing Lincoln's Inn Fields. The oldest part of the Inn is the attractive Old Hall, dating from 1490. The hall, which has a crypt, was sometimes used as a courtroom – the opening scene of Charles Dickens' *Bleak House* is set there – and a large painting by Hogarth, 'Paul before Felix', hangs above the place where the Lord Chancellor would sit. The poet and dean of St Paul's John Donne laid the foundation stone of the rebuilt chapel in 1620. The main Great Hall, incorporating the Library, is a 19th-century addition and has a large mural by G.F. Watts, entitled 'Justice: A Hemicycle of Lawgivers'.

Outside, beneath huge plane trees, office workers make the most of London's largest public square at lunchtimes in summer. The former rough pastureland was bought by a 17th-century developer, who, in 1629, reached an agreement with Lincoln's Inn that the centre should be left undeveloped. One of the earliest law firms in the square, Farrer & Co, established its practice in Newcastle House (No 66) in 1790 and is still there today. The Queen is among the firm's clients.
Lincoln's Inn, WC2 3TL. Holborn tube. Grounds open Monday–Friday 7am–7pm. Two-hour tours arranged; book at least two weeks in advance.

㉖ Hunterian Museum

More than four centuries of blundering, butchery, wrongheadedness and advances in the healing arts are on show at the museum of the Royal College of Surgeons. The country's largest collection of organs, tissues and human anatomy dates back to the bequest of the surgeon and collector John Hunter, in 1789. It was at one time a much larger, more rambling place. Even in recent times, artists could go there to draw cadavers. Since a thorough refurbishment in 2005, most exhibits are displayed in shining glass cases, which mask the aroma of formaldehyde and probably much else. The original collection of some 3,500 items amassed by Hunter is displayed in the atrium, where a gallery shows the paintings he collected, including work by William Hodges, the artist who sailed with Captain Cook and brought back specimens for Hunter. An upper gallery displays the Science of Surgery; the Silver and the Steel Gallery shows the development of surgical instruments. Videos of operations are screened, and visitors can try their hand at virtual keyhole surgery.

35–43 Lincoln's Inn Fields, WC2A 3PE. Holborn tube. Open Tuesday–Saturday. Free curator-led tour every Wednesday at 1pm.

㉗ The Seven Stars

In a quiet road behind the Royal Courts of Justice, the Seven Stars has decor to reflect its clientele – caricatures of lawyers, a wig and a gavel. Lawyers sometimes bring their clients to this tiny atmospheric pub after a successful case. The earliest customers were, however, Dutch seamen. That was when the pub was known as the League of the Seven Stars after the seven provinces of Holland. A street party was held in 2002 to celebrate its 400th anniversary.

53–54 Carey Street, WC2A 2JB. Holborn tube.

㉘ The Old Curiosity Shop

This beamed 16th-century shop is a literary landmark, the model for Charles Dickens' Old Curiosity Shop – or maybe not. 'The place … was one of those receptacles for old and curious things which seemed to crouch in odd corners of this town and to hide their musty treasures from the public eye in jealousy and distrust,' Dickens wrote. 'There were suits of mail standing like ghosts in armour here and there, fantastic carvings brought from monkish cloisters, rusty weapons, distorted figures in china and wood, and iron and ivory; tapestry and strange furniture that might have been designed in dreams.'

It could have been this little shop that was his inspiration, or it could as well be one of 'a good many little low-browed old shops of a wretched kind down that turning in the Blackfriars Road that has Rowland Hill's chapel on one side, and the likeness of a golden dog licking a golden pot over a shop door on the other'. Rowland Hill's chapel, now known as Surrey Chapel, is still there, but the shops and the golden dog are gone, and here is as good a place as any to conjure suits of mail, distorted figures and the furniture of dreams.

13 Portsmouth Street, WC2A 2ES. Holborn tube.

㉙ Conway Hall

'To thine own self be true' reads the sign over the concert-hall stage at Conway Hall, and it is hard to imagine a more honest-looking place. This is the delightfully unreconstructed home of the South Place Ethical Society, which moved into the building in 1929 from South Place Chapel in Finsbury. It is named after a South Place minister, American Mercure Conway, who was a fervent supporter of the abolition of slavery, a biographer of Thomas Paine and a friend of Dickens and Darwin. He also became London literary agent for Mark Twain, Walt Whitman and Louisa May Alcott, and leaned towards humanism after one of his sons died.

Today SPEC is an educational charity for 'the study and dissemination of ethical principles, based on humanism and free thought'. Lectures, meetings, performances and community events are held in the small hall and the three meeting rooms, as well as in the 500 seat concert hall. On Sunday evenings, like a prop for an amateur dramatic society, a Victorian standard lamp on stage awaits the arrival of musicians. Top chamber orchestras play in what is believed to be the oldest series of concerts in the world, held from October to April, going back to 1887.

37 Red Lion Square, WC1R 4RL. Holborn tube.

SIR JOHN SOANE'S MUSEUM

BLOOMSBURY

㉚ Pipers' Central London Model

An absorbing 1:1,500 scale model of contemporary London spreads out across the main gallery at the Building Centre.
About 12m (40ft) long, the Central London Model, by architectural model-makers Pipers, stretches from Paddington to the Royal Docks and includes not only existing buildings but also, in white, proposed developments, to show at a glance how the city's skyline is changing. On the wall are details of the proposed developments, borough by borough.

This large exhibition space on two floors is looked after by New London Architecture, and includes a Products Gallery and an Eco Zone Gallery, showing sustainable products and materials. The Building Centre was set up in 1931 to create awareness of quality building design. Events and exhibitions are held through the year.
26 Store Street, WC1E 7BT. Tottenham Court Road tube.

㉛ L. Cornelissen & Son

Artists' suppliers L. Cornelissen & Son's shop is wood-panelled and beautifully decked out with floor-to-ceiling cabinets containing jars of pigment powder, for sale by the gram. Watercolour tablets, oil tubes, inks, egg tempera, chalks and pastels make fanfares of colour among the polished cases and drawers. Canvases, easels, brushes, drawing blocks, gold leaf – it is impossible to imagine everything in their 20,000 item stock. The shop's first premises, in Covent Garden, were opened in 1855 by Louis Cornelissen, a Belgian lithographer who moved to London from Paris to escape the Franco-Prussian war. Artists Walter Sickert, Aubrey Beardsley and, more recently, Derek Jarman were among the clientele, and the shop was a port of call for every fine-art student in London. It closed when the last family member died in 1977, but was revived by Nicholas Walt, who brought the whole store, from its attractive shop front to its fitted interior, to Great Russell Street.
105 Great Russell Street, WC1B 3RY. Tottenham Court Road tube.

㉜ British Museum

Whatever a visitor's expectations, there are bound to be surprises: a Picasso from the huge collection of prints and drawings; an entire hall devoted to the Parthenon Frieze and showing its original bright colouring in a video; mummified cats (180,000 were imported from

QUEEN ELIZABETH II GREAT COURT, BRITISH MUSEUM

Egypt in the late 19th century to use as fertiliser); exquisite Greek vases on which flying gods resemble angels; and the sheer ordinariness of the Rosetta Stone, which was the key to the whole mystery of ancient Egypt. Sculptures from the Seven Wonders of the Ancient World are here, too, from the Mausoleum of Mausoleus and the Temple of Artemis, while the ethnographic collection has items from the Pacific and the Americas. The exhibits chosen for the BBC's series *History of the World in 100 Objects* are all identified, from the mummy of Hornedjitef to a solar-powered lamp and charger.
Great Russell Street, WC1B 3DD. Tottenham Court Road tube.

bookstacks. The Reading Room, built by Sydney Smirke, brother of the museum's architect, Robert Smirke, is 43m (140ft) in diameter and pioneered the use of concrete and cast iron with a papier-mâché ceiling. The place became an essential resource for writers, researchers and students, including Karl Marx, Oscar Wilde and Virginia Woolf. Two staircases wrap around the Reading Room, leading to the first-floor restaurant and Joseph Hotung Gallery, which has temporary exhibitions, and to a walkway to the upper Near East and Egyptian rooms.

The Great Court is adorned with 12 statues from the museum's collection, including a 9th-century BC stele of Assyria's Ashurnasirpal II, an Easter Island figure and two 17th-century Chinese guardians.

Great Russell Street, WC1B 3DG. Tottenham Court Road tube. The Great Court remains open after the museum has closed, until 10.30pm on Thursday and Friday.

㉞ Wellcome Collection

Setting itself up as a 'free destination for the incredibly curious', the Wellcome Collection is full of surprises and thought-provoking items. Born in Wisconsin in 1853, Henry Solomon Wellcome came to London as a young man, where he teamed up with New Yorker Silas Burroughs to create Burroughs Wellcome & Company (later merged into GlaxoSmithKline) to produce the world's first medicine in tablet form. His own curiosity led him to travel widely, and to develop an interest in archaeology as well as medicine. By the time he died in 1936, he had amassed a million items for his foundation.

A permanent collection of some 500 objects is housed here on the first floor, entitled 'Medicine Man'. It doesn't look cluttered; most items are kept in drawers and cabinets, which the inquiring visitor may open to discover the treasures within – unusual implements and finds, from amputation saws and artificial limbs to Nelson's razor and a lock of George III's hair. The Lightbox shows still and moving images from the collection, and the Medicine Now gallery concentrates on current medical topics, using a variety of perspectives, including art. Special exhibitions on the ground floor have included 'Sleeping and Dreaming' and 'High Society: Drugs in Victorian Britain'. Events are held regularly on the themes of medicine and wellbeing, and a café and bookshop make this free modern venue an intriguing place in which to contemplate the human condition.

183 Euston Road, NW1 2BE. Euston tube.

㉝ The Great Court

The size of a football pitch and covered with 3,312 separately designed panes of glass, the Great Court, by Foster and Partners, is the hub of the British Museum. It is the largest covered public square in Europe, and has information points, a shop and café. This is the best place to meet and take stock before a tour of the museum.

The Great Court was originally an open space, intended as a garden. Then in the 1850s, the Reading Room, which is the white drum at the Court's centre, was built and until the British Library (see page 49) was opened in 1998, the Great Court contained 3 miles of iron

㉟ Petrie Museum of Egyptian Archaeology

Here are 'firsts' of so many things: the oldest surviving dress (a beadnet creation worn by a dancer), the earliest examples of metalworking and glazing, the oldest papyrus wills and the oldest known calendar. A suit of armour from Memphis, Roman socks, and images of the astonishingly priapic god Min are also on display. With intimate daily objects, beautiful frescoes and public sculptures, the museum gives a vivid account of life on the Nile. Some 8,000 items were amassed by Flinders Petrie, 'the father of Egyptian archaeology', whose scrupulous methodology set a benchmark for research. Dating from 5000 BC, they cover the whole gamut of the great river's treasures, from the time of the pharaohs to the Nubian kings, Greek Ptolemys, Romans, Coptic Christians and Muslims. One of Petrie's best-known discoveries was the Merneptah stele, now in the Cairo Museum, which has the only known ancient Egyptian written reference to 'Israel'. Aware of his intellectual gifts, Petrie donated his own head to the London College of Surgeons, although it was lost in transit from Jerusalem immediately after his death in 1942.
Malet Place, WC1E 6BT. Euston Square tube.

㊱ Woburn Walk

A few inches of snow and a mail coach would turn Woburn Walk into the perfect Christmas card. Lit by central street lamps and especially atmospheric in the evening, this pedestrianised lane is a relief from the noise of Euston Road. The stucco-fronted Georgian buildings were designed by Thomas Cubitt in 1822. Beneath first-floor cast-iron ornamental balconies, shops have bow-fronts, each of 24 panes, offering glimpses into galleries, bookshops, a vintner and antiques dealer. Café tables are set out on its pavement. From 1895 to 1919 the Irish poet W. B. Yeats lived at No 5, where Ezra Pound and other literati would foregather in his sitting room on Monday evenings.
Woburn Walk, WC1H 0JL. Euston tube.

㊲ The School of Life

The shop for the School of Life is described as a 'chemist's of the mind'. On sale in the bow-fronted Georgian building are books, cards and novelty items as well as tickets for classes and weekend courses. The School of Life was founded by writer and philosopher Alain de Botton, to offer an antidote to academic disciplines, concentrating instead on 'things we all tend to care about: careers, relationships, politics, travel and families'. Another instigator, Sophie Howarth, was frustrated by the 'lack of dialogue between culture and self-improvement' when she worked at Tate Modern, where she found the cultural world 'just so snooty about everything to do with personal development'.

The place is a mix of philosophy school and literary salon, restaurant and dining club, all designed to fire the imagination. Luminaries give talks in a downstairs room, although classes often migrate to other locations around town, and there are organised 'Conversation' dinners and breakfasts.
17 Marchmont Street, WC1N 1AB. Russell Square tube.

㊳ The Foundling Museum

Keepsakes left by mothers with their abandoned babies are the most poignant items displayed in Captain Thomas Coram's Foundling Hospital. The philanthropic merchant, son of a poor Dorset family, made his money trading in North America. He set up the charity in 1790, at a time when 75 per cent of children died before the age of five and 90 per cent did not survive the workhouse. Bows and ribbons were tied to their clothes and swaddling cloth, which was sometimes embroidered, sometimes quite plain. The hospital carefully noted, and kept, 5,000 items from every one of the 200 or so children who arrived each year before dressing them in the foundling's own uniform, designed by William Hogarth, who was also Inspector of Wet Nurses.

Childless, William and Jane Hogarth fostered foundlings, and William was a governor of the hospital. He painted pictures to decorate its walls, and these are on display, along with works by Reynolds and Gainsborough. Artists were rewarded for their donations with a governorship.

The museum building was re-created from the original hospital when it moved out of London in 1926, and it includes the handsome rococo Governors' Meeting Room, where conversations among the artists helped to lead towards the founding of the Royal Academy. George Frideric Handel was another benefactor, giving concerts in the chapel, although he refused a governorship. A room of memorabilia includes his will and conducting score of the *Messiah*.
40 Brunswick Square, WC1N 1AZ. Russell Square tube. Closed on Monday.

㊴ The Russell Hotel

Late Victorian architecture reaches its wildest excesses at the Russell Hotel, built in 1900 in flamboyant French Gothic style and overlooking London's largest square. 'Embellished' is too tame a word to describe the arches, columns, busts of prime ministers, national coats of arms, galleries, balconies, towers and chimney stacks that fill its monumental terracotta and redbrick façade. The visitor stepping up to the main entrance beneath statues of four British queens (Mary, Elizabeth I, Anne and Victoria) by Henry Charles Fehr, enters the grand lobby to find a staircase in pink and blood-red marble that sweeps right to the top of the building. There is a wood-panelled bar, and the dining room is airy and elegant, with more grand pillars, stucco work and an ornate fireplace. The hotel's architect, Charles Fitzroy Doll, went on to design a similar restaurant on the *Titanic*.
1 Russell Square, WC1B 5BE. Russell Square tube

㊵ Coram's Fields

'No adults unless accompanied by a child', admonishes a notice at the entrance to Coram's Fields. A few years after Thomas Coram's Foundling Hospital left London, seven of the hospital's 23ha (56 acres) were bought, with the help of newspaper baron Lord Rothermere, to create Coram's Fields. The space is made for children. Geese, goats and sheep safely graze for the benefit of urban youngsters. There are football pitches and a basketball court, a playground, nursery, onsite staff and a community nurse, with after school and holiday activities. The Coram charity continues its work from offices in adjacent Mecklenburgh Square.
93 Guilford Street, WC1N 1DN. Russell Square tube

㊶ Charles Dickens Museum

How lively this simple, attractive Georgian House must have been when Charles Dickens and his wife Catherine and baby son moved in a year after they were married. By the time they left not three years later, in December 1836, they had two daughters to take with them, too. No idler, Dickens had used his time in Doughty Street to complete *Pickwick Papers* and *Oliver Twist*, to write all of *Nicholas Nickelby* and to begin *Barnaby Rudge*. He was 27. The rooms are full of his memories: the Victorian parlour, the small back boxroom where he finished writing about Mr Pickwick, the desk and the inkstand that fuelled his industrious pen, the pictures of his life and times, the room where Catherine's sister, Mary, died. The museum, which opened in 1925, has undergone a £3.1 million refurbishment to coincide with the 200th anniversary of the author's birth in 1812. It has added space to take account of 10,000 books, manuscripts and other documents relating to the life of the greatest storyteller London has ever known.
48 Doughty Street, WC1N 2LX. Russell Square tube.

㊷ The Walks, Gray's Inn

Sir Francis Bacon laid out the Walks in Gray's Inn in 1606, and they are even now a tranquil green haven. A broad gravel path runs the length of the 2ha (5 acre) gardens from the main Inn building up to Theobald's Road, shaded by plane trees and Indian bean trees, brought to these shores by Sir Walter Raleigh and planted by Bacon. A statesman, lawyer, historian, author and scientist, Bacon was treasurer of what was at one time the largest of the Inns of Court, but the summerhouse he built on the Upper Walks is no longer there. He put on a number of plays in the Inn's Great Hall – Shakespeare's *Comedy of Errors* was first performed there – and recent summer seasons of events in the Walks have included productions of Bacon's plays.
Theobald's Road, WC1R 5ET. Open Monday to Friday, noon–2.30pm.

㊸ British Library

The greatest permanent exhibition of the written word is in the British Library's low-lit Sir John Ritblat Gallery. The luminous 7th–8th-century Lindisfarne gospel, a Gutenberg Bible, Leonardo notebooks, the Magna Carta, fabulous maps, original music scores and literary works from Shakespeare's first folio to *Alice's Adventures Under Ground* are just some of the 200 exhibits. What is considered to be one of the greatest collections of works of the Enlightenment is here, too – some 65,000 volumes and 19,000 pamphlets amassed by George III, with the help of a full-time librarian and advice from writer and lexicographer Dr Johnson. The Library's philatelic collection is on permanent display in an upper gallery, as is an exhibition on the conservation of books and manuscripts. Changing exhibitions in the ground floor and basement galleries are invariably worth seeking out. These, together with the café and shop selling books and CDs from some of the Library's vast audio collection ensure the British Library is not just for students and researchers, but is a fascinating place for all to visit.
96 Euston Road, NW1 2DB. Euston tube.

CENTRAL

EDGWARE ROAD

Edgware Road

West End

High on his plinth, Eros sends city-goers out into the heart of theatreland to lose themselves in the excitement of Soho and Chinatown, while among the backstreets, away from the hubbub, quiet corners exert a magic of their own.

BAKER STREET

MARBLE ARCH

REGENT'S PARK

WARREN STREET

GREAT PORTLAND STREET

GOODGE STREET

TOTTENHAM COURT ROAD

OXFORD CIRCUS

BOND STREET

LEICESTER SQUARE

PICCADILLY CIRCUS

GREEN PARK

Euston Road

Marylebone Road

Marylebone High Street

Portland Place

Great Portland Street

Tottenham Court Road

Goodge Street

Oxford Street

Wigmore Street

Oxford Street

New Bond Street

Regent Street

Shaftesbury Avenue

Charing Cross Road

Piccadilly

Park Lane

Baker Street

Gloucester Place

SOHO & CHARING CROSS ROAD

❶ Burleigh Mansions

Passers-by are able to look clear through this building, from one street to another. A late-Victorian mansion block with two addresses, Burleigh House has a central corridor that runs parallel to Cecil Court for more than 90m (100yd) between Charing Cross Road and St Martin's Lane. With marble mosaic floor and potted plants, the hallway is lit by a ceiling of small glass squares, giving the illusion of daylight above.
95 Burleigh Mansions/20 Charing Cross Road, WC2H 0HU. Leicester Square tube.

❷ Notre Dame de France

Paintings in the Lady Chapel of this circular church are by the French filmmaker, artist and designer Jean Cocteau. He produced them in 1959 in a state of apparent religious ecstasy and fervour, in little more than a week. On arriving in the morning, Cocteau would light a candle before the statue of Our Lady of Lourdes, roll up his sleeves and start engaging with his characters, talking with them as he brought them into being. 'Oh, you most beautiful of women, loveliest of God's creatures, you were the best loved,' he told the Virgin Mary. 'I want you to be my best piece of work, too. I am drawing you with light strokes. You are the yet unfinished work of Grace.' The church dates from 1865 and was built for the working-class French of the area. It owes its circular shape to the fact that it occupies the site of the world's first 'panorama', a rotunda containing a huge circular painting. Devised in 1793 by Robert Barker, who coined the word, these panoramas became popular in the 19th century.
5 Leicester Place, WC2H 7BX. Leicester Square tube.

❸ Odeon, Leicester Square

The black granite façade of the largest single-screen cinema in Britain dominates the east side of Leicester Square, emphasised by a 37m (120ft) cubic tower outlined in blue neon at night. It was built on the site of the Alhambra Theatre as a flagship cinema for the Odeon chain, opening with *The Prisoner of Zenda* in 1937. The architect was Harry Wheedon, who was employed by Odeon's Oscar Deutsch to make his cinemas appeal to smart audiences. Its magnificent interior was renovated in 1967 and the faux leopard-skin seats have gone. It has two circles and capacity for nearly 1,700 people, with state-of-the-art technology for showing films in all media. The original Compton organ remains and there is an Art Deco safety curtain in front of the stage. A royal retiring room is provided for the royal film performance.
24–26 Leicester Square, WC2H 7JY. Leicester Square tube.

❹ Chinatown

Pagoda arches bookend Gerrard Street in the heart of Chinatown, distracting the eye from the 17th-century houses now given over to restaurants and supermarkets. On ground level this is a busy pedestrian thoroughfare; produce is constantly wheeled from store to shop, would-be diners browse menus and sightseers soak up the atmosphere. But from the first floor up, the street takes on a different look, and gives a glimpse of the activities of another age. This was an arty and sociable street of coffee houses, taverns and hotels. A blue plaque above Loon Fung supermarket shows that the poet John Dryden (1631–1700) lived here; he was often seen writing at his desk by a window onto the street. New Loon Supermarket at No 9 was the Turk's Head tavern where, in 1714, the writer Samuel Johnson and artist Joshua Reynolds founded The Club. The Nassau coffee house was in the Whettons Building on the corner of Gerrard's Place, built in 1734. This was where architect James Gibb lived. In 1900, writers G.K. Chesterton and Hilaire Belloc first met in the Mont Blanc, now the Golden Harvest, serving Cantonese food.

Chinatown spreads round to Little Newport Street on the east side and to Wardour Street on the west, where the Wong Kei restaurant occupies the ground floor of the wigmaker Willy Clarkson's premises, above which hangs his clock inscribed with the words 'Costumier' and 'Perruquier'. Metal plaques on the Art Nouveau building state that the actress Sarah Bernhardt laid the foundation stone in 1904, and her fellow actor Henry Irving laid the coping stone in 1905.
Gerrard Street, W1D. Leicester Square tube.

❺ Lex Garage

A piece of motoring history can be found in a former NCP on the corner of Lexington and Brewer streets. The four-storey Art Deco building with a yellow ceramic façade and copper-clad domed towers was designed by J.J. Joass and Robert Sharp in 1929, and is one of the earliest examples of a multi-storey car park with

CHINATOWN

ramps, as opposed to lifts. It could accommodate 1,000 cars, and was built to serve the entire West End. Each floor had a turntable, and there was a canteen where chauffeurs could wait while their employers enjoyed a night on the town. Bathrooms in each tower were used as ladies' changing rooms. There were also petrol pumps on the forecourt. In danger of being torn down for development in 2002, Lex was saved by English Heritage, which succeeded in having it listed as 'the largest and best-equipped building for the service of the motor car of its day'. As a result, its 3,716sq m (40,000sq ft) can now be seen as an extraordinary backdrop to fashion shows and other events that are held there. *Brewer Street, W1F 0LA. Piccadilly Circus tube.*

❻ Soho Parish School

To find a small Victorian primary school in the heart of Soho is surprising, to say the least. The chatter of children in the playground drifts over the blank wall and iron railings in Great Windmill Street, just a few doors away from the Windmill Theatre, famed for its nude review. The school has been there since the 1820s, when it was St James's and St Peter's Primary School. Small rooms limit class sizes to 20, and the total of around 140 four–to-eleven-year-olds speak more than a dozen languages between them. Empty wallets and other debris hurled away in the night sometimes have to be cleared from the playground in the morning, and until it was shut down by the authorities in 2010, girls in the next-door clip joint hid out of sight when parents gathered to pick up children in the afternoon. Christmas and summer fairs are the time to see the school's achievements. *23 Great Windmill Street, W1D 7LF. Piccadilly Circus tube.*

❼ Algerian Coffee Stores

It is takeaway only at the Algerian Coffee Stores, because there is nowhere to sit – or do much else. This small shop sells coffees and teas from the same wood counter and display shelves that have been there since it opened its doors in 1887. There are more than 80 coffees on sale, and around 120 teas, as well as teapots, and coffee-making equipment. If it could be bottled, the shop's aroma alone would be worth buying. *52 Old Compton Street, W1D 4PB. Piccadilly Circus, Leicester Square tube.*

WEST END

⑧ Ronnie Scott's

All the jazz greats who have come to London in the past half century have played at Ronnie Scott's, which claims to be the oldest jazz club in the world. The London-born saxophonist opened his first venue in Gerrard Street in 1959 and moved to the current address in Frith Street in 1965. The place had a recording studio and for a while Ronnie Scott's had its own label. The club was never the most elegant nightspot in town, but in 2006, ten years after Scott's death, it had a makeover. Today, intimate as ever, the main venue is plush and dimly lit, with dining tables right up to the stage, and seats lining the side walls as in a theatre. Glasses are now provided for beer. The rooms above, Ronnie's Bar Upstairs, are more informal, with sofa seating.
47 Frith Street, W1D 4HT. Leicester Square, Piccadilly Circus tube.

⑨ Little Italy

Nowhere else in London does coffee taste as it does in Bar Italia, and nowhere feels more Italian. The small Frith Street café has been run by the same family since it was opened by Lou and Caterina Polledri in 1949. Its red stools and Formica bar top are unchanged, and the Gaggia machine is the original. Bar Italia has always supported Italy's sporting heroes, and a picture of the heavyweight boxing champion Rocky

Marciano, who befriended the family, hangs behind the bar. A large screen occupies one end of the room, and the clientele spills on to the street any time the Italian national football team is playing. Bar Italia is open 24 hours a day, and does not sell alcohol.

Soho's Italian community pre-dates the Second World War, and when hostilities broke out, many resident Italians were rounded up and interned. Ennio and Isador Camisa were among them. They ran the family delicatessen, started in Brewer Street in 1929, and their business was confiscated. After the war, they had to work to buy it back. Today, a delivery bike is parked outside the shop in Old Compton Street, and Fratelli Camisa continues to be one of the most authentic delicatessens in town. Its narrow, dark interior, hung about with Parma hams, is redolent of olives, cheese and salami. Stepping inside is like entering a small-town grocer's in Italy, of around the same 1950s period as Bar Italia. This old-fashioned shop is matched by the lighter, brighter Lina Stores nearby, with its basil plants, fresh-filled pasta and sacks of polenta.
Bar Italia, 22 Frith Street, W1D 4RF. Fratelli Camisa, 61 Old Compton Street, W1D 6HS. Lina Stores, 18 Brewer Street, W1F 0SH. Tottenham Court Road, Leicester Square tube.

RONNIE SCOTT'S

10 Maison Bertaux

Cramped pavement tables and blue-striped awning mark this outpost of Paris in Soho. The patisserie, where everything is made on the premises, has been here since M. Bertaux escaped the French capital when it was being disrupted by the Commune in 1871. Michele Ward, the current owner, began working for the last Bertaux when she was 14. The café can be hired, and a small first-floor room is used as an art gallery and occasional performance space.
28 Greek Street, W1D 5DQ. Leicester Square, Piccadilly Circus tube.

11 Soho's Secret Tea Room

A polite English tea, complete with doilies and flowery china, and served by staff wearing waistcoats and aprons while a forties foxtrot plays in the background, is an unlikely enterprise for a pub that for 63 years was run by 'the rudest landlord in London'. The Coach and Horses is now called 'Norman's Coach and Horses' after Norman Balon, who retired in 2006, having written his memoirs entitled *You're Barred, You Bastard*. Such language would be quite out of place in Soho's Secret Tea Room, which is reached via stairs at the back of

the bar. This upstairs room has long been used by staff of magazine *Private Eye* for fortnightly lunches. Like the pub, it has changed little in half a century, and now tea-timers can sip a choice of teas and take their pick from the cake stands while imagining the writer and outrageous alcoholic the late Jeffrey Barnard locked overnight in the bar below – the scenario for Keith Waterhouse's play *Jeffrey Barnard is Unwell*.
29 Greek Street, W1D 5DH. Leicester Square tube.

12 The French House

Customers spill on to the pavement beneath the French flag outside this small Soho institution, which derives its name from Charles de Gaulle and the Free French who patronised it during the Second World War. The place started life in 1910 as a wine house run by a German, who was deported in 1914. It was then taken over by Victor Berlemont, a Belgian, who renamed it York Minster. His son Gaston, famed for his handlebar moustache, was born here, and became as much of an institution as the pub. Under his post-war gaze, artists such as Francis Bacon and Lucian Freud popularised it, while Dylan Thomas once staggered off leaving his only copy of *Under Milk Wood* on the floor. Stories of drunken behaviour are legion. There are few places to sit in the single room, which has a central dark-wood counter with brass fittings. Beer is served by the half pint only, and the pub sells more *pastis* than any other bar in Britain. Gaston may be gone but his regime remains – no mobile phones, no canned music, and no TV or other distractions from intellectual discourse and drunken blether. There is an upstairs restaurant.
49 Dean Street, W1D 5BG. Piccadilly Circus, Leicester Square tube.

13 Milroy's of Soho

Whisky bottles line the walls of Milroy's small shop, which stocks an astonishing 700 labels – some 400 from Scotland. Around 300 are available for tasting. Formerly a wine merchant's, the shop was taken over in 1964 by Scottish brothers' John (Jack) and Wallace Milroy, who became avid promoters of whisky, particularly single malts. Brandy and rum are also on offer, but whisky remains the most popular tipple, some of it from Milroy's own bottling. Today the business is owned by Jeroboams, London's largest independent wine merchant. Whisky evenings and tutorials are organised in the cellar.
3 Greek Street, W1D 4NX. Leicester Square tube.

⑭ Marshall Street Baths

The most beautiful indoor public pool in London reopened in 2010 after 13 years of disuse. Campaigning by locals finally paid off and the 9m (30ft) swimming pool in a Grade II listed leisure centre was restored to much of its 1930s glory. The original Sicilian marble of the pool, and the pale green Swedish marble walls, look glorious beneath the beautiful glazed, barrel-vaulted ceiling. It is a palatial setting. A public wash house stood here from the 1850s, and the later baths included a child welfare centre as well as a public laundry. Stars of aquatic shows trained in the pool, including one-time Tarzan Johnny Weissmuller. A bronze fountain of a child mermaid with dolphins by Walter Gilbert, cousin of Sir Albert Gilbert, who sculpted Piccadilly Circus's Eros, has been preserved, as has the original wooden ticket booth. Owned by Westminster Council, the baths are run by not-for-profit Nuffield Health.
Marshall Street, W1F 7EL. Oxford Circus tube.

⑮ Liberty's

A cross between a rambling country house and a Tudor theatre, Liberty's has creaking plank floors, bottle-glass windows, stone fireplaces, galleried open-timbered top-lit wells and oak staircases. It exudes warmth and care. But the distinctive half-timbered building is just part of the story. It was designed by Edward and Stanley Hall for the storekeeper Arthur Lasenby Liberty, who began by selling imported fabrics from India and Japan at East India House, his shop at 213 Regent Street. The store the Halls built in 1925 was half in Regent Street. The curved neoclassical façade had to be in keeping, so they included a 35m (115ft) frieze, titled 'Britannia and the Wealth of East and West', showing merchandise borne across the world to Britain by camel, elephant and sea, watched by three figures peeking over the roof parapet.

The more familiar building in Great Marlborough Street, which is the present store, used spars, planks and timbers from two obsolete three-deck warships, the 80 gun HMS *Hindustan* and the 121 gun frigate HMS *Impregnable*. Rising to four storeys, the building has a gabled roof with bargeboards and a connecting bridge across Kingly Street to the Regent Street building. Here is installed a colourful clock, by Hope Jones. Four angels represent the four winds, and St George and the Dragon are set to fight on the hour. Liberty's association with the Arts and Crafts movement, which resulted in the Art Nouveau

style in Italy being termed *Stile Liberty*, is still evident in the beautifully made materials and leather goods sold by the store.
Great Marlborough Street, W1B 5AH. Oxford Circus tube.

⑯ Courthouse Hotel

This was formerly the Great Marlborough Street Magistrates' Court, where the great and the good – and the bad – were summoned to account for themselves. John Lennon appeared on a charge of selling sexually explicit lithographs in 1970 (acquitted on a technicality). Mick Jagger and Keith Richards appeared on drugs charges. Oscar Wilde brought a case against the Marquess of Queensberry for criminal libel. Notorious showgirl Christine Keeler was summoned over allegations involving politician John Profumo in the 1960s. The case brought down the government and became a byword for scandal. Way back in 1835, Charles Dickens worked there as a reporter. Now, private tables in the bar occupy old holding cells. The restaurant, Silk, was No 1 Courtroom and the judges' bench, witness stand and dock have been preserved.
19-21 Great Marlborough Street, W1F 7HL. Oxford Circus tube.

⑰ St Barnabas House of Charity

For plasterwork in a domestic setting, the rococo interior of the House of Charity is hard to beat. The Georgian house was built in the 1740s and later acquired by Richard Beckford, uncle of eccentric novelist William Beckford, whose family made their fortune from sugar plantations in Jamaica. Beckford had it for just nine months in 1754, but was responsible for the decoration, notably the attractive first-floor Council Room, which overlooks both Greek Street and Soho Square. As Soho fell out of fashion, the house was used by the Westminster Commission for Works for Sewers, and this is where Sir Joseph Bazalgette began drawing up plans for his great Embankment schemes.

In 1862, the building was taken over by the nearby House of Charity to provide short-term accommodation for the poor. Those staying there were obliged to attend the charity's chapel in Manette Street, accessed through a private garden, where concerts are now occasionally held. Today, the charity offers life skills programmes, and the building, fully restored, is used by a private members' club.
1 Greek Street, Piccadilly Circus tube. Tours on Tuesday and Thursday.

FOR PLASTERWORK,
THE INTERIOR IS
HARD TO BEAT

ST BARNABAS HOUSE OF CHARITY

⑱ The Tottenham

Once known as The Flying Horse, The Tottenham is the only pub on Oxford Street. In the 19th century, there were 37. From the outside it does not look that promising, but the Victorian interior dazzles, with murals, carvings and etched and stained glass. The pub dates from around 1790 and used to cater for theatre-goers attending the nearby Tottenham Street Theatre, which in its day was one of London's finest music halls. The pub's saucy secret is a painting of three buxom ladies by Felix de Jong, a leading decorative artist in music hall.

6 Oxford Street, W1D 1AN. Tottenham Court Road tube.

⑲ Centre Point

Described by the architectural historian Nikolaus Pevsner as 'coarse in the extreme', Centre Point was once seen as an ugly symbol of corporate greed. Now a listed Grade II building, it has gained such respectability that the Royal Fine Arts Commission has referred to it as having 'the elegance of a Wren steeple'. The world's tallest pre-cast concrete structure when it was completed in 1966, it was London's first skyscraper, 36m (117ft) tall.

Centre Point was designed by Richard Seiffert for the property speculator Harry Hyams, who wanted to let out the whole building to a single tenant or nobody. As a result, it stood unoccupied

for more than a dozen years, during which time it was occasionally stormed and taken over by squatters. Shelter, the charity for the homeless, started in the same year that Centre Point opened, and three years later another charity for homeless young people, called Centrepoint, began at St Anne's Church in Soho. HRH Prince William is the charity's patron.

Now, Hyams' building is at the centre of the new Tottenham Court Road rail hub. The Paramount Restaurant occupies the 32nd floor, and the Paramount Bar, with a spectacular 360 degree view, is on the top floor, both open to the public, although visitors must phone or email ahead.
101–103 New Oxford Street, WC1A 1DD. Tottenham Court Road tube.

⑳ Tin Pan Alley

The 12 Bar Club is now the only place to hear regular live performances in Denmark Street, London's Tin Pan Alley. Once a stable and forge, the venue has a tiny stage and is one of the smallest in town. It was opened at No 26 in 1978 as a folk and blues club, by Andy Preston, who had a guitar workshop at No 28. The walls of Denmark Place, the alley beside it, are papered with notices from musicians requiring work and bands wanting players. Every building in this street of music has a story attached to it, some of them recounted in *New Musical Express* and *Melody Maker*, both first published from here.

Agents, publishers and instrument vendors started to inhabit the short street more than a century ago. Rose Morris, 'London's biggest music store', at No 11, began in 1919. In the 1950s songwriters and performers started getting together in the street, and by the 1960s, when studios were set up, it was a centre of the music world. Reg Dwight (better known as Elton John) was an office boy at Mills Music. David Bowie and other mods met at the small Giaconda Restaurant (No 9), which later became a haunt of punks, including the Clash. The Sex Pistols rented a flat at No. 6. The former Regent Sounds Studio (No 4) is where the Rolling Stones recorded their first LP, and were accompanied by record producer Phil Spector tapping a brandy bottle with a half-crown coin on 'Not Fade Away'. Now the Alley Cat bar and club occupy the basement. Tin Pan Alley Studios at No 22 has hosted an A-list of recording stars, including The Beatles, The Kinks, Jimi Hendrix, the Bee Gees and Stevie Wonder.
Denmark Street, WC2H 8NG. Tottenham Court Road tube.

㉑ Phoenix Artist Club

Costume designs, photos, prints, props and a model of the Old Vic are among the many artefacts that make this a nostalgic and engaging basement bar. Fronting Charing Cross Road, the Phoenix is one of the West End's most attractive theatres. Gilbert Scott had a hand in its design, and the interior is by the Russian director and designer Theodore Komisarjevsky, who was responsible for the spectacular Tooting Granada (see page xx). The theatre opened in 1930 with *Private Lives* starring Noel Coward and Gertrude Lawrence, giving Laurence Olivier his West End debut. The generous basement space once accommodated the rehearsal and dressing rooms. The Phoenix has staged a string of musicals in recent years, and soundtracks constantly play in the bar. It is open to all-comers before 8pm, and customers already there are not generally asked to leave after that time; it stays open until 2am. Music, cabaret performances and other events are sometimes arranged by the club's colourful director, Maurice Huggett.
1 Phoenix Street, WC2H OD2, Tottenham Court Road, Leicester Square tube.

㉒ Foyle's

When the Foyle brothers opened their five-storey premises on Charing Cross Road in 1929, it was the biggest bookshop in the world, with 30 miles of shelving. The shop was started by Gilbert and William Foyle, the Barnum & Bailey of the book world. William was a great showman, who sold books by weight at twopence a pound. He set up a Right Book Club in response to Victor Gollancz's Left Book Club. When Hitler ordered the burning of 'unGerman' books in the 1930s, William telegrammed the Fuhrer to suggest that Foyle's buy them instead, and offered to pay a good price. His daughter Christina instigated the lunches that became such an established part of the 1960s and 1970s literary world. The business is still in the same family's hands, and expanding. On sale are many books that are unavailable elsewhere, including second-hand and out-of-print titles. In 2002, Foyle's gave shelter to Ray's Jazz Shop and opened a first-floor jazz café, with a separate entrance and small stage for performances. The CDs and records ended up in Foyle's own music department. Now plans are afoot for Foyle's to move a few doors away, into the buildings vacated by Central St Martin's College of Art and Design, possibly in 2013.
113-19 Charing Cross Road, WC2B 0EB. Tottenham Court Road tube.

WEST END

Great names set in stone

From Inigo Jones to Norman Foster, visionary architects have shaped, styled and reshaped London, and their work stands as an enduring testament to their brilliance and vision.

It could have been so different. If the fire that broke out on the night of September 2, 1666 had not devoured the pitch-covered timbered buildings of the City, London might have continued to grow in an entirely raggle-taggle way. The voracious Great Fire consumed some 13,200 houses and 87 churches. The Tower of London, standing up wind, was saved only by 'the plucking down of houses' in the fire's path.

The flames failed to reach several other important buildings, and among those still standing are St Paul's Church and the Piazza in Covent Garden, the Banqueting House, the Queen's Chapel at St James's Palace, and – across the river – the Queen's House. All are the work of Inigo Jones (1573–1652), known as 'the first English architect'. Born in Smithfield, the son of a Welsh cloth worker, Jones had travelled to Italy, where he developed a passion for the ideals of the Renaissance architect Andrea Palladio. As Surveyor to the King's Works, Jones enjoyed the patronage of James I and Charles I, producing his brilliant, beautiful and costly edifices.

In the wake of the Great Fire, Charles II appointed Christopher Wren (1632–1723) as Surveyor General, to oversee rebuilding. Wren also looked to Rome, having been stirred by the writings of Marcus Vitruvius, an architect from the 1st century BC, and his theory of *venustas* (beauty), which he said could be learnt from 'the truth of nature'. Wren produced a town plan with open spaces ringed by radiating streets on which would stand 87 new churches. It was ambitious, glorious, visionary and completely unaffordable. Wren's office was commissioned to build 51 churches and the grand design was set aside. With Robert Hooke, Wren built the Monument to commemorate the fire, but his own monument is the sublime St Paul's Cathedral, which still dominates the skyline.

Baroque to Gothic

Other famous contributors to the city include Nicholas Hawksmoor (*c.* 1661–1736), who became Deputy Surveyor of Works at Greenwich. The six English baroque churches he designed under Wren, together with the twin towers of Westminster Abbey, are his outstanding legacy. William Chambers (1723–96) built the eccentric Pagoda at Kew Gardens, but his masterpiece was Somerset House, completed after his death by Robert Smirke (1780–1867). A leading exponent of Greek revival architecture, Smirke is best known for the British Museum. The work of Robert Adam (1728–92) can still be seen in the Admiralty Screen by Admiralty House, in Chandos House in Marylebone, in his remodelling of Kenwood House and in the interior of Syon House. What also remains is the influence of 'Adam Style' – a theory of 'movement' in architecture, based on his studies of antiquity. Adam's near contemporary John Nash (1752–1835) is famed for his grand schemes, designed for the Prince Regent (George IV in waiting) and still to be seen in the area of Regent's Park.

A pupil of Nash, Augustus Pugin (1812–52) repudiated classical architecture with its pagan symbolism, arguing that the Gothic style was the only one appropriate for a Christian country. He created the interiors for the Palace of Westminster, working with Charles Barry (1795–1860), and designed the tower in which Big Ben hangs – before descending into madness and dying.

New ideas

The Modern Movement of the 20th century shared Pugin's distaste for the classical. Out went Corinthian columns and acanthus friezes – out, too, Gothic barbs and spikes, portentous entrances with intimidating runs of steps, and all forms of historicism. Modernists, with foreign émigrés Berthold Lubetkin (1901–90) and Erno Goldfinger (1902–87) at the forefront, were on the march.

During the 1960s craze for demolition, high-rise flats and offices went up and fine old buildings came down. London imported a style of architecture known as brutalism, involving poured concrete and geometric shapes. The Royal National Theatre by Denys Lasdun (1914–2001) is among the best-known examples. The city's architecture might at that point seem to have travelled as far as it could from the Palladian aesthetic of Inigo Jones – but the journey is never-ending.

The City skyline today is a fantastical cluster of thrusting structures that clamour for attention. The viewer might feel awed by Lord Foster's Gherkin building at St Mary Axe, the Cheese Grater by his former partner Richard Rogers, the Shard by Renzo Piano and the Pinnacle by Kohn Pederson Fox, but by and by the eye slides westward and comes to rest on Wren's St Paul's, overshadowed but still unsurpassed. As Keats expressed it, paraphrasing Vitruvius, 'beauty is truth, truth beauty'.

FITZROVIA

㉓ The Sanderson's courtyard

Best seen when the magnolia is in bloom, this courtyard at the heart of Ian Schrager's boutique hotel and urban spa provides a magical retreat. Open to the sky, it brims with flowers, and its cleverly placed trees, plashing fountains, mosaics and reflecting pool give it a calm ambience. The courtyard was designed for the original building by Philip Hicks in 1958, and has been classified as a landmark 'Heritage Garden'. Before being converted to a hotel, the building was the headquarters of wallpaper manufacturers Arthur Sanderson. The company marked its centenary by moving there in 1960. The Honfleur, Pemberley, Pompom and Painter's Garden designs that were Sanderson's hallmarks are no longer in evidence, since the hotel's interior was designed by Philippe Starck, who does not use florals.
50 Berners Street, W1T 3NG. Tottenham Court Road, Oxford Circus tube.

㉔ Pollock's Toy Museum

To enter this little museum is like walking into a great, cluttered toy cupboard, which is also, in its way, a museum of childhood, a poignant evocation of generations past and of diverse cultures. Climbing three winding staircases, the visitor is watched by once-beloved wax and china dolls, staring glassy-eyed. Threadbare teddies, imbued with the dust of centuries, sag on shelves. A pervading sense of devotion reflects not only the affection of long-ago children, but of the museum's founder, Marguerite Fawdry.

Benjamin Pollock was a Victorian toy theatre printer in Hoxton, who enjoyed success in the latter part of the 19th and early 20th centuries, when toy theatres were very popular. 'If you love art, folly or the bright eyes of children, speed to Pollock's,' wrote Robert Louis Stevenson in 1887. By the middle of the 20th century, though, times had changed. The shop had been bombed, and the receiver was called in. That was when Marguerite Fawdry arrived and was told her only way of accessing an item for her son's toy theatre was to buy all the stock, which she duly did, displaying it first in a rented attic in Monmouth Street, Covent Garden. Now run by the founder's grandson, the museum and shop has occupied two houses in Fitzrovia since 1969, and is crammed with playthings – Edwardian board games, jack-in-the-boxes, traditional folk toys from around the world, puppets, nursery furniture, clockwork figures, dolls' houses, a Victorian nursery, and an Egyptian clay mouse from around 2000 BC. During school holidays, there are toy theatre performances – perhaps more for adults than for the online and gaming generation.
1 Scala Street, W1T 2HL. Goodge Street tube.

㉕ Heal's

Everything for the house beautiful and house functional is brought together under one roof – and two umbrellas. Ambrose Heal was the Terence Conran of his day. By the time he joined the family firm in 1893, Heal & Son had been in business for 83 years, selling beds and bedroom furniture, which they advertised in the novels of Charles Dickens. But it was Ambrose's genius for Arts and Crafts design that ensured the company became even more successful. Heal's published its first catalogue in 1898, establishing the simple vernacular 'Heal's style', then, in 1917, it moved into the premises that had been purpose built by Heal's friend and cousin Cecil Brewer, and put out the flags.

If Heal's captured the *Zeitgeist* of the early 1900s, it was Terence Conran's Habitat that revolutionised home and high street in the 1960s and 1970s. Conran's Storehouse group bought Heal's in 1984, and now the Heal's chain is owned by Wittington Investment. But Brewer's building, with its sweeping spiral staircases and its façade with blue spandrels depicting the tools of the craftsman's trade, is still the place to come for salad bowls and sofas, beds and bathrobes, mugs and rugs and ravioli trays.
196 Tottenham Court Road, London W1T 7LQ. Goodge Street tube.

㉖ Fitzrovia Mural and Glass Panels

The entire flank of a five-storey building, topped off with a long line of chimneypots, is devoted to what many regard as London's finest mural. This depiction of, and commentary

A POIGNANT EVOCATION OF GENERATIONS PAST

on, local life is more than 18m (60ft) high. It was painted in 1980 by artists Mick Jones and Simon Barber in a style reminiscent of Diego Rivera (1886–1957), the Mexican muralist, in close consultation with the residents of Fitzrovia. A butcher, builders, office workers, nurses and schoolchildren, among others, all crowd into the composition, which shows them at work and at leisure. The skyline represents buildings of the future. Wit and polemic mix in a highly figurative narrative style. The mural has faded over the years, and been defaced with graffiti, and a project to restore it is under way, backed by the London Mural Preservation Society.

Down below in Whitfield Gardens, in 2003, 12 free-standing illuminated glass panels, featuring full-colour artwork and etched glass, were erected in steel frames. Exquisite, intriguing and amusing, they represent the history of the area and the people who have lived there, from artist and satirical cartoonist William Hogarth to singer Boy George. The first three numbered panels are entitled 'Whitfield Gardens and the Reverend Whitfield', 'The Soul Catchers' and 'Hub of the Anti-Slavery Campaign'. The last one is called 'Our Glasses Public Art Club Land'. A 13th panel is an index of the characters portrayed. *Whitfield Gardens, off Tottenham Court Road, W1. Goodge Street tube.*

㉗ Royal Institute of British Architects

In 1834, the Institute of British Architects was founded by a small group of young men concerned by the lack of training within the profession. Its Royal Charter was granted by William IV in 1837, and in 1934 it moved into this handsome Art Deco building, which was officially opened by George V and Queen Mary. A competition to design the Royal Institute of British Architects' (RIBA's) headquarters had been won by George Grey Wornum in 1932, a year after he became the institute's president. The idea of designing a home for architects might have been a daunting one, but Grey Wornum, who had seen active service in the Great War, in which he had lost an eye, rose to the challenge.

Before entering, the visitor should pause and look up to see the two figures that stand on columns flanking the doorway. These are by James Woodford and, together with a third figure, by Bainbridge Copnall and located high on the façade, they represent the spirit of man and woman as creative forces in architecture.

Architects are, of course, not always seen as a force for good. It was at a dinner to celebrate

RIBA's 150th anniversary in 1984 that Prince Charles delivered his famous speech denouncing modern architecture in all its aspects. Instead of raising his glass to the institute, he poured scorn on what it had come to represent, saying of a proposed extension to the National Gallery by Ahrends Burton Korlek that it was 'like a monstrous carbuncle on the face of a much-loved and elegant friend'.

The remark caused much controversy and the carbuncle was never built. The National Gallery remains unblemished, and RIBA's elegant headquarters are entirely friendly to visitors. Mighty bronze doors, embellished with reliefs by Woodford, showing the Thames and some of the capital's most significant buildings, open on to various exhibitions, a library, a bookshop, a restaurant full of air and light with an outside terrace, and a café. *66 Portland Place, W1B 1AD. Regent's Park tube.*

㉘ Broadcasting House

Hailed by the *Architectural Review* as 'the new Tower of London' when it opened in 1932, the home of the BBC featured streamlined contours and a rounded, ship's prow frontage. Designed by George Val Myers and Watson Hart, Britain's first purpose-built broadcasting facility can genuinely claim iconic status – during the worst of the bombing in the Second World War, it stood as a symbol, not just of 'Auntie' (a nickname coined to describe an 'Auntie knows best' attitude), but of national unity. Like RIBA, its near neighbour and contemporary, it is a Portland-stone, Art Deco masterpiece. The statue over the entrance, by Eric Gill, is of Prospero and Ariel from Shakespeare's *The Tempest*. The naked Ariel provoked controversy. Questions were asked in the House of Commons on the affront to public decency. Another work by Gill stands in the reception area. Entitled 'The Sower', it is a metaphor for the broadcaster sowing seeds of ideas, information and entertainment.

In recent years, Broadcasting House has undergone extensive renovation, to be completed in 2013. A glass-fronted extension, connecting the original building to a new east wing, will allow passers-by to see the BBC going about its business, while a central piazza will offer such facilities as a café and performance space. 'Breathing', a glass-and-light sculpture on the new wing, commemorates reporters and crew killed in the line of duty. *Langham Place, London W1A 1AA. Oxford Circus tube.*

MAYFAIR

㉙ Bentley's Oyster Bar and Grill

This long-established oyster bar and seafood restaurant is tucked away in a Victorian building off Piccadilly. When Bentley's first opened in 1916, it must have been for Londoners a symbol of optimism in the dark days of the Second World War. The Bentleys had their own oyster beds in West Mersea, near Colchester, home to an annual oyster festival, and over decades they established a solid reputation as restaurateurs and purveyors of this much-prized mollusc. It is strange to think that in Dickens' time, oysters were food for the poor, a plentiful source of cheap protein, used to bulk out steak pies. In *The Pickwick Papers* Sam Weller remarks that to eat an oyster is an act of 'reg'lar desperation'.

The lauded Richard Corrigan took over for a stint as head chef at Bentley's in the early 1990s, and when the restaurant came up for sale in 2005 he did not hesitate to buy it. The dining rooms, over three floors, have been refurbished without any sacrifice of atmosphere. These days, the oysters are from Maldon and Loch Ryan. Whether in or out of fashion, oysters have long been a part of London history, and the resurgent popularity of the capital's old oyster houses today signals the triumphant return of the native.
11-15 Swallow Street, W1B 4DG. Piccadilly Circus tube.

㉚ Sotheran's

A bibliophile's heaven, this is the oldest antiquarian booksellers in the world, based in handsome premises off Piccadilly. Henry Sotheran set up shop in York in 1761, and the business gained a footing in London in 1815 – the year that 15,000 troops staged a victory parade in Hyde Park to celebrate the defeat of Napoleon. A visitor to this shop, whether passer-by or serious collector, may be lost in wonder for hours, and in the age of the soulless e-book reader and instant gratification, be reminded that a book can be a work of art, a labour of love, something to cherish and possess. Finds to browse may include Charles Kingsley's *The Water Babies* from 1915, with illustrations by William Heath Robinson, a Kate Greenaway *Mother Goose* from 1881, a volume of Hans Andersen tales illustrated by Arthur Rackham, Sir Richard Burton on Zanzibar – or Captain Hugh Clapperton's *Journal of a Second Expedition into the Interior of Africa, from the Bight of Benin to Socatoo* (1829). Classic children's literature forms the bulk of the stock, which ranges from architecture, travel and exploration to natural history (especially birds) and science. Although not all the books are antique, or expensive, being transported back in time through the written word is an absorbing occupation, illustrating how very much the world has changed.
2–5 Sackville Street, W1S 3DP. Piccadilly Circus tube.

㉛ Royal Institution Museum

Science has been the *raison d'être* of this learned institution since 1799, and in the museum, scientific progress, and the human stories of the men and women driving it, can be explored. Science begins with people fired by what American psychologist and philosopher John Dewey called 'audacity of imagination', and the ground floor is devoted to leading lights of the institution's history. Foremost among these is Michael Faraday, the 19th-century chemist and physicist, or 'natural philosopher', a former bookbinder's apprentice, who is regarded as one of the most influential scientists and best experimentalists in the history of science. Also featured is Faraday's boss, the 'arrogant yet charismatic' Humphry Davy, inventor of the eponymous safety lamp that saved the lives of countless miners; and Ada Byron, Countess of Lovelace, product of the brief marriage between the romantic poet and Isabelle Milbanke. Ada was an 'enchantress of numbers' and muse to Charles Babbage, father of the modern computer.

Downstairs, Faraday's laboratory, where he worked on his theories of electromagnetism, is preserved as it was in the 1850s – standing in contrast to the nanotechnology lab. Upstairs, displays recall some of the greatest events to have happened at the Royal Institute and the greatest scientists to have appeared in its lecture theatre over 200 years.
21 Albemarle Street, W1S 4BS. Piccadilly Circus tube. Admission free.

㉜ Albany

Britain's most exclusive apartment block has been home to many famous – and some infamous – residents since the 18th century. It was built as a Palladian mansion for Lord Melbourne by Sir William Chambers, in 1771–4, before Chambers embarked on Somerset House. Not 20 years later, on Christmas Day 1791, Melbourne House, as it was then called, passed into the hands of Frederick, Duke of York and Albany, in exchange for his leasehold house in Whitehall – Lord and Lady Melbourne having wildly overspent. The Duke was scarcely less extravagant, and within ten years turned

Albany House, as it had been renamed, over for development. Behind the mansion, in the former garden, two blocks of chambers were built by Henry Holland in 1802–3, the development providing 'elegant and convenient Sets of independent Freehold Apartments'. To exclude 'improper inhabitants', there would be no letting or sale of sets without general consent, and no profession or trade was to be conducted from within. The premises were to be called 'Albany' since 'The Albany' suggested a public house.

Then, as now, the sets, as they are still called, were intended only for men of wealth and standing – but at least one 'improper inhabitant' sidestepped the rules. In 1815, Lord Byron smuggled in his mistress, Lady Caroline Lamb, in the guise of a pageboy. What can be seen by the curious passer-by is not just an important Parisian-style building but, from time to time, the starry and distinguished people who dwell at this most sought-after address.

Albany, W1J 0AS. Piccadilly Circus tube.

㉝ Royal Academy of Arts

The Royal Academy of Arts was founded in 1768 by George III, described as 'an enthusiastic if undiscriminating patron of the arts'. Founding members included artist Sir Joshua Reynolds and architect Sir William Chambers, who designed Somerset House and, through his friendship with the king, gained permission for the new learned academy to occupy seven of the state apartments in that building. Reynolds became the academy's first president and laid down in his *Discourses* the conception of the Academy as a body of professionals that, 'besides furnishing able men to direct students', would form 'a repository for the great examples of the Art'.

The Royal Academy's first show, in 1769, was attended by Dr Johnson, who recorded: 'The Exhibition is eminently splendid.' Thus was established the RA's unbroken tradition of the Summer Exhibition, which today attracts some 10,000 works for selection by Academicians.

In 1836, the RA moved to what is now the National Gallery, then in 1867 to its splendid present home, built by Sir John Denham in 1664–5 and since extended and remodelled. Members of the Academy are all practising painters, sculptors, engravers, printmakers, draughtsmen and architects, elected by their peers. Past Academicians have included John Constable, Thomas Gainsborough and J.M.W. Turner, and current members include David Hockney, Tracey Emin, Antony Gormley, Anish Kapoor and the architects Norman Foster and Richard Rogers. The collection is largely devoted to British art and artists, with major works by Reynolds, Gainsborough, Turner, Constable, Alma-Tadema, Millais, Sargent, Spencer and Hockney. A permanent exhibition of architectural drawings and models donated by Academicians is displayed in the John Madejski Fine Rooms, the glittering former state rooms of Burlington House.

Burlington House, W1J 0BD. Green Park, Piccadilly Circus tube.

Summer Exhibition

ROYAL ACADEMY OF ARTS

BURLINGTON ARCADE

㉞ K2 Telephone Box

At the entrance to Burlington House, in the shelter of the arch, stands a red kiosk that may be familiar to older Londoners. This is Giles Gilbert Scott's original wooden prototype K2 telephone box, dating from 1924. In the days before numerical dialling codes, London telephone exchanges rejoiced in such names as Fountain (Streatham) and Frobisher (Earl's Court), Primrose (St John's Wood), Ambassador (Paddington), Empress (West Kensington), Avenue (City of London) and Grosvenor (Mayfair).

The K2 was one of four competing designs set up across London, and Gilbert Scott based it on Sir John Soane's tomb in the graveyard in St Pancras Old Church. He originally suggested that his box, with its classical overarching style, should be made of silver-coloured steel, but the Post Office overruled him and rolled them out in bright red cast iron. Only 1,500 K2s were made, all sited in London. Scott's more economical K3, made of reinforced concrete, cost half as much to manufacture, and was painted cream, which was deemed more suitable for the rural settings in which it would be located. A K6 model was designed to commemorate the Silver Jubilee of George V in 1935. British Telecom began to phase out red boxes in 1987, but Westminster Council reintroduced them to the streets of Central London, where they provide many a photo opportunity for visitors from abroad, although iPhones and BlackBerries mean they are of little practical use.
Burlington House, W1J 0BD. Green Park, Piccadilly Circus tube.

㉟ Burlington Arcade

Britain's first shopping arcade, and one of the most beautiful, has never ceased to impress. Commissioned by Lord Cavendish, who lived in Burlington House, this architectural masterpiece opened in March 1819, to provide a new shopping experience 'for the gratification of the public, and to give employment to industrious females'. It accommodated 47 leaseholders, and while a mere six of them were industrious females, according to the custom of the time, even male purveyors of fine hats and whalebone corsets were addressed as 'Madame'. The elegant little thoroughfare connecting Burlington Gardens to Piccadilly was policed by Beadles, who sat in armchairs at either end, rang hand bells at closing time, and stepped in when anyone broke the rules against whistling, singing, riding bicycles, opening umbrellas, carrying large parcels and discarding oyster shells in this hallowed precinct. Even today, the atmosphere is rarefied and the specialist shops expensive, strong on craftsmanship and service. Anyone in need of a Fabergé egg, a vintage Rolex, handmade shoes or a silver tea service need look no further. Piccadilly Arcade, an extension linking Piccadilly and Jermyn Street, dates from 1909 and is lined with 28 bow-fronted shops. A statue of Beau Brummell commemorates the arch dandy and arbiter of style in Regency London, who claimed to spend 5 hours dressing, and proposed cleaning one's shoes with champagne.
Burlington Arcade, W1J. Piccadilly Circus, Green Park tube.

㊱ Royal Arcade

Another fine example of a 19th-century shopping mall, this neo-Gothic High Victorian arcade dates from 1879 and is topped with an attractive glass roof. It connects Old Bond Street and Albemarle Street, and its elegant shops, separated by arches, sell luxury chocolates, cashmere sweaters, hunting jackets, flowers and heraldic stationery. Originally known as 'The Arcade', the mall received royal patronage when Queen Victoria chose H. W. Brettel's, still at No 12, to supply her riding skirts and undervests.
Royal Arcade, W1S, Green Park tube.

㊲ Geo. F. Trumper

In London's finest traditional barbers, customers are assured of privacy. Adjacent shaving booths have velvet curtains so gentlemen may sit with their heads swathed in hot towels in perfect seclusion. George Trumper established his gentleman's barbers and perfumers on Curzon Street in the late 19th century – a time when it was rare for men to shave themselves. The gentleman had his valet, his 'gentleman's gentleman'; the working man had his 'penny barber', and for the man about town there was Trumper, at his service.

James Bond's creator, Ian Fleming, knew this old shop with its original mahogany fittings and glass display cases; he was one of those members of the intelligence services who must have appreciated Trumper's discretion when he worked at MI5, which, at the time, was based on this street. As well as the dying art of the wet shave, services on offer include hair cutting and tinting, and moustache and beard trims; and a shaving school offers one-to-one tuition from a barber of long experience. Trumper's also sell its own range of soaps, colognes and 'grooming requisites'.
9 Curzon Street, W1J 5HQ. Green Park tube.

WEST END

㊳ Handel House Museum

This house was the home of George Frideric Handel, the great baroque composer, from 1723 until his death in 1759. St James's Palace, where Handel was 'Composer of Musick of His Majesty's Chappel Royal', appointed by George II, was a short stroll from his doorstep; and the King's Theatre, Haymarket, the focus of his opera career, was not far. As a composer, Handel has been described as 'a magnificent opportunist', and so it seems he was in life. As well as living, working and composing on the premises, he did business from it, and subscribers could collect scores 'from the Author in his House in Brook-Street, Hanover Square'.

On Handel's death, his servant John du Burk succeeded to the tenancy and bought his master's goods and chattels for £48. The building has since undergone alteration, but the interior is furnished faithfully in the Georgian style that Handel would have known, and prints and paintings from the Handel House collection are exhibited. There are regular recitals.

Balthasar Denner's portrait of Handel hangs in the National Portrait Gallery, and the composer's harpsichord is in the V&A. The largest collection of Handel memorabilia is in the Foundling Museum (see page 48).

In the adjoining house in Brook Street, No 23, a selection of manuscripts and printed scores is also on display. This is where rock musician Jimi Hendrix lived with his English girlfriend Kathy Etchingham from 1968 until his untimely death two years later.
25 Brook Street, W1K 4HB. Bond Street tube.

㊴ Claridge's

'Not that I intend to die,' the late Spencer Tracy once declared, 'but when I do, I don't want to go to Heaven. I want to go to Claridge's.' Since the ghost of that craggy old Hollywood actor has yet to be reported, fans must hope he has settled for the next best thing. In the 1950s, Mrs Spencer Tracy, Katharine Hepburn, made her exits and her entrances via the staff door rather than conform to the dress rule that barred women in trousers from the foyer. There can be no more self-regarding hotel in London than this Art Deco treasure, and with reason.

The Claridge's story began in the early 1800s with a small hotel on Brook Street, run by William and Marianne Claridge. In 1854, they took over the five adjacent houses that together were the Mivart, and ran it as 'Claridge's, late Mivart's' until 1856. In 1893, since his electrically lit Savoy Hotel was such a brilliant success, and Gilbert & Sullivan revenues were increasing, Richard d'Oyly Carte decided it was time for an encore. He took over Claridge's and commissioned C. W. Stephens, designer of Harrods, to rebuild it.

The new hotel opened in 1898, and in the 1920s Basil Ionides, a pioneer of Art Deco who had worked at the Savoy, was brought in to redesign the restaurant. In 1929, Oswald Milne designed a new main entrance, and a façade of Roman stone and a mirrored foyer in the jazz moderne style were incorporated. Centrepiece of the present foyer, made over in modern Art Deco style by the New York designer Thierry Despont, is a chandelier by Dale Chihuly, an artist specialising in glass.

A cream tea in Claridge's Reading Room is an exercise in pure decadence.
Brook Street, W1K 4HR. Bond Street tube.

㊵ Brown Hart Gardens

In 1888, communal gardens were laid down in Duke Street for the benefit of residents of surrounding flats, but in 1902 the Duke of Westminster leased the land to the Westminster Electricity Supply Company to build a substation. London streets had been lit by gas, but electricity was the coming thing, and it had to be generated somewhere, somehow. The gardens – an important public amenity or the haunt of 'disorderly boys', 'verminous women' and 'tramps' – were closed, and the furniture, fountain and shelter distributed around other sites. By 1905, the fine substation, built in the baroque style from Portland stone by Charles Stanley Peach, stood on the site. It had a kiosk and steps up at either end, a balustrade around it, and Diocletian windows to light the engine-room galleries. On its roof was a new, paved garden, with trees in tubs.

The word 'gardens' today might mislead the visitor; this is not one of London's green spaces, but a raised terrace open to the public, a place of recreation and entertainment, where children play, workers eat their lunchtime sandwiches, and free concerts and open-air theatre are staged. Disorderly boys are not welcome; this is perhaps the only place in the city where quarrelling is forbidden by law.

The flats for which the original Duke Street Gardens had been planted were built on the site of two 18th-century streets of small houses, Brown Street and Hart Street, which had been cleared to make way for them; hence the current name of the gardens.
Brown Hart Gardens, Duke Street, W1K. Bond Street tube.

MARYLEBONE

41 The British Dental Association Museum

This quaint collection began in 1919, when Lilian Lindsay, the first female in Britain to qualify as a dentist, gave the Association a cache of dental equipment, which she had stored in her bedroom. Since then, the number of exhibits has grown to around 30,000, including dental instruments and equipment, photographs, archives and works of art. On display are walrus-tusk dentures, 19th-century floss, toothache cures, some wicked-looking dentist's chairs, a clockwork drill, extraction keys and forceps, and an electromagnetic dental mallet to set the teeth on edge. A lovely oil painting of Lilian Lindsay dates from 1959. Less enchanting is a mezzotint, 'Ludicrous Operator or Blacksmith Turn'd Tooth Drawer', which shows the extraction of an 18th-century peasant's last remaining tooth by a typical quack of the day. A gripping, at times hilarious, archive of dental-health films includes *Oral Surgery Part 2* (1948) – not for the squeamish.
64 Wimpole Street, W1G 8YS. Regent's Park, Bond Street tube. Tuesday and Thursday 1–4pm, and by appointment.

42 Wallace Collection

In leafy Manchester Square stands a grand private house, where the visitor can walk through room after room filled with art treasures. In 1882 the house was altered by its new owner, the Francophile philanthropist Sir Richard Wallace, whose true parentage was a matter of speculation, but who was nonetheless favoured and received a lavish inheritance. Living in Paris, Wallace had amassed a magnificent collection of paintings, armour, furniture and *objets d'art*. He married, in 1871, a French officer's daughter, to whom he left his collection on his death in 1890. She, in turn, bequeathed the house and the Wallace Collection to the British nation.

Visitors can enjoy this largesse without charge. In 25 galleries, sumptuous displays of French 18th-century paintings may be seen, together with Old Masters, miniatures, suits of armour, gold boxes, Sèvres porcelain, French furniture, clocks and ornaments. Works by Titian, Rembrandt, Velázquez, Canaletto and Gainsborough are on show. Frans Hals' 'Laughing Cavalier' is here, and Poussin's 'A Dance to the Music of Time' and Fragonard's exuberant 'The Swing'. A brasserie is open in the lovely setting of the Sculpture Garden.
Hertford House, Manchester Square, W1U 3BN. Bond Street tube.

43 Daunt Books

Natural light slants through roof glass upon a handsome oak-galleried Edwardian interior filled with fresh flowers, William Morris prints and smiling, passionately engaged staff. Daunt Books feels as if it might have put down roots here a century ago, but it was started in the 1980s by James Daunt, a former investment banker at J.P. Morgan, who wanted to combine his twin passions for reading and travel. In Daunt Books for Travellers (as it then was), the first of a small London chain, the browser would find an eclectic selection of titles, since Daunt would stock only those books that he would like to own himself, on the principle that 'there are far too many bad books'. Today, customers don't come for discount bargains, but for quality, time out and intelligent, responsive service.
83 Marylebone High Street, W1U 4QW. Baker Street, Bond Street tube.

44 Royal Academy of Music

The world-renowned Academy trains almost 700 students from more than 50 countries and welcomes the public through its doors. The ethos is warm and friendly, and the facilities are wonderful. Masterclasses and frequent free concerts are held in the three concert halls, including the 450-seat Duke Hall. The museum houses the Academy's collection of priceless instruments, busts and batons, paintings, manuscripts and memorabilia. During term time, craftsmen in the piano and stringed-instrument workshops can be seen in action, regular exhibitions are staged, and daily demonstrations given on historic pianos. Past students include Arthur Sullivan, Henry Wood, Simon Rattle, Elton John, Annie Lennox and Katherine Jenkins.
Marylebone Road, NW1 5HT. Regent's Park, Baker Street tube.

45 Cabbages and Frocks Market

Refreshingly free from the worthy ethos of the average farmers' market, this fun Saturday event mixes food, designer and vintage clothing, fresh produce, cottage industries and crafts. Foodies go for cup cakes and cappuccino, Japanese snacks, artisan breads, olives and oils, hog roast, *crêpes*, *galettes* and Bedouin fare. The market enjoys a particularly pleasant setting, at the north end of Marylebone High Street, in the grounds of St Marylebone Parish Church.
Marylebone Road, NW1 5LT. Baker Street, Regent's Park tube. Saturday 11am–5pm.

Westminster & St James's

The seat of government established next to the home of royalty ensures that British pageantry at its finest is on show. Green spaces are peaceful, but liveliness rules a stone's throw away, where other notable institutions surround the hub of Trafalgar Square.

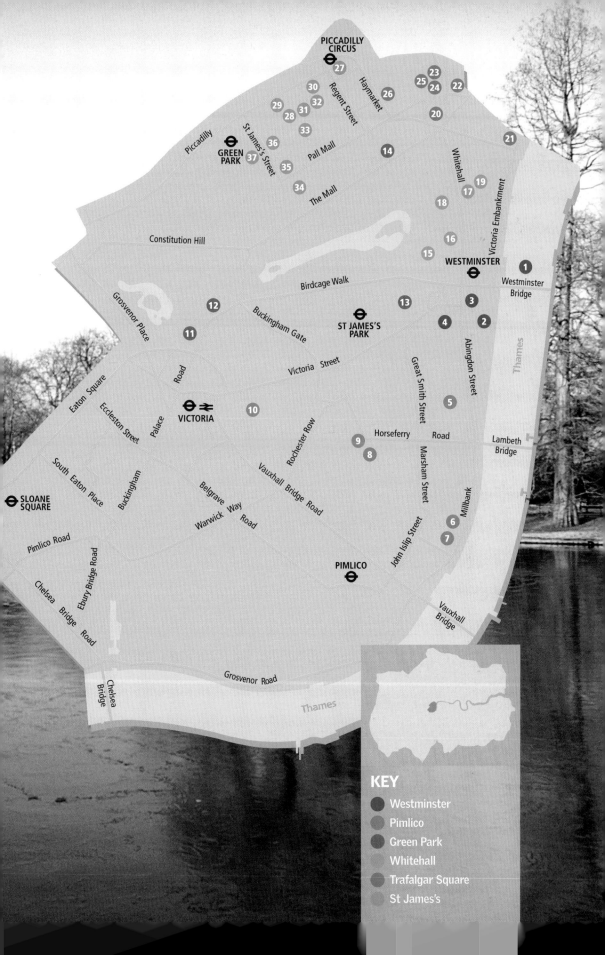

PICCADILLY
CIRCUS

27

23
25
24
22

30
26

29
32
31
28
20

33

21

36
GREEN
PARK
37
Piccadilly
St James's Street
35
Pall Mall
14
Whitehall
19
17
18

34
The Mall
16
15
WESTMINSTER
1
Westminster
Bridge

Constitution Hill

Birdcage Walk

Victoria Embankment

Thames

12
13
3

11
Buckingham Gate
ST JAMES'S
PARK
4
2

Grosvenor Place

Road
Victoria Street
5

Abingdon Street

Eaton Square
VICTORIA
10
Great Smith Street

Eccleston Street
Palace
Rochester Row
9
Horseferry
Road
Lambeth
Bridge

South Eaton Place
8

SLOANE
SQUARE
Buckingham
Belgrave
Vauxhall Bridge Road
Marsham Street

Warwick Way
Road
6

Pimlico Road
7

Ebury Bridge Road
John Islip Street
Millbank

Chelsea Bridge Road
PIMLICO
Vauxhall
Bridge

Grosvenor Road

Chelsea
Bridge
Thames

KEY
Westminster
Pimlico
Green Park
Whitehall
Trafalgar Square
St James's

WESTMINSTER

1 Westminster Bridge

'Earth hath not anything to show more fair: Dull would he be of soul who could pass by A sight so touching in its majesty.'
The bridge itself may be unremarkable, but Wordsworth's early morning prospect of the river remains one of the best views in the city. Until it was unveiled with a huge hullaballoo in 1750, the only other crossing of the Thames in the capital was London Bridge, and such was the nation's pride in the new bridge that it was decreed that anyone found defacing it would be executed without benefit of clergy. The bridge opened up the whole of rural south London for pleasure and urban expansion. Over it went William Blake as a young boy, out for a day of angel-spotting among pastureland and the Surrey Hills, and over it went all the institutions London was keen to be rid of – hospitals, workhouses, orphanages. The bridge was rebuilt in 1862 with Gothic input from Charles Barry, architect of the Houses of Parliament. *SW1J 2JH. Westminster tube.*

2 Houses of Parliament

The interior of the Palace of Westminster is in a time warp, locked in the preoccupations of parliament at the time of its rebuilding between 1837 and 1860, when the Gothic revival style looked back to the days of chivalrous knights. The most overblown of Augustus Pugin's high Gothic is the Queen's Robing Room, which she uses just once a year for the State Opening of Parliament. Gilt drips from the ceiling and paintings of Arthurian legends by William Dyce

WESTMINSTER BRIDGE

decorate the walls. In the Royal Gallery, frescoes of Waterloo and Trafalgar by Daniel Naclise, each 13.7m (45ft) long, confirm Britain's triumphant position in the world, although their colours are fading. Another triumph recalled is the defeat of the Spanish Armada, and in 2007 five panels depicting the encounter, each 3.6 x 4.3m (12 x 14ft), were placed high in the Prince's Chamber. Painted by Anthony Oakshett, they are copies of tapestries that were lost in the fire of 1834, which destroyed all but the Hall of the Palace.

The Palace of Westminster is bookended with two towers. The Victoria Tower with the Lords' entrance is on the south side and was the tallest building in the country when it was erected as part of Sir Charles Barry's rebuilding following the fire. At the other end, by Westminster Bridge, is the Clock Tower, where the 13.5 tonne Big Ben bell strikes the hour.

Houses of Parliament, SW1A 0AA. Westminster tube. UK citizens can write to their MP for a tour of parliament; overseas visitors are restricted to tours on Saturdays. Anyone can queue for a seat in the Strangers' Gallery in the House of Commons.

❸ Westminster Hall

'Save, oh save the Hall!' The chant came from the crowd as fire raged through the Palace of Westminster on the night of October 16, 1834; and all effort was directed at keeping the flames from the most ancient and best-loved part of the Palace. The largest hall in Europe was built for William II, son of the Conqueror, in 1099. Over the years the Hall served many purposes. Parliament sat here for a while, and this was where the treason trials of Charles I, Guy Fawkes and Thomas More were held. The head of Oliver Cromwell, who had led the parliamentary forces against the king, was impaled on a spike above the Hall. After the restoration of the monarchy, his body had been exhumed from Westminster Abbey and posthumously hanged before being decapitated. In 1894, the 300th anniversary of his birth, a statue of Cromwell by Hamo Thorneycroft was erected in front of the House of Commons. His head is bowed in order, it is said, to avoid looking at Charles I, whose bust is in a niche on St Margaret's church opposite.

Today Westminster Hall is the starting point of any tour of parliament, and visitors are likely also to be given free entry to the Jewel Tower on the far side of Westminster Abbey, which was the only other building from the Palace of Westminster to survive the fire.

Houses of Parliament, SW1A 0AA. Westminster tube.

❹ Westminster Abbey

Appropriately enough, the place where England's monarchs are crowned is also London's crowning glory. A beautiful abbey church, French influenced, its flying buttresses support its Gothic elegance around a nave taller by far than any other in the country. It brims with memories of the great and good. Statesmen, scientists and literary figures rest here, including Charles Darwin, Isaac Newton, Geoffrey Chaucer and Ben Jonson – buried upright in the nave – and a special corner is reserved for poets. Edward the Confessor, who founded the Abbey in 1065, was the first to be buried here. His magnificent tomb stands behind the high altar, and his coronation chair is still used today. George II was the last monarch to be interred here, in 1760, and authority still radiates from the marble effigies, particularly from Elizabeth I.

The medieval tiled floor of the Chapter House, which has images of animals, musicians and the Westminster salmon, a tithe claimed from Thames fishermen, is exceptionally well preserved. This is where the Abbey's monks met each day to read chapters from the Rules of St Benedict and conduct their business. The Undercroft Museum contains funerary wax effigies and other curiosities, although its highlight may not be obvious at first. Badly damaged by time, the Westminster Retable measures 1 x 3.5m (3 x 11ft) and is divided into five panels. It is thought to have been the main altarpiece of the Abbey, and it dates from around 1260, making it the oldest surviving altarpiece in Britain.

The architectural apogee of Westminster Abbey is the Lady Chapel behind the altar. Created for Henry VII and begun in 1503, it is described by the Abbey as 'the last great masterpiece of medieval English architecture'. The ceiling is the high spot in every way: beautiful fan vaulting cascades down around carved pendants, and seems to float on air, although the stones must weigh many tonnes. Who its creators were, nobody is sure. Around the wall are statues of 95 saints. The king is buried behind the altar with his queen, Elizabeth of York; their gilt bronze effigies are by the Florentine sculptor Pietro Torrigiano. Above the oak stalls and carved misericords hang the flags of the Order of the Bath, which have been here since 1725. The Royal Airforce Chapel is at the east end. Looking back through the church from the Lady Chapel is to journey through hundreds of years of English architecture.

Broad Sanctuary, SW1P 3PA. Westminster tube. Monday–Saturday; Sunday services only.

WESTMINSTER & ST JAMES'S

PIMLICO

❺ St John's, Smith Square

Music is the glory of this English baroque masterpiece in Westminster's political heartland. Its wonderful acoustics and airy space attract musicians from all over the world. The architect was Thomas Archer and an apocryphal tale is told that when he asked Queen Anne how she would like the church designed, she kicked over a footstool and said, 'Like that!' He put towers at each corner, like the upturned piece of furniture, and it became known as 'Queen Anne's footstool'. It was rebuilt to be used as a concert hall after being gutted by an incendiary bomb in the Second World War and Sir Hugh Casson subsequently described it as being 'as cool and evocative as the inside of a seashell'. The Smith Square Bar and Restaurant, open at lunchtimes and for concert evenings, is in the brick-built crypt where photographs show the wartime damage.
Smith Square, SW1P 3HA. Westminster tube.

❻ Clore Gallery

A whole wing of the Tate Gallery was built for Britain's great landscape painter James Mallord William Turner. The Covent Garden-born artist left all his works to the nation on his death in 1851, and after being housed in the National Gallery, the collection was moved to the Tate, although it was not until the 1980s that proper space was made for it in a new wing. The design by James Sterling was controversial. The chairman of the Turner Society called it 'diabolical and dire' and the art critic Gavin Stamp wrote: 'I have a strong impression that an architect is showing off at the expense of England's greatest painter.' Once inside the gallery, however, the debate is soon forgotten as it fulfils its function to display some of the 300 oil paintings, 30,000 sketches and watercolours and 300 sketchbooks that made up the Turner Bequest. The only missing elements are the nudes and pornographic works, which were destroyed by John Ruskin on Turner's death.

Turner's techniques are explored in an upper gallery, where his heavily annotated copy of Goethe's *Theory of Colour* is part of an exhibition about his working methods. A wooden copying desk, with eight of his drawings in gold frames and sheets of blank paper, is just like the one that students at the National Gallery used to sit at to copy his work, in the same way that Turner had to learn his art by copying the masters. Visitors are encouraged to pick up a pencil and, with helpful tips, start sketching.
Millbank, SW1P 4RG. Pimlico tube.

❼ Tate Britain

The most comprehensive collection of British art, from 1500 to the present, occupies a saccharine-white building, appropriate to its benefactor, Sir Henry Tate, who became rich after inventing a machine to cut sugar into cubes. Built on the site of Millbank prison, it has a Greek temple portico crowned with a statue of Britannia. Tate was a collector of paintings, many by the Pre-Raphaelites, and his initial donation of 65 works included *Ophelia* by John Millais, whose statue has subsequently been relegated to the back of the building, and J. W. Waterhouse's *The Lady of Shallott,* which continues to be the gallery's best-selling postcard. The spacious sculpture gallery, paid for by art dealer Joseph Duveen and opened in 1937, has changing exhibitions. Works contending for the annual Tate Prize are put on show in Tate Britain.

In the basement, a delightfully fanciful mural by Rex Whistler, *The Expedition in Pursuit of Rare Meats,* decorates the restaurant. When the mural was unveiled in 1927, the place was described as 'the most amusing room in Europe'.
Millbank, SW1P 4RG. Pimlico tube.

❽ Regency Café

There is nothing Regency about this old-fashioned café, with its tiled walls, gingham curtains, Formica tables and deco exterior – but then, it takes its name from the quiet, residential backstreet on which it stands, not from its architecture. It opened in 1946 and has been a favourite for the Great British Breakfast ever since. The walls are hung with framed photos of boxers and footballers; the menu is chalked up on blackboards. Orders are taken at the counter and customers find a table and wait for the call of 'Two fried eggs, tomatoes and bubble' (bubble-and-squeak: potato and cabbage mashed together and fried), or 'Sausage, egg, bacon, two toasts', boomed out by the man behind the till. 'This is probably the best old-style café in London,' is the judgement of no less an authority than Michel Roux, the owner and head chef of Michelin-starred Le Gavroche, 'serving the perfect mug of tea, real brewed coffee, a good bacon sarnie, with a choice of breads, and service with a smile.' Such is his admiration for the Regency that he brought eight hopeful trainees here to do a hand's turn for an episode of his television programme *Michel Roux's Service*. One of London's oldest greasy spoons is also one of London's finest.
17–19 Regency Street, SW1P 4BY. Pimlico tube.

9 The London Scottish Regimental Museum

'A soldier is a man hunter. As a deer stalker chooses the least visible of colours, so ought a soldier to be clad.' So said Lord Elcho, Earl of Wemyss and March, the founder of the London Scottish Regiment, who decreed that their uniform should be Hodden Grey. This homespun, undyed Scottish cloth would ensure no clan loyalties were served by the regiment, which was raised in 1859. Today they wear regular combat uniforms, with Tam o'Shanters, and are kilted only on special occasions. The whole colourful history of the regiment is laid out in this exceptional drill hall where the Pipes and Drums meet for practice every Thursday evening. The hall has memorials from the Boer War and the two world wars, and rises to two galleries, where there are exhibits from the Regimental Museum. To maintain drill space on the ground floor, the galleries have no supporting pillars but are suspended from arched cast-iron booms. Among those to have served in the regiment were Ronald Coleman, Alexander Fleming, Kenneth Grahame, Eric Newby and Victor Silvester. The museum is open on three days a week, but because the building belongs to the Ministry of Defence, visits must be made by appointment. *95 Horseferry Road. St James's Park tube.*

10 Westminster Cathedral

A magnificent church and art-house, Westminster Cathedral rises like a vision of the East between the commercial glass blocks of Victoria Street. The Neo-Byzantine building was designed by John Francis Bentley in red brick banded with white Portland stone. The 82m (270ft) campanile is reached by a lift and topped with a cross containing a relic of what is believed to be the true cross. It has a single bell, named Edward, after Edward the Confessor to whom the tower is dedicated. The bell was a gift from the Duchess of Norfolk, a member of England's premier Catholic family, and the cathedral represents the re-establishment of the Catholic church in England 300 years after the Reformation. More than 120 varieties of marble from all over Europe have been used in the interior, and it is radiant with mosaics that dance in the light. These were added after the cathedral's completion in 1903 when Sir Edward Elgar conducted the oratorio of *Dreams of Gerontius*, to which he had set the poem by Cardinal Newman. The cathedral took just seven years to build, and the decoration has been added to ever since. Most notable are the 14 stations of the cross by Eric Gill, early work he made between 1913 and 1918, not long after converting to Catholicism. *Morpeth Terrace, SW1P 1EP. Victoria tube.*

ROYAL MEWS

GREEN PARK

⓫ Royal Mews

The palatial quarters of the royal horses, a fairytale golden coach and the royal fleet of streamlined cars can all be seen here. One of the finest working stables in the world lies behind a giant entranceway flanked by Roman columns and topped with a clock. Within, the Riding House dates from 1760 – 60 years before the mews itself was built by John Nash. A pedimental carving, 'Hercules Capturing the Thracian Horses', was added in 1859 by William Theed. Also known as the 'The Mares of Diomedes', the four horses – The Fast, The Shining, The Blonde and The Terrible – were vicious and untamable, their madness attributable to being fed on human flesh. The horses in the mews have, by contrast, impeccable manners, thanks to a more suitable diet. These magnificent Cleveland Bays and Windsor Greys can be seen out and about being exercised in Hyde Park, and pulling the brougham that delivers mail from Buckingham Palace to St James's Palace. They swing by St James's Palace, pulling a covered brake, to collect the Yeomen of the Guard for investitures at the palace, and turn out for such pageants as the Trooping the Colour. The horses are a great attraction, but there is more for the visitor to see, including the miniature carriages designed for Queen Victoria's children, among them the Prince of Wales and future Edward VII, the first member of 'the firm' to ride in a motorcar – a Daimler belonging to Lord Montague.

13 Buckingham Palace Road, SW1W 1QH. Victoria, Green Park, Hyde Park Corner tube. Closed at certain times during the year.

THE HORSES HAVE IMPECCABLE MANNERS
ROYAL MEWS

⑫ The Queen's Gallery

Paintings by Rembrandt, da Vinci, Canaletto, Van Dyck and Stubbs, Fabergé eggs, Sèvres porcelain, exquisite miniatures, chinoiserie, armour, fans, clocks, silver sculptures … here are just some of the treasures amassed by kings and queens over more than five centuries, and on display to the public in regularly changing exhibitions. The gallery, on the southwest front of Buckingham Palace, began life as a chapel designed by John Nash, and has been developed from its bombed-out shell. It opened in 1962 to display part of the Royal Collection – works owned by the Queen 'in trust' for the nation – and by the time it closed for remodelling in 1999 it had received some 5 million visitors. In the largest building project at the palace since the great ballroom was created for Queen Victoria in the 1830s, architects John Simpson & Partners added a Doric entrance portico and a new complex of rooms, providing almost four times the gallery space. It was opened by the Queen in May 2002 to coincide with her Golden Jubilee, and in 2004 won the Best Modern Classical Building Award from the Georgian Group.
Buckingham Palace, SW1A 1AA. Victoria, Green Park, Hyde Park Corner tube.

⑬ Methodist Central Hall, Westminster

The view of the Houses of Parliament and Westminster Abbey from the dome of Central Hall is a highlight of the free tour offered at the Methodists' principal building. The fact that it is marginally taller than the Abbey was a contentious issue when the hall was opened in 1912. Funding for the building was started in order to celebrate the centenary of the death of John Wesley, the founder of Methodism, and congregations were asked to contribute a guinea (£1.05p) each towards the Million Guinea Fund. No religious artefacts decorate the building, which was a stipulation of the competition held to find an architect. Candidates had to submit plans anonymously. The winners were Henry Lanchester and Edwin Rickards, who went for Viennese Baroque. John Betjeman

described the white Portland stone building as 'a splendid foil to the towers of Westminster and the Houses of Parliament'. The Great Hall, Lecture Hall and Library are the largest of 30 rooms, some of them used for public inquiries. In the Great Hall, which seats 2,160, suffragettes campaigned for the vote, Mahatma Ghandi addressed the Temperance Movement, and General de Gaulle founded the Free French. It also hosted the first meeting of the UN General Assembly in 1946. Exhibitions are often held in the hall, and Wesley's Café on the lower ground floor is quiet and convenient for anybody visiting Parliament Square.
Storeys Gate, SW1H 9NH. Westminster tube.

⑭ ICA

The dream of an anarchist is fulfilled at one of London's swankiest addresses, in a Roman-classical-style mansion designed by John Nash. In 1947, the poet, art critic, historian and champion of surrealism Herbert Read had the idea for a 'laboratory' or 'playground' for innovative modern arts, and together with a group of artists and patrons, he launched the Institute of Contemporary Arts (ICA) as a place where artists, writers and scientists could meet and debate. The first exhibitions were held in rented premises and organised by Roland Penrose, surrealist painter and friend of Picasso's. Meetings were held in the basement of the Academy of Cinema on Oxford Street before more permanent premises were found in 1950, on Dover Street, in what was once the home of Horatio Nelson. The ICA stayed there for 18 years and then moved to elegant Nash House.

In the early years, the institute exhibited the works of Picasso and Jackson Pollock; it launched Pop art, Op art and British Brutalist architecture, and it continues to push the boundaries. Exhibitions in the two galleries are free. There are two cinemas, a theatre, a reading room and bookshop. This was one of the first venues to present original punk rock band The Clash. It hosted the debut London gig of American alternative band the Scissor Sisters, and the debut show of the contemporary artist Damien Hirst.
12 Carlton House Terrace, SW1Y 5AH. Charing Cross tube.

WESTMINSTER & ST JAMES'S

Land of pomp and glory

London is an ancient city, enraptured by history, celebrating it at every opportunity. Centuries-old customs are alive and well, staged as colourfully and distinctively as ever.

Swish, swish, swish, swish – what can this be? A man in a top hat and white smock approaches, carrying a birch broom with which he sweeps the street of 'foulness'. Behind him come men in top hats and tailcoats, men in Tudor caps and ermine, all clutching little posies, which they may sniff when overcome by the stench of ordure. It is the first Thursday after July 4, the Feast of the Translation of St Martin, and the annual Procession of the Worshipful Company of Vintners is under way. Once one of the wealthiest of the City Livery Companies, the vintners have had headquarters on Upper Thames Street since 1446. An earlier Vintners Hall burnt down in the Great Fire of 1666, but a new one was built and it was business as usual for the flourishing wine trade.

This annual parade to the church of St James Garlickhythe is just one charming cameo in a city very big on pageantry. The 2011 wedding of the Duke and Duchess of Cambridge was said to have been watched by 2 billion people around the world and London staged a dazzling display. In some aspects, the city is one long-running pageant. Every morning, within the sheltering walls of the Tower of London, 36 men put on their 'undress' uniform – a sort of dark blue frock with red trimmings – and Tudor bonnets.

The Queen watches soldiers of the Household Division on Horse Guards Parade, performing the traditional ceremony in honour of her official birthday.

TROOPING THE COLOUR, HORSEGUARDS PARADE

Their red-and-gold uniform, or Tudor State Dress, is kept for State occasions and has been little modified since the 16th century. These are Yeoman Warders, former servicemen and women with honourable records, nicknamed 'Beefeaters', a detachment of the Yeoman of the Guard with a history stretching back to the reign of Edward IV (1461–83). To the Ravenmaster falls the job of caring for the seven glossy corvids (the statutory six ordered by Charles II, plus a 'spare') on which the nation's fate depends. Legend has it that if they leave the Tower, England will fall. The day at the Tower ends at 10pm, as it has since the 14th century, with the Ceremony of the Keys, when the gates are locked and the safety of the Crown Jewels within is assured for another night.

Over at Buckingham Palace, meanwhile, the morning spectacle is of men in red jackets and towering bearskins performing the Changing of the Guard. In June, Trooping the Colour is staged by Her Majesty's personal troops, the Household Division, to celebrate the sovereign's official birthday, with the Queen in attendance to take the salute. This tradition dates from the reign of Charles II in the 1600s, when fighting men were rallied to their regimental 'colours', which because of their size and brightness, could be seen even in the chaos of battle.

The first mention of the sovereign's birthday being 'kept', by the Grenadier Guards, can be traced to 1748. When George III became king in 1760, it was ordered that annual parades should mark the day. From the accession of George IV, the tradition has been unbroken with just a few exceptions, including the two world wars. For years, the Queen would appear on horseback, riding sidesaddle and wearing the uniform of the regiment whose flags were being trooped (an honour granted in rotation). Since 1987, she has attended in a carriage. More than 1,400 men parade, with 200 horses, ten bands and corps of drums, processing along a route that extends from Buckingham Palace down the Mall to Horse Guards Parade. Afterwards, members of the royal family gather on the palace balcony to watch an RAF flypast.

The Lord Mayor's Show

Each year, 500,000 people line the streets to watch the spectacle and join the fun of the biggest annual party of all. The tradition dates from the reign of King John. The Lord Mayor was originally appointed by the sovereign, but towards the end of John's reign, in 1215, the king granted a charter to the people of London to allow them to elect their own mayor – a man equal in stature to the powerful barons – on the condition that the new incumbent present himself to the sovereign each year to swear loyalty to the Crown.

For 800 years the Lord Mayor has made the journey, at first by ceremonial barge, and in more recent times by gilded state coach, with more and more of a sense of carnival. The world's oldest civic procession extends, today, for more than 3 miles – almost twice the length of the route it follows, from Mansion House to Victoria Embankment, with a stop-off at the Royal Courts of Justice, where the Lord Mayor swears allegiance before the Lord Chief Justice and the judges of the Queen's Bench. The procession includes more than 6,000 invited participants, more than 140 decorated floats, and numerous talented performers. It is preceded by an RAF flypast, and the day ends with a fireworks display from a barge moored between Blackfriars and Waterloo bridges. Charles Dickens advised that 'the best point of view is from the window of a friend who occupies rooms along the lie of route, more especially if he have liberal ideas on the subject of lunch.'

WHITEHALL

⑮ Churchill Museum and Cabinet War Rooms

This heavily fortified Whitehall basement, a few yards from No. 10 Downing Street, is where Winston Churchill, members of his Cabinet and his chiefs of staff spent most of their time during the unremitting aerial bombardment of London, which lasted from September 1940 to May 1941. A million London buildings were destroyed or damaged, including the Houses of Parliament and Westminster Abbey, and 20,000 people lost their lives. Below ground, Churchill and his colleagues worked in a warren of cramped rooms, and it was from here that they directed operations all through the Second World War. Here is the Cabinet Room, the typing pool, the telephone with a 'secure' line to the American president, and the Map Room, where battles were plotted and followed. In Churchill's bedroom is the desk from which he broadcast.
King Charles Street, off Whitehall, SW1A 2AQ. Westminster, St James's Park tube.

⑯ Durbar Court, Foreign and Commonwealth Office

This most gorgeous of government buildings is seldom open to the public; an opportunity to see it should not be missed. Matthew Digby Wyatt's confection of red and grey granite and marble paving in the India Office is at the heart of the Foreign and Commonwealth Office. It rises to three storeys of pillars, from Doric to Ionic and Corinthian. An Indian water garden is mapped out on the floor of the court in coloured marble from Greece and Sicily. The Sultan of Turkey was the first overseas visitor to be received here, in 1867, and in 1902 it was decorated to use for state receptions for the coronation of Edward VII. In Delhi, the coronation was celebrated with a two-week durbar, or reception, organised by Lord Curzon, and the office's name was changed to Durbar Court.
King Charles Street, SW1A 2AH. Westminster tube.

⑰ Banqueting House

Charles I, who was executed in front of Banqueting House in 1649, commissioned nine works from Peter Paul Rubens to celebrate the life and rule of his father. Among them was *The Apotheosis of James I*, confirming the divinity of Stuart kings. These are enormous pieces, painted on canvas and pasted to the ceiling, and they are the crowning glory of the only building to survive the fire that burned down the Tudor palace of Whitehall in 1698. The Banqueting House, a later addition finished in 1622, had been built for court entertainments. Today, Inigo Jones's Palladian masterpiece is open to all, although few seem to notice it among the other edifices on Whitehall, despite its lavish grandeur. Beneath it is a wonderfully atmospheric vaulted basement, the Undercroft, which was once used as a drinking den by James I and his cronies, and by Charles II, the reinstated Stuart king, to hold lotteries.
41 Whitehall, SW1A 2ER. Embankment, Charing Cross tube.

⑱ Horse Guards

When the black-clad royal family, walking behind the bier carrying the body of Princess Diana, passed beneath the arch of Horse Guards, London seemed the most extraordinary setting for a drama. The central arch of William Kent's building, guarded by two mounted troopers on the Whitehall side, is still the formal entrance to St James's Palace and Buckingham Palace at the opposite end of the park. Troopers mount guard from 10am to 4pm, and are changed at 11am (10am on Sundays). Horse Guards Parade, the tiltyard of the former Whitehall Palace, where knights from all over Europe jousted, is now used for ceremonial occasions, in particular for Trooping the Colour on the Queen's official birthday. It was also chosen as the venue for the beach volleyball competition in the 2012 Olympic Games.
Horse Guards, Whitehall SW1A 2AX. Westminster, Embankment, Charing Cross tube.

⑲ Henry VIII's Wine Cellar

The wine cellar of the original Tudor Whitehall Palace survived the fire of 1698, and is now incorporated into government buildings. It was built as part of York Place, the official London residence of the Archbishops of York. After Archbishop Thomas Wolsey had enlarged the house, become a Cardinal and fallen from favour, Henry VIII took over York Place and renamed it Whitehall Palace. Although the cellar's vaulting pillars and brickwork have been faithfully preserved, the whole is something of a delusion. It used to be at street level. When it was threatened with destruction before the Second World War, to make way for a new MoD building, engineers moved the 800-tonne edifice 2.7m (9ft) along and 5.8m (19ft) down in one undisturbed piece, encased in a steel frame and transported on rollers. The cellar, 21m (70ft) long, can be visited by appointment.
Horse Guards Avenue, Westminster, Embankment, Charing Cross tube.

A CONFECTION OF RED AND GREY GRANITE

DURBAR COURT, FOREIGN AND COMMONWEALTH OFFICE

TRAFALGAR SQUARE

⑳ Britain's Smallest Police Station

A miscreant required by a member of the constabulary to accompany him to the station would have had to wait outside – this pillbox of a cop shop has room for one only. Trafalgar Square has always been a rallying point and place of protest, and this police lookout post was built into the plans. It is a hollowed-out granite lamppost, now used to stash street-cleaning supplies. A faded list of bylaws posted on the side forbids camping or caravanning, busking, washing and drying clothes, exercising – or using any 'foot-propelled device' upon the square without permission from the mayor.
Trafalgar Square, WC2N. Embankment, Charing Cross tube.

㉑ Pop-up Urinals

Just as the male visitor searches for a convenience, one rises out of the pavement in front of him. Telescopic urinals have been installed around the West End, the first one having made its appearance on Villiers Street near the Embankment. Made by a Dutch company, Urilift, the stainless-steel urinals are 2m (6½ft) tall, fully plumbed and strictly nocturnal. By day they disappear into the pavement.
Villiers Street, WC2N. Embankment, Charing Cross tube.

㉒ St Martin in the Fields

A handsome presence on Trafalgar Square, James Gibbs's building makes an emphatic statement. It has a classical-style pediment, Corinthian columns and a high steeple topped with a gilt crown. The coat of arms over the portico proclaims this as the royal family's parish church. The claim that it is 'one of the most significant ecclesiastical buildings in the English-speaking world' is not made lightly; Gibbs's style has been copied in North America and elsewhere. Older by a century than the National Gallery, St Martin's stands on the site of a 13th-century monastery, which was rebuilt by Henry VII.

Handel played here on the 1727 Schreider organ, and music is the heart and soul of this church. Its Christmas carol services are internationally renowned, and there are free lunchtime concerts and jazz in the crypt, where there is also an art gallery. In the First World War 'the church of the ever-open door' offered shelter to soldiers on their way to France. In 1948 St Martin's fight against homelessness was marked by the foundation of the Social Service Unit. That work continues today through the Connection at St Martin's; around 7,500 people are cared for each year. Charles II's mistress, his 'pretty, witty' Nell Gwynn, is buried here, as are the artists William Hogarth and Joshua Reynolds. The choir, dressed all in red, are a fine sight, but the most colourful event is a harvest festival of the Pearly Kings and Queens, which is held at St Martin's every year.
Trafalgar Square, WC2N 4JJ. Embankment, Charing Cross tube.

㉓ National Portrait Gallery

The great, the good, the bad and the ugly all have a place here in the world's most extensive collection of portraits. The gallery was founded in 1856 to bring together portraits of famous British men and women. The driving force behind the initiative was Philip Henry Stanhope, backed by Thomas Babington Macaulay and Thomas Carlyle, whose busts are set into the wall above the entrance. As the 5th Earl Stanhope put it to the House of Lords, there should be 'a gallery of original portraits, such portraits to consist as far as possible of those persons who are most honourably commemorated in British history as warriors or as statesmen, or in arts, in literature, in science'. It was established on the principle, still applied today, that the status of the sitter would be the most important thing, not the art, yet there is art here of a most affecting kind, dating from the Tudors – a portrait of Henry VII is by an unknown hand – to the present day, including paintings of the author P.D. James and the actor Sir Ian McKellen. Among the portraits, the visitor will find many of those who created and chronicled this amazing city – Sir Christopher Wren, Inigo Jones, Sir John Vanbrugh, Decimus Burton, Samuel Pepys, Samuel Johnson, Charles Dickens, Victoria and her beloved Albert.

The gallery has occupied Ewan Christian's Florentine-Renaissance-style building since 1896. By the time it opened it was already too small to house the collection and it has been extended. The view from the rooftop restaurant is one of the best in London. Diners look out past Nelson's Column, across Whitehall to the Houses of Parliament and Big Ben. There are paintings of Nelson, of course, and the seductive Emma Hamilton, and of Sir Edwin Landseer, whose lions protect that granite column and E.H. Baily's 5.5m (18ft) statue of the hero of Trafalgar.
St Martin's Place, WC2H 0HE. Embankment, Charing Cross, Leicester Square tube.

㉔ National Gallery

At the very centre of London, one of the greatest collections of Western European paintings in the world can be seen for free. The idea for a national art gallery began with the acquisition of 38 pictures that had belonged to John Julius Angerstein, a London merchant, Lloyd's underwriter, patron of the arts, and friend of George III and the prime minister William Pitt the Younger. These were to be the core of the collection, and were exhibited in his house at 100 Pall Mall. In 1831, parliament agreed to fund a building for a national gallery, and Trafalgar Square was chosen as the location because it was deemed to be the centre of the capital, and accessible to all. There would be no charge to enter, and extended opening hours would mean that working people could visit.

The gallery, which opened in 1838, occupied the site of the King's Mews, and the architect William Wilkins used many of the construction methods of the Mews building. The fine neoclassical edifice, which has a grand central portico, provides a dramatic backdrop to Trafalgar Square. Seven new exhibition rooms and a dome were added in 1876. In 1907, barracks at the rear were cleared to enable the building of five new galleries. In November 1940, incendiary bombs destroyed Hamptons, the next-door department store, and in its place now stands the Sainsbury Wing, which was opened in 1991 to display the early Renaissance collection. The Wilton Dyptich, jewel of early English church painting, is there. Not only are the paintings at the National Gallery among the city's greatest treasures, but it offers world-class art cinema, too.
Trafalgar Square, WC2N 5DN. Embankment, Charing Cross tube.

㉕ National Gallery Collection

Hundreds of wartime evacuees are today back home at the National Gallery. With great percipience, on the eve of war, it was decided that the gallery's priceless collection should be sent out of London. Most of it went to Wales, and eventually a disused slate mine was converted to house the paintings. It was to a gallery stripped of its treasures that Myra Hess performed lunchtime concerts in the foyer. The bomb that hit the gallery on October 12, 1940 would have destroyed the Raphaels.

Building on the collections of John Julius Angerstein and Sir George Beaumont, the trustees began to acquire works according to their tastes and with no formal policy. From 1855, however, the new director, Sir Charles Eastlake, travelled through Italy, buying many Italian Renaissance works, such as Botticelli's *Adoration of the Kings* and Uccello's *The Battle of San Romano*, widening the gallery's scope. In 1871, the bequest of the late prime minister, Sir Robert Peel, endowed the gallery with 77 mainly Dutch and Flemish paintings.

Today the visitor can see Velázquez's *Rokeby Venus*, Constable's *The Haywain*, Raphael's *Madonna of the Pinks*, Boticelli's *Venus and Mars*, Titian's 'Bacchus and Ariadne', Turner's *Fighting Temeraire* and van Gogh's *Sunflowers* as well as bathers by Monet, Seurat and Cézanne. Family visits are encouraged, and the effect of so many great works is mesmeric.
Trafalgar Square, WC2N 5DN. Embankment, Charing Cross tube.

㉖ Theatre Royal, Haymarket

Gilded opulence, a resident ghost and first-class stagecraft distinguish this West End theatre. In 1720, a carpenter John Potter opened a modest theatre beside a cannon and musket gun shop. He called it the Hay Market. A century later, John Nash shifted the theatre south, rebuilding it with a spectacular frontage of decorated windows, a portico and Corinthian columns. Backstage tours of this spectacular playhouse include the No 10 dressing room, which was John Gielgud's office in the Blitz, and the No 1 dressing room, where actor-manager and friend of Dickens' John Buckstone (*d.* 1879) is apparently sometimes heard rehearsing his lines. The tour takes visitors on stage for an actor's eye view of this magnificent auditorium. The first scheduled matinee was staged here. For the £1.3 million refit in the 1990s, 1,200 books of 24 carat gold leaf were used.
18 Suffolk Street, SW1Y 4HT. Piccadilly Circus tube.

THERE IS ART HERE OF A MOST AFFECTING KIND
NATIONAL PORTRAIT GALLERY

CRITERION

ST JAMES'S

㉗ Criterion

Croesus would have felt at home here among the gilded mirrors, mosaics, plaques, drapes and general air of affluence, but the visitor on a more modest budget can still sit over a drink in the bar and marvel. Since it opened in 1873, the Criterion has attracted many famous diners, and it unabashedly drops names. Arthur Conan Doyle must have been a customer. In *A Study in Scarlet*, he had Dr John Watson – a casualty of the second Afghan war, scraping by on 11 shillings and sixpence (58p) a week – raising a glass at the long bar, where a chance meeting would lead to a fateful introduction and the literary world's first glimpse of a strange character named Sherlock Holmes. In 1908 the restaurant hosted the first meeting of the Actresses' Franchise League, champions of women's suffrage, whose members included Ellen Terry, Lily Langtry and Sybil Thorndike.

Now London's only neo-Byzantine-style restaurant is owned by entrepreneurs from Georgia, formerly a part of the USSR. Recently it figured in films *Batman: The Dark Knight* and *A Good Year* starring Russell Crowe.
224 Piccadilly, W1J 9HP. Piccadilly Circus tube.

㉘ John Lobb

'The most beautiful shop in the world' is frequented by clients who take their shoes seriously. This bootmakers' business was founded in 1866 by John Lobb, a Cornish farm boy who learnt the skills of a cobbler and gained a royal warrant under Edward, Prince of Wales. Today, the firm holds two royal warrants – from the Duke of Edinburgh and the Prince of Wales – and retains not just historic ledgers but the lasts of all customers past and present, hand-carved from maple, beech or hornbeam into contoured models of the customer's feet. Among the meticulously stacked lasts are those of George Bernard Shaw, Guglielmo Marconi, Laurence Olivier, Rex Harrison and Roald Dahl.
88 Jermyn Street, SW1Y 6JD. Green Park, Piccadilly Circus tube.

㉙ Fortnum & Mason

At 4 o'clock it is time for Mr Fortnum and Mr Mason to step out of the clock that hangs over the door of their emporium, and to bow to one another to the chimes of 18 bells. This store is like no other, a grocer's *par excellence* that has been in business for three centuries. The clock, 122cm (4ft) tall and weighing 4 tonnes, is a modern addition, dating from 1964, since when it has chimed every 15 minutes, and every hour the courtly pair of mechanical figures have emerged. The whole institution feels frightfully British. Scotch eggs, Dundee cake, potted Stilton, English mustard, Sir Nigel Playfair's vintage marmalade, Colonel Skinner's mango chutney are all for sale, but alongside them is an abundance of produce from around the world. They are very big on hampers for events such as Royal Ascot, the boat race, Henley Regatta and Wimbledon. Window shoppers will find entrancing displays. Food is served all day and in the evening in five elegant and tranquil dining rooms. A pianist plays in the St James's restaurant.
181 Piccadilly, W1A 1ER. Green Park tube.

㉚ Waterstone's, Piccadilly

The Waterstone's flagship store occupies a prime West End position in the premises of a former, much-loved London landmark, Simpson's of Piccadilly. It is the largest bookshop in Europe. Six of its eight floors are today dedicated to books – 8½ miles of shelving hold more than 150,000 titles. The Art Deco interior is largely intact. The natural wood surfaces and Travertine marble steps have been retained, and there are comfortable armchairs and very good rest rooms. The atmosphere is closer to that of a private house than a warehouse. Event space is put to imaginative use for readings, discussions, signings and cookery demonstrations. Indeed, this is a top place for author appearances, the first and sometimes only choice of many big names, including Keith Richards, David Beckham and Bill Clinton. A fifth-floor bar and restaurant affords great views across London.
203–6 Piccadilly, W1J 9LE. Piccadilly Circus tube.

㉛ Floris

'Perfumers to her Majesty the Queen', Floris dates from 1730, and this magnificent shop is fitted with Spanish mahogany showcases bought at the Great Exhibition of 1851. The firm boasts of being 'Purveyors of the Finest Perfumes and Toiletries to the Court of St James's', and has counted many famous names among its clients. The business was founded by Juan Famenias Floris and his wife Elizabeth, and received its first royal warrant in 1820 as comb maker to George IV. Displayed in such fine surroundings, the soaps and perfumes, scented candles and toiletries for men and women may prove irresistible.
89 Jermyn Street, SW1Y 6JH. Green Park, Piccadilly Circus tube.

WESTMINSTER & ST JAMES'S

㉜ Paxton & Whitfield

Blessed are the cheese makers, for they have been supplying Paxton & Whitfield since Harry Paxton and Charles Whitfield sealed their partnership in 1797. Indeed, the business goes back still further, to a stall in Aldwych market set up by Sam Cullen in 1742. When Paxton & Whitfield were appointed cheesemongers to Queen Victoria, it was the first of many warrants the company would hold. They have been established in St James's for more than 200 years and in the present premises for 100. In 2009 they teamed up with Fromagerie Androuet, so that now their English cheeses are sold in six shops in Paris, while the century-old Androuet supplies French cheeses to Paxton & Whitfield. *93 Jermyn Street, SW1Y 6JE. Green Park, Piccadilly Circus tube.*

㉝ London Library

'In books lies the soul of the whole past time,' said the author and historian Thomas Carlyle, whose vision inspired this great London literary refuge in 1841. Such reverence for the printed word endures – rarely has a book been thrown away at the world's largest independent lending library, where a million or so well-thumbed books reside on 15 miles of open shelving, including collections dating from the 16th century.

Tucked away in the northwest corner of St James's Square, the library is a fine example of Victorian enlightenment. Its first president was a politician, the Earl of Clarendon, its first auditor William Makepeace Thackeray, Carlyle's friend and fellow author. William Gladstone and Sir Edward Bunbury were on the first committee. Early members included Charles Dickens and George Eliot. Past presidents and vice-presidents include Alfred, Lord Tennyson, Rudyard Kipling and T.S. Eliot. Anyone can buy a day ticket and sit and read, soaking up the clubby atmosphere. *14 St James's, SW1Y 4LG. Green Park, Piccadilly Circus tube.*

㉞ Queen's Chapel

This elegant little chapel was designed by Inigo Jones to be an integral part of the Tudor redbrick St James's Palace. Originally, it was to be for Maria Anna, the Infanta of Spain, on whom James I had his eye as a suitable match for his son and heir, the future Charles I. However, the promise of a chapel of her very own was not enough to win over the Infanta, who set her face against marrying a Protestant. So it went, instead, to Henrietta Maria of France, a Catholic with a more spacious religious view.

Built in 1623–5, it has stucco walls, stone quoins, a simple pediment and England's first Venetian window at its eastern end, and it remains one of the facilities of the British monarch's personal religious establishment. Although it was originally an adjunct to the palace, when adjacent apartments burnt down in 1809, they were not replaced, and in 1856–7, Marlborough Road was laid down between palace and chapel. Here, on her death in March 2002, the body of Queen Elizabeth the Queen Mother was placed in preparation for her lying-in-state in Westminster Abbey. She had lived to 101. Charles I was just 49 when he spent the night of Monday, January 29, 1649, his last on this earth, in St James's Palace. The next day he was taken to Whitehall, where, in front of Banqueting House, he declared, 'I shall go from a corruptible to an incorruptible Crown, where no disturbance can be,' before signalling to the executioner and laying his head on the block.

The public can attend services between Easter and the end of July, on Sundays and some weekdays. Outside, the bronze memorial on red granite is by Alfred Gilbert, the sculptor of Eros, and is believed to be London's only Art Deco monument. On the plinth is written: 'Faith, Hope, Love, The Guiding Virtues of Queen Alexandra.' *Marlborough Road, SW1Y 5HX. Green Park tube.*

㉟ Berry Bros & Rudd

Now an oenophile's paradise, Britain's oldest wines and spirits merchant began life as a grocer's, the Coffee Mill. The shop was opened by the Widow Bourne in 1698 – the sign still hangs inside – and the framed prints, dark panelling and bare boards are much as they would have been then. By 1765, Berry's not only supplied coffee to the surrounding coffee houses, which later became gentlemen's clubs, such as Boodle's and White's, but would weigh customers on its giant weighing beams. They still have the records of customers' weights – including that of Lord Byron and William Pitt – penned with a quill in Morocco-bound ledgers.

The enterprise has been in the same families for generations and has supplied wine to the royal family since the reign of George III. Today it has royal warrants from the Queen and the Prince of Wales. There is a wine school, offering tastings, lunches, dinners, master-classes and tours of the cellars, which extend to St James's Palace. *3 St James's Street, SW1A 1EG. Green Park tube.*

BERRY BROS & RUDD

36 Fox of St James's

The world's oldest cigar shop has been supplying tobacco products and smokers' accessories from the same premises for more than 200 years. Robert Lewis began trading tobacco on St James's Street in 1787. James J. Fox set up almost a century later in Dublin, in 1881, and the company opened its first London shop in 1947, buying the business of Robert Lewis in 1992. The shop front and dark interior are beautiful, and a small cigar museum includes old ledgers – Winston Churchill is paid up to date, but Oscar Wilde still owes a small sum. This is one of a very few shops to be exempt from the smoking ban.

19 St James's Street, SW1A 1ES. Green Park tube.

37 Spencer House

The only surviving 18th-century aristocratic family palace in London ranges in style from Rome to Athens – and from the sublime to the exuberantly ridiculous. It was begun by architect John Vardy in 1756 for the first Earl Spencer, a forebear of the late Diana, Princess of Wales, and has been recently restored. The house was conceived as a showpiece of classical design, sparing no expense. The exterior, including the Palladian façade with its decorative pediment and seven upper bays split by Tuscan columns, along with the ground-floor interior, is Vardy's work. Then in 1758 the sculptor and architect James Stuart, a pioneer of neoclassicism newly returned

from Greece, stepped in to work on the upper floor. Some of the state rooms – the Morning Room, the Music Room, the Ante Room (the Spencers' 'Little Eating Parlour') and the Library – although very grand, have the authentic feeling of a family home.

The entrance hall sets a lofty tone, featuring a Doric frieze derived from the Temple of Jupiter the Thunderer, splendid busts and an oval relief over the chimneypiece. This represents Antinous, the beautiful Greek boy who was the Emperor Hadrian's minion and 'slave of his unlawful pleasures'. In Vardy's Palm Room are carved and gilded palm trees, symbolic of marital fertility. A frieze of griffins was inspired by the Temple of Antoninus and Faustina in Rome. To this fantastical salon the gentlemen would retire after dinner, while the womenfolk made their way up to Lady Spencer's Room on the first floor. The ceiling of her ladyship's drawing room is based on one in the Baths of Augustus in Rome, while the frieze is adapted from that of the Erechtheum in Athens. The Painted Room, designed and executed by Stuart, is one of the most famous of the period in England. It draws on sources from Herculaneum to classical landscape painting, via Rome and the Vatican. The decorative theme celebrates marriage, the Triumph of Love and the Spencers' own happy union. Now, at last, the glory that was Greece and the grandeur that was Rome have been revived for visitors to see on Sundays, by arrangement and by way of a guided tour, except in January and August and subject to some variations.

27 St James's Place, SW1A 1NR. Green Park tube.

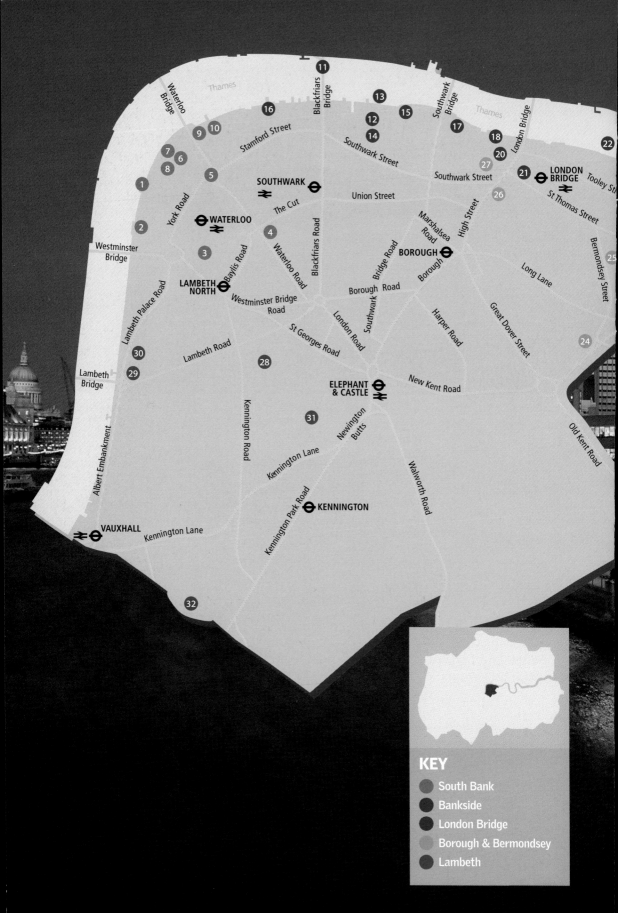

Tower
Bridge

9

23

South Bank & Beyond

The precincts of the South Bank pulsate with life all year round as crowds are drawn to its myriad cultural attractions. Slightly farther afield, echoes of a not-so-distant past can be found in the galleries of the Imperial War Museum.

SOUTH BANK

❶ London Eye

Brand names attached to the London Eye come and go, but the slowly spinning wheel, once threatened with closure, has proved remarkably enduring. It is a major addition to the London skyline, and it is hard now to imagine the city without it. A marriage of art and technology, with a funfair flavour, the wheel is one of the capital's tallest structures at 135m (450ft). The visitor steps inside one of 32 glass pods – the same number as there are boroughs in the city – and one circuit takes 30 minutes. Views extend up to 25 miles all around, and from the top, Hampstead Heath and Crystal Palace seem lowly places. Landmarks can be spotted by day, and by night the city is laid out in all its sparkling finery.
Riverside Building, County Hall, Westminster Bridge Road, SE1 7PB. Waterloo, Westminster tube.

❷ Sea Life London Aquarium

Strange to think that the seat of London's government for 64 years, from 1922, is now swimming with sharks. The aquarium is on the ground floor of what was once County Hall. It is one of the major attractions in a collection of entertainments that can make the Thames Walk beside it seem like a seaside promenade on a Bank Holiday. The Sea Life Centre claims to be one of the largest collections of marine life in Europe, with 500 species in 14 themed zones. There are Cuban crocodiles and Gentoo penguins as well as fish; four species of shark swim below visitors' feet on the shark wall.
County Hall, Westminster Bridge Road, SE1 7PB. Waterloo, Westminster tube.

❸ Scootercaffe

Lower Marsh has the feel of a street that the 21st century has forgotten. Nothing smart or fashionable is to be found among the market stalls and small shops, the knitting club, the sex parlour or the period pieces in Radio Days. However, just a glance at the rare British-built Vespa Piatti in the window, lit by a red glow from within, is all it takes to be drawn inside Scootercaffe, where coffee is made on an authentic 1957 Faema machine. This used to be Scooterworks, a bike repair shop, but after New Zealand-born owner Craig Dwyer started cranking up his Faema, customers dropped by just for the good coffee. Scooterworks moved on to Bermondsey, but Craig stood by his machine. Cakes and wine and beer are sold. Customers wanting anything more substantial can bring their own meals as long as they buy a drink. It opens from 8.30am until late and is closed on Sunday.
132 Lower Marsh, SE1 7AE. Waterloo tube.

❹ The Old Vic

From the outside, the large plain façade gives little clue to the rich interior of one of London's great theatres. Decorated in red and gold, it seats just over 1,000, and has much more space than 19th-century rivals across the river. The Old Vic stands alone just south of Waterloo Bridge, which was built at the same time. It opened in 1818 as the Royal Coburg Theatre, named after its patrons, Princess Charlotte and Prince Leopold of Saxe-Coburg Gotha, and the entertainment was initially popular rather than dramatic. When the great Shakespearean actor Edmund Keane crossed the river to educate the South London audience with six performances of the Bard, he declared, 'I have never acted to such a set of ignorant, unmitigated brutes as I have before me.'

Renamed The Royal Victoria shortly after the young queen came to the throne, it soon became known as The Old Vic. The interior was redesigned by Emma Cons, whose niece, Lilian Baylis, followed her as manager from 1912 to 1937. She made a home for The Old Vic Company, founded by Sir John Gielgud, which ran from 1929 to 1963. It was replaced by Laurence Olivier's National Theatre company, which subsequently moved to the South Bank. The Old Vic owes much of its continuing success to the American actor Kevin Spacey, who has been artistic director since 2002.
103 The Cut, SE1 8NB. Waterloo tube.

CUSTOMERS DROPPED BY JUST FOR THE COFFEE
SCOOTERCAFFE

SCOOTERCAFFE

⑤ BFI IMAX

The British Film Institute's 3-D cinema has digital surround sound to go with the largest screen in the country, making watching a film here an unforgettable experience. Characters leap out of the 26 x 20m (85 x 66ft) screen. As well as films for children, there are opera screenings and concerts via satellite. In 2011, *Frankenstein* was the first play from the National Theatre to be shown live on the IMAX screen. This 500 seat cinema is a short walk from BFI Southbank, formerly the National Film Theatre, and is housed in a glass drum in the centre of the roundabout at the southern end of Waterloo Bridge. It was built by Avery Associates to withstand traffic and train vibrations, and is reached through underpasses.
1 Charlie Chaplin Walk, SE1 8XR. Waterloo tube.

⑥ Poetry Library

The facility to read a book while sitting in a quiet space overlooking the Thames is one of the attractions of the Poetry Library.
Founded in 1953, the library now has the most comprehensive collection of contemporary poetry, written since 1912, in Britain. It moved to its current home, on Level 5 of the Royal Festival Hall, in 1988. The library holds more than 95,000 books, magazines, song lyrics, posters and cards. Recordings of poets reciting their own work can be heard in listening booths, and books can be borrowed or read in the room. There is an exhibition space, workshops, readings and events for children. It also runs an information service. Funded by the Arts Council, it is free to join.
Royal Festival Hall, SE1 8XX. Waterloo tube.

BOXES LOOK LIKE DRAWERS IN A DALI PAINTING

ROYAL FESTIVAL HALL

❼ Royal Festival Hall

Light, airy and accessible, the Royal Festival Hall projects a mood of optimism. The feeling is confirmed when, in the JCB glass lift, visitors' journeys are – rather delightfully – accompanied by scales in four-part harmony. The recording begins with a bottom E from the baritone at the ground floor, and rises to a sharp A from the soprano at the sixth. This singing lift is an echo of the cheerfulness that accompanied the building's opening for the 1951 Festival of Britain, which celebrated a new, peaceful world, and the centenary of the Great Exhibition in Hyde Park.

Concerts in the main hall, where boxes look like drawers in a Dali painting, can be inexpensive, and the neighbouring, smaller Queen's Hall and Purcell Room allow for a variety of performances. Seats are comfortable, there are no sightline problems and the acoustics are uniformly good. The foyer, where there is a bar and café, is always open, and various events are put on there – free Sunday music in the Clore Ballroom, photographic exhibitions, or paintings in the basement gallery. Outside on the concrete walkway art installations are not unusual, and time may be idled away at café tables, watching the river traffic plough by.
Royal Festival Hall, SE1 8XX. Waterloo tube.

❽ Feliks Topolski's Century

Between Waterloo Bridge and Hungerford Bridge, two whole railway arches are filled with a 183m (600ft) mural. It was executed with preternatural energy and passion by the Polish Expressionist artist Feliks Topolski, and tells the story of his life from his birth in Warsaw in 1907 through to his travels in Latin America in the early 1980s, including major world events. By turns witty, dramatic and humane, the painting, made on hardboard panels 6m (20ft) high, encompasses the Blitz, the Black Panthers and the royal family. The whole fairground of paintings reflects his life as a tireless war artist, portrait painter of the famous and publisher of his own *Chronicles* – some 3,000 works described by actress Joyce Carey as 'the most brilliant record we have of the contemporary scene, as seized by a contemporary mind'.

Topolksi set up his studio beneath the arches after arriving in London in 1935. He began his epic narrative painting in 1975, and it was unveiled by Prince Philip, Duke of Edinburgh in 1984. On Topolksi's death in 1989, he bequeathed it to the nation. After major refurbishment, it can be viewed on pre-booked tours and by appointment.
150–2 Hungerford Arches, SE1 8XU. Waterloo tube.

❾ BFI Mediateque

If a film is held in the British Film Institute national library, anybody can view it in the Mediateque on the Southbank. This room in the centre of the BFI building is equipped with monitors and seats for two, with headphones, so visitors can scroll through the archives, or pick out any feature film or documentary they might want to see, from early government information films on how to use a telephone to recent releases. The archive is updated every month, and films can be found online and booked in advance.

Opposite the Mediateque is the BFI bar, a comfortable place with sofas, and a bookshop. There are three cinemas in the building. Second-hand book stalls beneath Waterloo Bridge, by the pavement bar and restaurant on the river side of the building, help to make the BFI a good retreat on a rainy day.
Belvedere Road, SE1 8XX. Waterloo tube.

❿ Royal National Theatre

Immaculately designed by Denys Lasdun, the Royal National Theatre is an unadorned, Brutalist masterpiece. Stairways, floors, balconies and terraces seem to be positioned at all angles, sometimes leading to dead ends, sometimes to views high above the lobby. Bars, bookshop and restaurants are stumbled upon, and art and photographic exhibitions are often staged on the upper floors. Musical notes drift up from free pre-performance concerts, which take place in the lobby at 6pm and at lunchtime on most weekends. The terraces are a successful feature, rising like steps around the building, which is crowned with two big boxes – the flies of the main theatres into which scenery magically disappears. Along with the foyer, the terraces are used for occasional performances, and in summer art and theatre enliven the open-air forecourt.

Several times a day, visitors are guided around backstage to see technicians, scene painters and prop-makers at work in Britain's largest theatre complex. The National has three stages. The Olivier, named after Sir Laurence Olivier, the theatre's founder, is the largest, seating 1,120 on deeply raked, lavender-coloured seats (the actor's own choice); technology allows for dramatic scenery changes. The Lyttleton, named after Oliver Lyttelton, first chairman of the National, seats 890 and has a conventional layout with an orchestra pit. The smallest, the Cottesloe, is to be renamed the Dorfman, following a £10 million gift from financier Lloyd Dorfman.
Belvedere Road, SE1 9PX. Waterloo tube.

Sounds of the city

The capital is a magnet for world-class musicians, young hopefuls and gifted buskers alike. Music fills the air as players, professional and amateur, showcase their talents.

The South Bank Centre stages a thousand paid performances, and more than 300 free foyer events each year, and is one of the world's largest arts complexes. Add to this the city's role as host to a great classical music festival – the Royal Albert Hall's Proms – and the fact that the O2 Arena sells around 2.5 million tickets annually, and it is easy to see why London claims to be the capital of live music. This is the city where hopefuls come to make their mark and where top musicians can be heard every day. Mozart, aged nine, composed his first symphony while living in Ebury Street, SW1, and Chopin gave his last concert recital at the Guildhall. The world's first purpose-built recording studio was built by EMI in Abbey Road and the first Hard Rock Café, with rock memorabilia, opened in Piccadilly.

THE SCOOP, CITY HALL

Comfortable and acoustically reliable halls and recital rooms have swelled to the sounds of all the great performers, and for nearly two centuries conservatoires have produced world-class composers and players. Students are regularly booked for free recitals in entrance halls, museums and galleries, including the National Theatre and the National Gallery's Sainsbury Wing, to ensure music, not Muzak, fills the air. Bands that may have been spotted busking are hired for late evenings at the V&A.

If music is an aid to contemplation, a recital must be the best way to see some of the capital's memorable buildings, from Southwark Cathedral to

the Arab Hall in Leighton House, and of course at the Handel House Museum. Most impressive of all, and most distinctive of London, are the free lunchtime concerts that can be heard every weekday in the City's churches. Who better than Bach or Vivaldi to enhance an appreciation of the finer elements of Wren's masterpieces, played by duos or quartets, or sung by choirs of enthusiastic city workers? St John's Smith Square and Hawksmoor's St Luke's in Old Street are among several churches that have turned themselves over entirely to music.

Summer festivals and al fresco events include free opera in Covent Garden's Piazza, courtesy of the Royal Opera House. Screens go up in Trafalgar Square, Hyde Park, Somerset House and The Scoop outside City Hall, and amplifiers are hauled onto stages in the parks. The biggest event of the season is the Proms where promenaders pay the least money for the best place. 'The proximity of this huge standing crowd, listening in impeccable silence, has a galvanising effect on the finest musicians. They play out of their skins,' wrote *The Times*' music critic Richard Morrison.

Intimate venues

For the devoted follower, a handful of traditional small venues around the capital provide similarly intimate proximity with performers. At the Wigmore Hall, for instance, the Sunday Coffee Morning Concerts, with free coffee and sherry, can bring to mind pre-war Vienna. In Oxford Street, Glenn Miller was just one of the wartime Americans in uniform to make the 100 Club swing – Bo Diddley and the Rolling Stones would come later. At Ronnie Scott's, the late saxophone-playing owner's jokes are still occasionally dusted off in the newly spruced-up club: 'It's just like home – filthy and full of strangers.' Rating the Troubadour in Earl's Court as one of 2011's Top 10 restaurants in London, the *Daily Mail* described the 1950s coffee house as 'a towering bohemian behemoth held together by the glue of time'. It is little changed since Bob Dylan came by, aged 21, and Jimi Hendrix deafened the cellar crowd.

Music in the city benefits from an ethnic mix that can call on Irish fiddles, Turkish ney flutes, Arabic ouds, Indian sitars, Balinese gamelans, Mexican trumpets, Caribbean drums and Aboriginal didgeridoos. It would be quite feasible to see a different band perform every night of the year. The curtain raiser for the 2012 Cultural Olympiad, overseen by Jude Kelly, Artistic Director of the South Bank Centre, is the River of Music, with free performances by musicians from all 205 participating countries at landmark sites along the Thames. It is nothing less than one would expect from the city of live music.

BANKSIDE

⑪ Blackfriars Station

Platforms span the river, so passengers can choose on which side to alight – at the original Blackfriars Station, near St Paul's on the north side, or at the new Bankside, not far from Tate Modern on the south side. Such a length of platform, around 305m (1,000ft), means that trains 12 carriages long can use the station. Opening in 2012, it is quite a feat of engineering.

Blackfriars Station was called St Paul's when the first rail bridge – St Paul's Bridge – was opened in 1864 for the London, Chatham and Dover Railway. After that was removed in 1985, the abutments on the south bank, with colourful insignia, remained and were listed Grade II. Its iron-red pillars also remained and have proved a help in building the new bridge. While the work was being carried out, a bale of straw was hung from the new bridge, a traditional Thames device to indicate work is in progress. A ticket office with lifts up to platforms is situated on the Thames Path on Bankside.

Thames Walk, SE1. Blackfriars tube.

⑫ Tate Modern and Tate Project

The Turbine Hall in Tate Modern is such a mind-altering space, it has helped to change the way people think about art. This is no place to hang paintings, or even attempt a mural. It is a place to experiment – with sculpture, sound, light, even performance. As each new installation becomes news, it has helped to induce a generation of Londoners to reappraise their attitudes towards art, and to make Tate Modern the most visited art gallery in the world. On entering the immense space of the Turbine Room, visitors seem like plankton swallowed by a whale. Tall, cathedral-like windows illuminate the bolted pillars and industrial lifts, and the hum of the transformer station – still operating on the building's south side – creates a low background chant. The rest of the internal space, on seven floors, with shops and cafés, affords views over the river.

Bankside power station was designed by Sir Giles Gilbert Scott between 1947 and 1963, its 4.2 million bricks rising to a central chimney 99m (325ft) tall, where peregrine falcons have been known to nest in spring. The building was converted to an art gallery to relieve the Tate Gallery at Millbank of its renowned collection of international art from 1900 until the present day. Around 2 million visitors a year were expected; 5 million turned up. As a result, the original architects, Herzog and de Meuron, have been invited back to design the Tate Project, a brave and brand new building rising over the space vacated by the vast oil tanks that once fuelled the power station at the back of the Bankside building. Eleven floors rise in angular shapes to 65m (213ft) with a perforated brick latticework exterior to make it light up like a giant chequerboard. The galleries will have greater variety of size and shape than in the linear Tate Modern, and there will be larger spaces for contemporary exhibitions. The public terrace on Level 11 has the best views.

Bankside, SE1 9TG. Southwark tube.

TATE MODERN AND LONDON MILLENNIUM FOOTBRIDGE

⑬ London Millennium Footbridge

The first pedestrian bridge to be built over the Thames in central London since Tower Bridge was both a feat of engineering and a bold act of planning, which connected Bankside with the City, opening up a wonderful view between icons traditional and contemporary – St Paul's and Tate Modern. Sir Norman Foster's design got off to a wobbly start when it opened in June 2000, an estimated 80,000 to 100,000 pairs of feet causing it to sway. It took more than a year and £5 million to put right. Just over 305m (1,000ft) in length, the Millennium Bridge has an aluminium deck 4m (13ft) wide that hops across two piers. Eight suspension cables haul it into the banks. Designed with the help of the sculptor Sir Anthony Caro, it is immensely airy, giving clear views up and down the river. The architects describe it as 'a thin ribbon of steel by day … a blade of light at night'.
SE1. Southwark tube. EC4. St Paul's tube.

⑭ Monument to an Unknown Artist

Passers-by are surprised to find a 6m (20ft) tall bronze statue behind Tate Modern, copying their movements. The animated statue of an artist, scarf flowing, brush in hand, interacts with people walking past. It was commissioned by Land Securities, who have developed the surrounding glass blocks, and designed by the art collective Greyworld. An inscription reads: *non plaudite modo pecuniam* – 'don't applaud, throw money'.
Sumner Street, SE1 9JX. Southwark tube.

⑮ Shakespeare's Globe

Built by master craftsmen using 6,000 bundles of Norfolk water reed, 36,000 hand-made bricks and oak timbers, Shakespeare's Globe is as near as can be to the original 'wooden O' of 1598. Shakespeare was both a shareholder and a player at the Globe, where, until his death 18 years after it opened, The King's Men put on his plays. Owned by Cuthbert and Richard Burbage, it was swiftly erected using timbers from a playhouse in Shoreditch that had been abandoned after a dispute with the landlords. With a central well open to the elements, three galleries of seats rise around the sides, leaving 'the groundlings' to stand in the pit in front of the covered stage, where they could make their feelings known to the players. It burnt down in 1613 when cannon fire set it alight during a performance of *Henry VIII*, but was rebuilt and opened the following year. It was finally closed and demolished by Puritans during the Civil War in 1644.

The reconstruction was completed in 1992, largely due to the efforts of the American film-maker Sam Wanamaker, and a year-round exhibition attempts to bring Shakespeare's London to life. Visitors can add their own voices to pre-recorded scenes of his plays and hear actors read familiar lines – including many different deliveries of the famous soliloquy from *Hamlet*, 'To be or not to be'.

The summer season of plays at the Globe begins on April 23, Shakespeare's birthday. In Shakespeare's day, the company performed at Blackfriars Theatre in the winter months. Now the Globe plans year-round performances with a new indoor theatre that will occupy the pink brick building to the left of the Globe's main foyer entrance. This will be in the Jacobean style that followed Shakespeare's Elizabethan age.
21 New Globe Walk, SE1 9DT. Southwark tube.

⑯ Oxo Tower

The most blatant flouting of a ban on riverside advertising led to the letters OXO being spelt out at the top of this prominent tower. Oxo started life as a liquid beef extract devised by the German chemist Justus von Liebig and produced by the Liebig Extract of Meat Company. As a healthy additive to poor diets, it was praised by Florence Nightingale and the company was the official caterer to the 1908 London Olympic Games, when Oxo was given to athletes.

The tower was a power station, built to supply a local post office, and the Liebig company bought it to develop as a wharf for landing and storing cargoes of meat. The Art Deco design was carried out by the firm's architect, Albert Moore, between 1928 and 1929, with the Oxo branding in glass on all four sides of the chimney, which would be lit up at night.

The whole of the Oxo Tower Wharf was part of a 1990s development, an award-winning scheme that brought restaurants, craft shops and apartments to the area. A free public viewing area is accessed from the 8th floor, where Harvey Nichols' bar, brasserie and restaurant are located. Above it, years after the company vacated the building, the word Oxo is illuminated at night in red lights, still cheekily promoting the bouillon cube to the world.
Oxo Tower Wharf, SE1 9PH. Blackfriars tube.

LONDON BRIDGE

⓱ The Anchor

A map would be useful to help guide new customers around the nooks and crannies of this popular riverside pub. A Cask Ale Bar, snugs and minstrels' gallery ramble up to the first-floor terrace and restaurant, which somehow manages to look down on the Shakespeare dining room, even though it is not on the ground floor. Old oak beams, exposed brickwork and open fires make this pub a tourist's heaven, especially as it has the best riverside seating in Central London, and there is enough space in the smaller rooms to avoid the music and football screens that dominate the larger bars.

A pub has stood here since the 15th century, so of course Shakespeare would have known it, and there are stories of how miscreants would hide in its cubby holes, desperate to escape the nearby Clink prison. The Anchor is also presumed to be the 'little ale house on bankside' referred to by Samuel Pepys in his diary, from where he watched the Fire of London grow.

Henry Thrale, the brewer and friend of Dr Johnson, once owned the place, when Thrale's Brewery was one of the largest in London. The Anchor Brewhouse spread over 4ha (9 acres), and Thrales Intire Porter was known 'from the frozen regions of Russia to the burning sands of Bengal'. Today, the beer comes from Fullers, the only traditional family brewery left in London, and the company has recently spent £2.8 million on refurbishing the pub.
34 Park Street, SE1 9EF. Southwark tube.

⓲ *Golden Hinde*

The full-sized replica of Drake's original ship, which went right around the world in 1577–80, has made the same trip. So it is instructive to climb aboard to see just how the sailors lived. Twenty gentleman officers and around 50 crew crammed onto this 37m (121ft) brightly painted galleon, including musicians hired to keep spirits high. Family sleepovers organised on the Cannon Deck can give just a small idea of the discomfort of the voyage.

Originally named *The Pelican*, the *Golden Hinde* displayed a shining deer at its prow. Four other privateers made up the fleet, and they plundered so much treasure from Spanish vessels during the trip that the booty was used for ballast. It made millionaires of every sailor and enriched the nation, as half of it went to a grateful Elizabeth I. It was the French Ambassador, however, who knighted Drake on board the ship, to avoid antagonising the Spanish. The Queen

insisted the *Golden Hinde* afterwards remain at Deptford, where it became the world's first maritime museum.
Pickfords Wharf, SE1 9DG. London Bridge tube.

⓳ City Hall

The off-centre glass globe beside Tower Bridge gives the mayor and his cohorts good river views. 'It expresses the transparency and accessibility of the democratic process,' says its architect, Sir Norman Foster, who came to it after completing the refurbishment of the German Reichstag (parliament) in Berlin. The 45m (148ft) tall sphere, leaning southwards, is designed for maximum solar gain and minimum heat loss. A sweeping ramp more than half a kilometre (a third of a mile) long spirals up to the ninth floor and there are solar panels on the roof. The second-floor assembly chamber has seating for 250 members of the public, who can use the Just Deli Café in the basement on week days. There are regular free exhibitions, and in The Scoop, an oval amphitheatre in front of the building, free music and performances.
The Queen's Walk, SE1 2AA. London Bridge tube.

⓴ Southwark Cathedral

The fact that both Anglicans and Catholics possess two cathedrals in London, one each side of the river, is confirmation that North and South London are treated as two separate communities. The Catholics have Westminster Cathedral and St George's in Southwark; the Anglicans have St Paul's and the Cathedral and Collegiate Church of St Saviour and St Marie Overie, better known as Southwark Cathedral. Although ancient, it was not designated a cathedral until 1905, when it was given the coat of arms displayed on the standard that flies above its tower. It is a lovely church. There is nothing high and mighty about it. 'Overie' derives from 'over the river' and was the name given to the priory of St Mary Overie established in the 12th century, part of which has been uncovered at the back of the building. On the Dissolution of the Monasteries, it was renamed St Saviour's and later sold to the congregation.

Its proximity to playhouses gives it thespian connections. The Shakespeare memorial and window, with scenes from the plays, are in the south aisle, and Shakespeare's brother is thought to be buried somewhere in the church. Sam Wanamaker, the American actor who resurrected the Globe Theatre, has a memorial tablet, and there is a plaque to Oscar Hammerstein II, who

in memory of William Shakespeare for several years an inhabitant of this parish b 1564 d 1616

endowed the choir. The American connection is most visible in the John Harvard Chapel. This commemorates the founder of Harvard College, who was born nearby and baptised here. Other colourful memorials include a vivid red, green and blue tomb to John Gower, friend of Chaucer and court poet to Richard II and Henry IV. There is often music in the cathedral, sometimes drama, and five services are held every day.
London Bridge, SE1 9DA. London Bridge tube.

㉑ Old Operating Theatre Museum and Herb Garret

A bricked-up operating theatre for women was discovered in the roof of St Thomas's Church in 1957, almost a century after it had ceased to function. Dried opium poppy heads in the rafters were evidence that this had also been a herb garret. The church was built in 1703 by Thomas Cartwright, master mason to Christopher Wren, who was a governor of St Thomas's hospital. The rest of the hospital left for its current site by Westminster Bridge when the railway company wanted the land to develop London Bridge station. It is the oldest surviving operating theatre in Europe, dating from 1822, before anaesthetics and antiseptic surgical

procedures were in use. Tiers of seats surround the wooden operating table, and the surgery would be watched by students. The museum has a collection of surgical objects, including knives, saws, leech jars and a primitive vibrator, used to control 'hysterical' women.
9A St Thomas Street, SE1 9RY. London Bridge tube.

㉒ HMS *Belfast*

A giant floating, fighting machine, HMS *Belfast* is a survivor of the Second World War and the Korean War. The ship may seem archaic today, but to stand on the bridge, to see the navigation room and gyro compass binnacle, to stand by the 6 in guns and note their shells and cordite charges, is to feel close to some real action. She could hit targets 12 miles away. The giant engines down on Deck 5 could take the ship up to 32 knots, steered blind by the helmsman four decks down behind the main armour, directed by the Officer of the Watch. This powerful and efficient light cruiser was on active duty for 32 years, serving in the Arctic convoys and on D-Day. Life on board is relived with sleepovers in original bunks in the renovated mess decks.
Morgan's Lane, SE21 2JH. London Bridge tube.

BOROUGH & BERMONDSEY

㉓ Butler's Wharf

A once neglected and forgotten area lives again as a smart enclave with waterfront dining and an unmatched view of Tower Bridge from below. Terence Conran tells how, in the 1980s, he was cruising down the Thames aboard a pleasure boat, when he noticed 'a wonderful collection of Victorian warehouses clustered on the south bank … Although derelict and abandoned, these 19th-century commercial buildings had tremendous appeal, not to mention a terrific location just across the river from the City and the Tower of London.'

One Design Museum, one 'Gastrodome' and so many smart shops and loft apartments later, the area is thriving, despite all the nay-sayers who assured Conran that money 'wouldn't cross the river'. Cobbled Shad Thames Street is flanked by brick warehouses with old winches and Victorian signage. It is crisscrossed with iron walkways high above the street, which were once used for rolling barrels between the Butler's Wharf and Cardamom buildings. The area has provided a backdrop for several films, including *The Elephant Man*, *The French Lieutenant's Woman*, *A Fish Called Wanda*, and, way back in 1968, *Oliver!* – most appropriately, since Charles Dickens chose the eastern end as the location for the villainous Bill Sykes's den in *Oliver Twist*.

The Blueprint Café is rather more than its name suggests. In fact, it is a smart restaurant on the first floor of the Design Museum, from where diners can train the blue binoculars provided on every table, across the river to the City. It is especially magical at night when Tower Bridge is ablaze with lights. Even Oliver could not have asked for more.
Blueprint Café, 28 Shad Thames Street, SE1 2YD. London Bridge, Tower Hill tube; Tower Gateway DLR.

㉔ M. Manze's

London's oldest pie and mash shop has been in the same family, and serving the fare of the city's working classes, since 1902. The Manzes came to London from Ravello in southern Italy in 1878, settling in Bermondsey and trading as ice merchants, then as ice-cream makers. Michele Manze married a widow, Ada Poole, and set up shop here, serving jellied eels and hearty pie and mash with liquor, just eight years after the opening of Tower Bridge.

The pie man was a fixture on the streets of the capital in Victorian times, with his tray of meat and eel pies for anyone who chose to grab a bite. The eel pies were sold with vinegar, or pea or parsley sauce, and provided ballast for hungry labourers. The first eel and pie shop opened in the 1850s and as others followed, a style was established, both handsome and practical. The tiled interior of Manze's is typical and unspoilt. The exterior is featured for a few blinks of the eye in Elton John's video *Made in England*. The food, cooked fresh every day, is a taste that some might never acquire, but the flavour of the past is just delicious.
87 Tower Bridge Road, SE1 4TW.

㉕ Museum of Fashion and Textiles

Once synonymous with its weekly antiques market, Bermondsey now basks in its new image as one of London's trendiest villages. Bermondsey Square is 'south London's coolest quarter', according to no less an authority than *Vogue*, and this fashion museum is sitting pretty in a once run-down but now impossibly hip hinterland. Founded by fashion designer Zandra Rhodes (never knowingly understated), it shares with eight apartments, a building designed by Mexican Ricardo Legorreta – one of his few European projects – and painted in 'exhilarating' pink and orange. The museum was conceived as a 'cutting-edge centre for contemporary fashion, textiles and jewellery'. It hosts regular exhibitions and is on a mission to inspire 'creatives'.

Visitors feasting their eyes should leave room for a Devon cream tea in the nearby café. Along the road at No 50 is the Delfina Studio Café, which opened in 1994 as a canteen for resident artists, since when it has evolved into a thriving and still 'arty' restaurant.
83 Bermondsey Street, SE1 3XF. London Bridge tube.

㉖ George Inn

When the stagecoach *Commodore*, reeking of damp straw, bore Charles Dickens to London from his boyhood home in Kent, it would have been at such an inn that he was deposited. The George is the sole survivor in London of the galleried inns that sprang up from the mid 17th century in response to the emergence of the regular coaching service. It was rebuilt in 1676 after a fire that devastated most of medieval Southwark, and in its previous incarnation was, it is said, known to William Shakespeare. Certainly it was known to Dickens, for it has passing mention in *Little Dorrit*. He had lodgings around the corner in Lant Street – a back attic in the house of an insolvent court agent, with a pleasant prospect of a timber yard

– while he laboured by day in a blacking factory by Hungerford Stairs off the Strand. His father, meanwhile, was languishing in nearby Marshalsea debtors' prison, a place that would as loom large in *Little Dorrit* as it did in the writer's memory. A remnant of the wall still stands, marked with a commemorative plaque.

At one time, the inn building surrounded the cobbled courtyard on three sides. But as steam replaced horsepower, the Great Northern Railway used the building as a depot, and in 1899 pulled down the central and northern wings to make way for warehousing. In the inn's heyday the galleries served as stalls from which customers could watch performances in the yard, and still today Shakespeare's plays are sometimes staged here. The interior is poky in the nicest way, consisting of a series of connecting rooms. The Old Bar was the waiting room, the Middle Bar the coffee room. If Dickens had indeed looked in here, the landlord might have hesitated to serve him. As the writer himself recalled: 'I was such a little fellow … that frequently, when I went into a strange public house for a glass of ale or porter to wash down the saveloy and the loaf I had eaten in the street, they didn't like to give it me.' But then he was, after all, just 12 years old.

77 Borough High Street, SE1 1NH. London Bridge tube.

㉗ Borough Market

A gastronome's heaven is to be found under the railway viaducts and among a maze of backstreets on the south side of London Bridge. This is London's premier 'foodie' market – its emphasis is on the quality and provenance of its wares. Many of the stallholders grow, raise or bake what they sell, and chef demonstrations are regular crowd pleasers.

There was a market here way back in 1014 – perhaps before – where traders would sell their produce and livestock. In the 13th century they were herded off to what is now Borough High Street. When that market was closed by order of parliament in 1755, residents got together to raise the money to re-establish a market on land that was known as 'The Triangle', where the churchyard of St Margaret, the Patron Saint of Expectant Mothers, was once situated. Today, the Triangle is still at the heart of the market, which accommodates wholesalers as well as stallholders. Organic fruit and vegetable sellers, cheesemongers, fishmongers, butchers and bakers and all manner of other specialists are to be found here, and the vendors' enthusiasm is infectious.

8 Southwark Street, SE1 1TL. Thursday, Friday, Saturday. London Bridge, Borough tube.

LAMBETH

㉘ Imperial War Museum

In 1917, in the thick of the fighting during the First World War, the government decided that a museum should be founded to commemorate this Great War. Formally opened in the Crystal Palace in June 1920, it settled in its present home in 1936 – less than three years before a second cataclysmic war, which would furnish it with many more exhibits. Fittingly, the building was the surviving central portion of the Bethlehem Royal Hospital, the world's oldest hospital for the insane, the dire institution that endowed the language with the word 'bedlam'.

The interior was grim until renovated in 1989, including the addition of a top-lit exhibition hall with barrel-vault roof. Here is no gung-ho celebration of war, but an opportunity to explore its causes, meaning and impact, whether through the re-creation of a front-line trench on the Somme in 1916 – complete with special lighting, sounds and smells – or the reconstruction of an air-raid shelter and a blitzed street in 1940.

Plenty of heavy-duty vehicles and weaponry are on display, from a British infantry tank used in France and the western desert in 1940–1 to a Polaris missile. A Spitfire and a Sopwith Camel can be viewed, along with a German one-man submarine and, poignantly, the *Tamzine*, the smallest surviving fishing boat to have taken part in the evacuation of Dunkirk in 1940. It is chilling to see a V2 rocket, as tall as a two-storey house. This was the world's first ballistic missile and 500 of them rained down on London in August 1944. The V2 superseded the V1, which Joseph Goebbels, the Nazi Minister of Propaganda, had named *Vergeltungswaffe Eins* (Revenge Weapon 1). Londoners nicknamed it the 'Bob Hope', because when one approached, you just bobbed down and hoped. The fortitude of ordinary people in the face of war is an important focus and one of the most touching aspects of the collections.

Visitors overwhelmed by an emotional Blitzkrieg can retreat to the Tibetan Peace Garden, opened by the Dalai Lama in 1999, or to the flower-scented inner garden, for some quiet contemplation.
Lambeth Road, SE1 6HZ. Lambeth North tube.

㉙ Garden Museum

The tomb of John Tradescant and his son, also called John, plant hunters and gardeners to Charles I, came to light in the churchyard of medieval St Mary-at-Lambeth in 1977. The discovery inspired John and Rosemary Nicholson to save the church from the wrecking ball and to found what was then the Museum of Garden History within its confines.

This is one of London's best small museums, and a fitting homage to the Tradescants, the first people to grow pineapples and nectarines in England. Father and son were travellers, horticulturalists and collectors. They rented a house in nearby South Lambeth Road, and there put on display their specimens and souvenirs. A German visitor, Georg Christoph Stirn, in 1638, described the exhibits he saw there, which included 'a salamander, a chameleon, a pelican, a remora, a lanhado from Africa, a white partridge, a goose which has grown in Scotland on a tree, a flying squirrel, another squirrel like a fish … a number of things changed into stone … an ape's head, a cheese, etc … the hand of a mermaid, the hand of a mummy … a sea parrot, a toad-fish … a hat band of snake bones'.

Today the Garden Museum has nothing so rare as a toad-fish or a mermaid's hand, but its collection is a heart-warming and diverting celebration of British gardeners and gardening, with paintings, posters, early gardening implements and artefacts. Regular events include talks, fairs and festivals, garden visits and annual Rhubarb Day. There is a garden, of course, a shop, and a good vegetarian café.
Lambeth Palace Road, London SE1 7LB. Lambeth North tube.

㉚ Lambeth Palace

A mix of medieval, Jacobean and Tudor buildings, this palace has been the official residence of the Archbishop of Canterbury since the reign of King John at the beginning of the 13th century. The chapel and the crypt survive from that time at the ancient beating heart of the complex, but the image of the palace

THE ATMOSPHERE IS ONE OF PEACE AND HARMONY
LAMBETH PALACE

that the passer-by receives is of a sturdy Tudor redbrick gateway with twin five-storey battlemented towers and mullioned windows above the entrance.

Over the centuries, Lambeth Palace has been subject to additions and alterations, and has endured many vicissitudes, including war damage and downright vandalism. Wat Tyler's rebels overran it in 1381, torching books and smashing furniture. The chapel and Lollards Tower took a direct hit from an incendiary bomb in May 1941 and were gutted. Scorch marks are still visible on the floor. And yet the atmosphere overall is one of peace and harmony. The tranquil formal garden, lovingly tended, produces fruit, flowers and herbs, as it has done for centuries.

In the grounds of the Palace, the Great Hall houses the Lambeth Palace Library. One of the earliest public libraries in Britain, it was founded in 1610, and for its 400th anniversary it put on display such exhibits as the MacDurnan Gospels, written and illuminated in Ireland in the 9th century, a Gutenberg Bible printed in 1455 (the first great book in Western Europe to be printed from movable metal type), and the warrant for the execution of Mary, Queen of Scots. The library is the principle repository of the documentary history of the Church of England, but its collections roam around such subjects as architecture, genealogy and colonial and local history. More than 46,000 manuscripts – 600 of them medieval – are freely available for research *Lambeth Palace Road, SE1 7JU. Lambeth North tube. Guided tours are booked far in advance.*

③ The Cinema Museum

Tucked away in a Kennington cul-de-sac, close to Elephant and Castle, this collection is fittingly housed in the Lambeth workhouse where Charlie Chaplin and his half-brother, Sidney, found themselves in 1896. It was brought together by Ronald Grant, who co-founded the museum with Martin Humphries in 1986. The memorabilia on show encompasses all aspects of cinema-going, including ushers' uniforms and exhortations to 'applaud with hands only' and, in the interests of public safety, not to spit.

Grant's passion for cinema began in childhood, and at 15 he was apprenticed as a projectionist with Aberdeen Picture Palaces Ltd. In the 1960s, he moved to London and worked at the British Film Institute and the Brixton Ritzy. Back in Aberdeen, on a visit, he saved from destruction numbers of artefacts from the James F. Donald cinemas. As the movie industry declined and cinemas began to close around the country, his

collection grew. He rescued furnishings and equipment that was being ripped out of picture palaces – seating, carpets, ashtrays. He also acquired more than 17 million feet of film, including fake Boer War footage shot in the countryside outside Blackburn and reflecting events in the Transvaal, in 1899, when cameras were too hefty to get in among the action. He and Martin Humphries still tend the delightful trove of treasures they have amassed and their passion for the subject is palpable. There is a great sense of organised chaos, with bank on bank of filing cabinets stuffed with archive material – 'drawer full' warns a note on GULAG–GUNS.
The Master's House, 2 Dugard Way, SE11 4TH. Kennington tube. Open for guided tours.

㉜ The Oval

In 1845, one William Baker obtained a lease to convert a market garden into a cricket ground on land owned by the Duchy of Cornwall, and 10,000 turfs were brought from Tooting Common at a cost of £300. At a dinner at the Horns Tavern that August, following a match between the Gentlemen of Surrey and the Players of Surrey, it was agreed to found the Surrey County Cricket Club and that The Oval would be its permanent home. (In the Raffles novels, author E.W. Hornung had his suave burglar play for the Gentlemen, reasoning that 'if you can bowl a bit, your low cunning won't get rusty, and always looking for the weak spot's just the kind of mental exercise one wants.')

It was at The Oval, in 1862, that Edgar Willsher stormed off the pitch after being 'no balled' six times for bowling 'high' above the shoulder – an incident that led to the legalisation of overarm bowling within the rules two years later. The club's first paid secretary, Charles Alcock, was also secretary of the Football Association and – unthinkably today – the first FA Cup final was played on these hallowed Tooting turfs, in 1872.

It was at The Oval, also, on August 29, 1882, that England lost to Australia for the first time on British soil, prompting a mock obituary for English cricket in the *Sporting Times*, which lamented: 'The body will be cremated and the ashes taken to Australia.' Galled by such sneering effrontery, a few days later, a team captained by the Hon. Ivo Bligh set off for Australia with the avowed intent to return with 'the ashes'. Captain Bligh came home triumphant with a small, symbolic terracotta urn and honour bright – and the 'Ashes' have been contested ever since.
Kennington Oval, SE11 5SS. Oval, Vauxhall tube.

KEY

● Hyde Park

● Chelsea

● Kensington &
Holland Park

● South Kensington

Holla

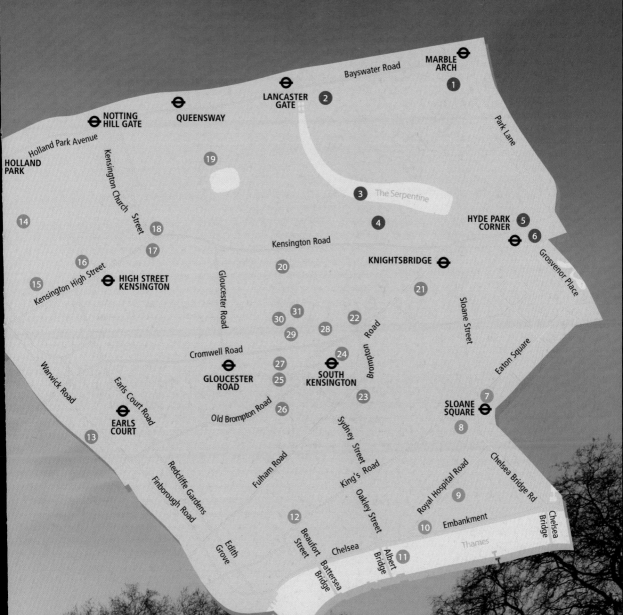

Kensington

Extensive parks and the long, curving lake of the Serpentine bring a taste of the country to the city. All around, smart shops serve well-maintained mansions, while world-famous museums are a lasting legacy of the Victorian age.

HYDE PARK

❶ Speakers' Corner

Treasonable talk is prohibited, as are incitements covered by common law, but otherwise people can say what they like in this democratic corner of Hyde Park. The fact that this applies to just about everywhere else in the country isn't the point; nor is the fact that blogs and Twitters might communicate with a far larger public. The point is that this is where people come when they have something to say, and are prepared to talk face to face. This is not the place for sound bites – old-fashioned arguments happen here. Marx and Lenin both spent time on soapboxes, so did the author George Orwell and Kwame Nkrumah, president of Ghana. Sunday morning is the best time to go.
Northeast corner of Hyde Park, near Marble Arch, W2 2UH. Marble Arch tube.

❷ Hyde Park Pet Cemetery

George Orwell called it 'perhaps the most horrible spectacle in Britain', and anybody who wants to see it has to book a week ahead. This is a peculiarly British enterprise, begun in 1888 when a dog named Prince, favourite of the wife of George, Duke of Cambridge, was run over. By the time it closed for burials in 1903, more than 300 animals had been interred, including not just cats and dogs but birds and even a monkey. Emotions expressed are real and raw. Shed a tear for Wee Bobbit, 'for six years our loving and most devoted friend'. Here, too, lie Dear Old Priny, Pomme de Terre, Chips, Scamp – and Emma, 'faithful and sole companion of my rootless and desolate life'.
Victoria Gate Lodge, Bayswater Road, W2. Lancaster Gate tube.

❸ The Serpentine

Rowing boats, pedaloes, a lido, a solar-powered ferry boat, fountains, fish, a lakeside café – the Serpentine sums up London at leisure. No wonder it was chosen for the swimming section of the triathlon for the 2012 Olympic Games. It covers 9ha (22 acres) and takes about 90 minutes to walk around, with plenty of diversions along the way. The lake was created by damming the Westbourne River, which came down from Hampstead, passed through Hyde Park and entered the Thames at Chelsea. The name derives from the fact that it was among the first artificial lakes to take on a natural rather than a symmetrical shape. Queen Caroline had it laid out in 1730 in the gardens of Kensington Palace, and two royal yachts sailed its waters. Eighty-four years later it was used for a re-enactment of the Battle of Trafalgar, when guns blazed and the French fleet in miniature was sunk.

The bridge at its centre marks the division of Hyde Park and Kensington Gardens, and the part of the Serpentine that falls in Kensington Gardens is rightfully called the Long Water. Here the lake is more natural, and wildlife habitats line its shores. Swans nest, rabbits hop and red-eared terrapins bask in the sun. The reeds attract dragonflies and moths. Also on the shore is the statue by Sir George Frampton of J.M. Barrie's Peter Pan, who magically whisked away the Darling children from their Kensington home.

The lake spills out over the eastern end between the café and Fisherman's Keep, which is the place on the southern bank where anglers can reel in roach and carp. Beneath the Queen Caroline Memorial and Dell Bridge, the water falls away into the Dell, one of the most attractive corners of Hyde Park.
Lancaster Gate, Hyde Park Corner tube.

❹ Rotten Row

This largely empty, dusty track was once one of the most fashionable avenues in London. When the reigning monarchs, William and Mary, moved into Kensington Palace, they had the 1½ mile stretch laid out along the southern length of Hyde Park as a safe route into town. But highwaymen were still at work, and to add to the monarchs' security, 300 lamps were hung from trees along the way, making it the first road in England to be artificially lit. Soon all society was making use of the avenue, and it became a place to stroll and ride, to show off in fancy carriages, much as Parisians did in the Bois de Boulogne. Some say the name derives from *rue de roi* – the king's road. John Timbs, in 1855, suggested it came from *rotteram*, to muster, adding: 'It is for saddle horses who can gallop over its fine loose gravel without danger from falling, and it is crowded with equestrians between 5 and 7pm.'

Today, as the park's South Ride, it is used by the Household Cavalry to exercise their horses, and for their daily trot to Horse Guards from the Knightsbridge Barracks, where they are billeted in Basil Spence's 1970 tower block. Hyde Park Stables make use of it, too. Anyone can hire horses at the stables, and enjoy 5 miles of bridleway in the park.
Hyde Park Stables, 63 Bathurst Mews, W2 2SB. Lancaster Gate, Paddington tube.

❺ Apsley House

A nude statue of Napoleon by Canova is an unlikely figure to greet visitors to the home of the Duke of Wellington, especially since it's 3.5m (11ft) tall. The duke, Arthur Wellesley, was already the most famous person in England when he bought the property from his brother in 1817.

The house was the first in London inside the Knightsbridge toll gate, so its address was No 1 London. It had been built by Robert Adam, and the duke had it enlarged by Benjamin Wyatt to accommodate his increasing collection of art. A Tory MP and twice prime minister, he used the house as a showcase home, where he could conduct affairs of state. It was not just titles and honours that were bestowed on him. Sèvres porcelain came from Louis XVIII, a 1,000 piece silver service from the grateful Portuguese and, most prized, paintings captured from Joseph Bonaparte's fleeing caravan in Vitoria. More than 80 works were seized from the Spanish royal collection, paintings by Goya, Rubens and Velazquez among them. Some are hung in the Waterloo Gallery, 27m (90ft) long and based on Versailles' Hall of Mirrors. Military memorabilia include both his and Napoleon's swords from Waterloo, and the Canova, *Napoleon as Mars the Peacemaker*, at the bottom of the staircase, another gift from Louis XVIII.

149 Piccadilly, W1J 7NT. Hyde Park Corner tube. Closed Monday.

❻ Wellington Arch

Anybody who wishes to peek into Buckingham Palace gardens should take the lift up to the viewing platforms of the monumental arch in the middle of the big roundabout at Hyde Park Corner. The arch was designed by Decimus Burton to celebrate the end of the Napoleonic wars, and it was originally topped by an outsized equestrian statue of the Duke of Wellington made of melted French cannon captured at Waterloo. It was intended to provide a triumphal entrance into London and Buckingham Palace, which was about to be occupied by royalty for the first time. There are three floors of exhibition space inside the arch, which once housed a police station.

Hyde Park Corner, W1J 7JZ. Hyde Park Corner tube.

APSLEY HOUSE AND WELLINGTON ARCH

CHELSEA

❼ Royal Court Theatre

This premiere theatre for new plays is one of the most important in Europe, in the judgment of the *New York Times*. There has been a theatre here, on the site of a dissenters' chapel, since 1870, when it was called the New Chelsea Theatre. Rebuilt in 1952, it was taken over by the English Stage Company under the artistic directorship of the inspired George Devine, whose mission was to discover 'hard-hitting, uncompromising writers', and to create a company that would put a rocket under British theatre. The company employed several talented young actors, including Alan Bates and Joan Plowright. An advertisement in *The Stage* brought in a flood of scripts, but one in particular was 'hard-hitting, uncompromising'. It was by a Fulham-born 27 year old, in the genre that would come to be known as 'kitchen sink' drama. The playwright was John Osborne, the play his debut, *Look Back in Anger*, starring Bates, and it had one great champion in the *Observer*'s Kenneth Tynan, who said: 'I doubt if I could love anybody who did not wish to see *Look Back in Anger*.' Since that time, the Royal Court has never looked back. Following redevelopment work, it reopened in triumph in February 2002, and continues to promote new talent.
Sloane Square, SW1W 8AS. Sloane Square tube.

❽ Saatchi Gallery

When John Sanders designed the Royal Military Asylum as a school for the children of soldiers' widows, he can have had no notion that it would one day be a showcase for young artists. Yet the building, completed in 1801, might have been made for just that purpose. After a little refurbishment of what had become the Duke of York's Barracks, by the architects Paul Davis & Partners and Allford Hall Monaghan Morris, in 2008 Saatchi was able to move in. Fifteen light, high, equally and beautifully proportioned spaces provide a perfect home for Charles Saatchi's protégés. Café Mess, with vaulted ceilings, exposed brickwork and outdoor seating, serves up fare that is perhaps easier to digest.
Duke of York's Headquarters, King's Road, SW3 4SQ. Sloane Square tube.

❾ Royal Hospital

The 'Men in Scarlet', Chelsea Pensioners, are unique to this city and have an abiding place in Londoners' hearts. In 1681, recognising the necessity for some provision for the 'succour and relief of veterans broken by age and war', Charles II commissioned Sir Christopher Wren to design a building for them. Wren's original idea was for a single quadrangle, known as Figure Court, flanked by accommodation blocks, with the Great Hall and Chapel on the third side. Before building began, however, it became clear that this was insufficient, so Wren added two further quadrangles. The annual Royal Hospital Founder's Day, when the veterans are usually reviewed by a member of the royal family, is held on, or close to, May 29, the birthday of Charles II and – what a birthday gift! – the date of his restoration as king in 1660. It is also known as Oak Apple Day, commemorating Charles's escape after the Battle of Worcester in 1651, when he hid in an oak tree to evade capture by Parliamentarians. For the celebrations, the gilded statue of Charles II in Figure Court is decorated with oak leaves and all participants of the parade, as well as spectators, wear sprigs of oak. The veterans are proud to give guided tours of their fine accommodation, by arrangement, and visitors and small groups are welcome to drop by.
Royal Hospital Road, SW3 4SR. Sloane Square tube.

❿ Chelsea Physic Garden

One of London's most unusual gardens, a centre of education, beauty and relaxation, lies behind a high brick wall on busy Royal Hospital Road. The 1.5ha (3.8 acre) garden was established in 1673 by the Worshipful Society of Apothecaries as a place where apprentices could cultivate and study medicinal plants. The soil was rich, the riverside position propitious – not only did it create a warmer microclimate, but river travel was safer and quicker than road, and the apothecaries could moor the barge they used for 'herborising' expeditions. In August 1685 the diarist John Evelyn wrote of his visit to the 'Apothecaries' garden of Simples at Chelsea', where he saw 'the tree bearing Jesuits' bark, which has done such wonders in quartan agues', and marvelled at the innovative subterranean heating of the greenhouse. Some of the first cedars of Lebanon seedlings in Britain were cultivated here.

The statue at the garden's centre is of Dr Hans Sloane (recalled in Hans Crescent and Sloane Street), who bought the Manor of Chelsea from Charles Cheyne in 1712, took over the freehold of the garden, and granted the tenants a lease on the land for £5 – still paid to his descendants. Today, the soil nurtures the largest outdoor fruiting olive tree in Britain. The oldest rock garden in the country on view to the public was

built here in 1772, using stones from the Tower of London, Icelandic lava, fused bricks and flint – one of the more unusual structures to have Grade II listing. An historical walk has been laid out to introduce the visitor to the seminal figures in the garden's development, including Sir Joseph Banks (Banksia) and William Forsyth (Forsythia). The work of the apothecaries was not always understood and they were at times the subject of derision. Plant finders and botanists today, acknowledging our debt, feel only respect. Lavender scones and homemade lemonade and ginger beer are served in the café.
Royal Hospital Road, SW3 4HS. Sloane Square tube.

⑪ Albert Bridge

The 'Trembling Lady', London's prettiest bridge was built at the urging of Prince Albert, to link Chelsea on the north bank of the Thames to Battersea on the south. It opened in 1873 as a toll bridge – the octagonal tollbooths are still in place – but it was never commercially viable. The bridge was designed by Rowland Mason Ordish, a leading architectural engineer, who had worked on the Royal Albert Hall, St Pancras station and the Crystal Palace, and was built according to his patented Ordish-Lefeuvre Principle – an early form of cable-stayed bridge design. However, it proved to be structurally unsound and had to be strengthened. The work took place between 1884 and 1885, overseen by Sir Joseph Bazalgette, and incorporated some of the elements of a suspension bridge. It was never conceived for the heavy traffic that plies across the river today, and is still in fragile condition. Plans to demolish it in the 1970s were vigorously opposed by conservationists led by John Betjeman, and it is Grade II listed. Its attractive appearance is partly functional. Ice-cream shades of pink and green ensure its visibility to river traffic in murky weather, and at night it is enchantingly lit with 4,000 low-voltage bulbs for the same purpose. Notices at either end warn marching soldiers from nearby Chelsea Barracks to break step so as not to damage the structure.
Albert Bridge, SW3/SW11. Sloane Square tube.

⑫ Bluebird Garage

An Art Deco garage built in 1926 to house 300 cars has become a Terence Conran 'gastrodome'. On site is a café, forecourt and barbecue, restaurant and bar, food store, bakery and wine cellar.
350 King's Road, SW3 5UU. Sloane Square, South Kensington tube.

KENSINGTON

CHELSEA PHYSIC GARDEN

KENSINGTON & HOLLAND PARK

⑬ Earl's Court Exhibition Centre

A volley of arguments is under way over this landmark exhibition space and prime music venue. Since it opened in 1937, Howard Crane's striking building, with its wide Art Deco, come-one-come-all frontage, has helped to define this part of London. A giant Ferris or 'observation' wheel – a kind of early London Eye – once stood on the site, where, in the late 19th century, 'Buffalo Bill' staged his Wild West show, drawing crowds of 15,000. The halls have hosted the Motor Show, beer festivals and the Brit Awards. Pink Floyd and Led Zeppelin played here in the 1970s. Plans to flatten it and to redevelop the 28ha (70 acre) area on which it stands are an exciting opportunity for regeneration or an unmitigated disaster, according to differing points of view. For now, as the chosen venue for 2012 Olympic volleyball, it has been reprieved.
Warwick Road, SW5 9TA. Earls Court, West Brompton tube.

⑭ Holland Park

Peacocks, opera and the Orangery all help to make this the most romantic park in London. Built in 1605 by James I's Chancellor of the Exchequer, Holland House was an elegant manor with a large garden that John Tradescant helped to plant. The dahlia was introduced to Britain here by Elizabeth, Lady Holland, who was a great socialite. She and her husband, the Whig politician Henry Vassell-Fox, 3rd Baron Holland, whose statue stands in the grounds, instigated 'the Holland House set', an influential literary and political circle, aided by the baron's uncle, Charles James Fox.

Before the war, this was the scene of London's last remaining game shoot, and at a ball here in the summer of 1939, Queen Elizabeth and George VI were among a thousand guests. It was a last hurrah. The manor was all but destroyed by incendiary bombs one night in September 1940. Bought with public funds in 1952, the house and 22ha (55 acre) park were opened to the public. What was left of the East Wing is now a youth hostel, while the remaining front terrace provides a lovely backdrop for a summer theatre and opera season. The grounds are compartmentalised into formal gardens, Japanese garden, a wild area, cricket pitch and woodland. The Belvedere restaurant in Holland House's former ballroom is a place for special occasions, and the Orangery in the formal gardens, which the peacocks favour, is a popular venue for wedding receptions.
Youth Hostel, Holland Walk, W8 7QU. Holland Park, High Street Kensington tube.

15 Leighton House Museum

Behind a restrained Italianate façade is an orientalist fantasy – interior decoration run riot. Frederic, Lord Leighton, was not just one of the most acclaimed but one of the most financially successful artists of the Victorian age – rich enough to commission a fine house for himself, and ask his friend Lord Aitchison to design interiors that bedazzle. From the time of its construction in 1864, until Leighton's death in 1896, the house was a work in progress, continually being added to and embellished. European, Asian and North African influences mix and mingle. The *pièce de resistance*, the Arab Hall of 1877, is lined with hundreds of 16th and 17th-century tiles from Damascus, inlaid with Egyptian woodwork. A gilt mosaic frieze depicts scenes from mythology. A fountain gently plays. A statue from the House of the Faun in Pompeii recalls a Roman villa quite as much as a Moorish palace in Andalusia.

The artist's studio is a hall 18m (60ft) long, washed in daylight from a huge north window, with a gilt dome and apse and marble inlaid fireplaces. Should Lord Leighton have put down his paintbrush and focused on interior design? Maybe. His house stands as his greatest legacy.
12 Holland Park Road, W14 8LZ. High Street Kensington tube.

16 Linley Sambourne House

This late-Victorian townhouse remains just as its owner left it on his death in 1910. Edward Linley Sambourne, a political cartoonist for the satirical magazine *Punch*, lived here with his family from 1874, and the visitor has the sense of trespassing on their private domain while they, perhaps, have just popped out for a stroll in Holland Park. It is as if the clock had stopped 100 years ago and time stood still. The cluttered interior is scarcely changed, complete with books, ornaments, velvet drapes, William Morris wallpaper, and a Victorian lavatory. Occasional tables are crammed with Chinese porcelain, plush chairs are strewn with cushions, everything crowds in. The walls are hung with framed original Sambourne cartoons, and with the erotic photographs (innocent by today's standards) that displaced drawing as the artist's passion. Perhaps a love of photography was passed down in the genes. Edward's great-grandson is Lord Snowdon, one-time husband of the late Princess Margaret (see below, Maggie Jones's).
18 Stafford Terrace, W8 7BH. High Street Kensington tube. Guided tours only.

17 Whole Foods at Barker's

The American organic and natural food retailer opened its first London superstore in this French Art Deco building in 2004. P.E. Culverhouse's 1930s steel-frame and Portland stone creation, complete with bronze and glass towers and reliefs of cars and aeroplanes, may seem an unlikely home for a supermarket opposed to air miles. Yet it rather nicely contrasts with the company's high ambitions to convert the world to a healthier and more sustainable way of life. Sustainability is not, it must be said, the first word that springs to mind when confronted with such visions of superabundance.
63–69 Kensington High Street, W8 5SE. High Street Kensington tube.

18 Maggie Jones's

The late Princess Margaret and her husband Antony Armstrong Jones used to come here, allegedly, when they were courting, hence the name. The decor is unchanged since the mid 1960s. Intimate nooks and large tables for parties have dried flowers and candles jammed in wine bottles, and the menu offers potted shrimps and steak-and-kidney pie.
6 Old Court Place, W8 4PL. High Street Kensington tube.

KENSINGTON

⑲ Kensington Gardens

William III, a martyr to asthma, found the clean air of Kensington beneficial to his health, so he commissioned Sir Christopher Wren to embellish and extend Nottingham House, a Jacobean Mansion on the West side of Hyde Park, as befitted a royal residence. When his cousin Anne became Queen in 1702, she lavished money on the grounds and ordained the creation of a 'greenhouse', to serve as a 'summer supper house' and place of entertainment. This was the Orangery, designed by Nicholas Hawksmoor, possibly in a unique collaboration with Sir John Vanbrugh. Behind its fine brick façade, Corinthian columns stand beside tall windows through which the sunlight floods, lighting up the long white interior, which today serves as a palatial café and restaurant.

The best time to see the gardens is in spring, when the visitor can stroll through a sea of waving tulips of every hue. Among the sights of the park are the high-Victorian Gothic extravaganza that was Queen Victoria's memorial to Prince Albert. Round Pond has been home to the oldest model yacht club in the country since 1876. The green woodpeckers that nest in the park might show themselves. Kensington Palace has, of course, been home to another William, the Duke of Cambridge, who has chosen to take his bride, Kate Middleton, to live there in a 'perfect' cottage.
Kensington Gardens, Kensington Palace, W8 4PX. High Street Kensington tube.

⑳ Royal Albert Hall

Since it opened in March 1871, this hall has provided a platform for great performers and figures of world stature. It was built to fulfil the desire of Prince Albert for a central hall that would serve to promote understanding and appreciation of the arts and sciences – a space not only for concerts but for exhibitions and public events, ceremonies and discussions. To these ends, it works magnificently. The Who and The Beatles, among many others, have performed here. Sir Winston Churchill, Nelson Mandela, and Bill Clinton have all taken the stage.

When Albert died prematurely, of typhus, at just 42, Henry Cole, one of his collaborators in the Great Exhibition of 1851 and a future director of the V&A, drove the project forward. The building's design and structure were inspired by Cole's visits to ruined Roman amphitheatres and work on it was begun by Captain Francis Fowke, a Royal Engineer, and completed, on Fowke's death, by Lt Col Henry Darracott Scott. The foundation stone was laid by Albert's widow, Queen Victoria, in May 1868.

A vast auditorium with a glazed dome and wrought-iron girders is at the heart of the hall, which was, at the time, the largest structure of its kind in the world. From 1921 to 1933 it was substantially modified. The unmissable exterior, incorporating 6 million bricks and 80,000 tonnes of terracotta, drew inspiration from Italy. Above a 24m (80ft) terracotta frieze of allegorical figures bent on artistic, scientific and cultural endeavours, the legend declares: 'This Hall was erected for the advancement of the Arts and Sciences and works of industry of all nationals in the fulfilment of the intention of Albert Prince Consort …'

In the mind of Londoners, the Hall is indivisibly associated with the 'Proms' – an annual season of 'Promenade Concerts', jubilant, flag-waving affairs, for which many of the 'Prommers' buy cheap tickets for standing room.
Kensington Gore, SW7 2AP. South Kensington tube.

㉑ Harrods Food Hall

From tea merchant Charles Henry Harrod's small grocer's shop, bought in 1849, has grown one of the world's most famous stores, a byword for luxury and good taste. The present store, built in 1889 and still one of the largest in Europe, has a terracotta-tiled exterior, embellished with cherubs and topped with a baroque dome. London's first 'moving staircase' – a continuous leather belt – was installed in 1898, with an assistant on hand to dispense cognac and smelling salts for nervous shoppers. Modern-day visitors, entering the carved and gilded Egyptian Room to be confronted by a giant gold sphinx, might be similarly overcome, fancying they have been transported to ancient Luxor. Stepping aboard the escalator, they should look up at the ceiling to see images of the night sky and Zodiacal figures, adapted from decorations at the Temple of Dendera.

It used to be said that customers could buy anything they wanted from Harrods, even an elephant, although there was never much call for those; hence the motto *Omnia Omnibus Ubique*, 'Everything for Everyone Everywhere'. This is London's third most popular destination for overseas visitors. The food halls are palatial, with mosaic friezes and, it seems, every kind of foodstuff under the sun. The dress code bans high-cut, Bermuda and beach shorts, swimwear, athletic singlets, cycling shorts, flip-flops and thong sandals, bare midriffs, bare feet, and dirty, scruffy clothes.
87–135 Brompton Road, SW1X 7XL. Knightsbridge tube.

A BYWORD FOR LUXURY AND GOOD TASTE

HARRODS FOOD HALL

SOUTH KENSINGTON

㉒ London Oratory

This was the first large Roman Catholic place of worship built in London after the Reformation, and the beautiful Church of the Immaculate Heart of Mary remained the largest Catholic church in London until the opening of Westminster Cathedral. The London Oratory is home to a community of priests named 'The Congregation of the Oratory of Saint Philip Neri', or simply, 'Oratorians'. The Oratorians' first London home was in premises variously described as a former 'whisky store', 'gin shop' and 'dance hall', just off the Strand. After three years, a house and temporary church were erected in an area of fields and lanes known as Brompton, and in 1874 an appeal was launched for funds to build something altogether finer. A competition was initiated to choose a designer. Herbert Gribble, 29, a recent convert from Devon, won the honour and a £200 prize. His neobaroque building was consecrated in 1884.

Among the church's treasures are Rex Whistler's paintings of the martyrs Sir Thomas More and John Fisher, and many mosaics and carvings. St Winifred's Chapel has a splendid high altar and an Italian altarpiece inlaid with precious stones, and marble statues of the apostles from Siena Cathedral. Chevalliaud's marble statue of recently beatified Cardinal Newman commemorates the man who brought St Philip's Oratory from Rome to England.

St Philip, who founded his congregation in the 1500s, stressed the importance of the beauty of divine worship and the exalting power of sacred music, and the Oratorians maintain the tradition. The organ, constructed on neoclassical lines by J.W. Walker & Sons in the 1950s to the designs of the organist Ralph Downes, is one of the finest to be built since the Second World War. *Brompton Road, SW7 2RP. South Kensington tube.*

㉓ Bibendum

The spectacular old white faience Michelin building, a mix of Art Deco, Art Nouveau and tyre motif, was restored by Terence Conran in 1987 and houses everything from the Conran Shop and a restaurant and oyster bar, to a crustacea stall and an airy café. This was where Conran pioneered the idea of bringing together eateries and retail outlets, as he would continue to do in Butler's Wharf. The brilliant building, by François Espinasse, dates from 1905–11. Motorists used to pull in for tyre changes in fitting bays at the front. Tile panels explore motoring history

BIBENDUM

and early racing cars. Etchings of Parisian streets on some upper windows are a nod to Michelin's role as mapmakers. Joyous references to the Michelin man are all over the building – one mosaic depicts him raising a glass of nuts and bolts. He has been promoting tyres since 1898 and, if not the world's oldest corporate mascot, he is one of the most loved. In his early incarnation he was known as 'the road drunkard' and his name, Bibendum, means 'drinking to be done'. *81 Fulham Road, SW1 6RD. South Kensington tube.*

㉔ No 5 Thurloe Square

From the end, the small mansion block on the southwest corner of upmarket Thurloe Square looks a fake, a façade put up in a film lot. Four-storeys tall and topped by chimney stacks, it is the width of a few red bricks. The ground-floor front window gives a clear view through the rear one. It seems incredible that it is occupied. But then, of course, it is not really that thin, but wedge-shaped, getting wider towards neighbouring Victorian houses on the eastern side. The building stands on the site of three houses (numbers 1, 3 and 5) that stood here until they were demolished in 1867 to make way for the railway line just outside South Kensington Station. In their place, 20 years later, this block of seven artists' studios was squeezed in, utilising the last few inches of space. *5 Thurloe Square, SW7 2TA. South Kensington tube.*

㉕ Bute Street

A London street with a strong French accent is to be found close to the Institut (right). Here is Nicolas for fine French wines, Bute Street Boucherie, the French Book Shop, La Bonne Bouchée and Rotisserie Jules, plus Oddono's great Italian ice-cream parlour – but no branch of French Connection. Two minutes' walk away on Cromwell Place is the double-fronted Cave à Fromage, where expert cheesemongers Eric Charriaux and Amnon Paldi offer a range of more than 200 farmhouse cheeses. Where better in London to find what James Joyce called a 'really footy brie'? *SW7. South Kensington tube.*

㉖ Christie's, South Kensington

Christie's have been in the auction business since the 1760s, so they should know if an old vase from the attic is priceless 18th-century Qianlong dynasty porcelain or 20th-century Woolworth. The country's busiest salesroom is open seven days a week, and holds 100 sales a year of more than 20,000 lots, attracting 200,000 visitors from around the world. The atmosphere is friendly, the salesroom bright, and there are exhibition spaces. Three times a month interiors sales are dedicated to home furnishings. The auctions can make for exciting spectacle, and include items within the reach of those of fairly modest means. *85 Old Brompton Road, SW7 3LD. South Kensington tube.*

㉗ Institut Français

***Entente* was never more *cordiale* than in this place of culture, learning and relaxation. Founded in 1910** by a young French woman, Marie d'Orliac, to introduce Londoners to French artists, writers and culture, the Institut is one of the oldest of 150 worldwide. It moved several times after it was first established at Marble Arch House, before finding a permanent home in this Art Deco building commissioned from the architect Patrice Bonnet.

The visitor stepping inside finds a cast of Rodin's *L'Age d'Airain* (The Age of Bronze) and a tapestry by Sonia Delaunay. Up the sweeping staircase, on the first floor, is Ciné Lumière, opened as a cinema by Catherine Deneuve in 1997. The library, converted from a ballroom in 1950, has a panelled reading room. It was refurbished in 1995, with open-access shelving, and inaugurated in 1996 by President Jacques Chirac. The Institut offers courses in French language and wine-tasting. Its Médiatèque holds the largest free-access collection of French material in the country – films, documentaries, music, poetry, novels and children's books. There is a pleasingly simple bistro for the hungry and thirsty to take *café au lait* and a *croque* or a glass of wine. *17 Queensberry Place, SW7 2DT. South Kensington tube.*

KENSINGTON

TILE PANELS EXPLORE MOTORING HISTORY

BIBENDUM

Eminently Victorian

London is deeply, extensively – in parts overwhelmingly – Victorian. So much of the fabric, the infrastructure, the very guts of the city were created in the Victorian era.

During the 64 year reign of Queen Victoria, London was the capital of a vast and expanding empire, the largest ever seen, and Britain's sense of itself as a world superpower, coupled with burgeoning industry and rail travel, translated into ambitious construction projects.

In those six decades from 1837 to 1901 the population of London mushroomed – from under 2 million in 1841 to more than 4.5 million in 1901 – and the city grew with it, swallowing up outlying villages from Clapham to Kilburn. Aided by the growth and affordability of the railways, omnibuses and trams, which for the first time allowed workers to live farther than walking distance from their place of employment, terrace upon terrace of bay-fronted houses was constructed for the working and lower-middle classes. Today, estate agents' windows are filled with pictures of these same houses, offered for sale or to let, and they are universally considered to be 'desirable'.

High-rise philanthropy

Meaner back-to-back terraces were built in the East End for the most oppressed and put-upon workers, but these came to be frowned upon, and cosier cottage-style residences began to take their place. Philanthropists such as the American banker and dry-goods merchant George Peabody commissioned some of London's oldest surviving high-rise apartment blocks, for 'artisans and the labouring poor'. The handsome Peabody Estate on Lawrence Street, Chelsea, was built to the Italianate design of Henry Astley Darbishire in 1870. Peabody was concerned 'to ameliorate the condition of the poor' and to benefit their health – to which end, vaccination was mandatory for tenants. Passages, steps, closets and lavatory windows had to be washed every Saturday, and passages and steps swept every morning before 10am. The heiress and philanthropist Angela Burdett-Coutts, a close friend of Charles Dickens, engaged Darbishire to build Holly Village (1865), eight rustic Gothic-style dwellings for her servants, in Highgate; she also had him build model dwellings on Columbia Road, E2, spearheading the Metropolitan Association for Improving the Dwellings of the Industrial Classes.

If, as Goethe said, architecture is frozen music, Victorian public architecture is 'God Save the Queen'; it is 'Pomp and Circumstance' in bricks and mortar. Victorian buildings – the seat of government, Gothic churches, schools, museums, railway stations, town halls, temperance halls, public libraries, almshouses, bathhouses, workhouses, public lavatories, gardens, burial parks – all sing of patriotism and civic pride.

In the early years of Victoria's reign, most new building was in the classical style, as in the Regency period, but the soaring popularity of the Gothic novel, Romanticism, and the influence of architects such as Pugin fired up the Gothic revival. Prince Albert of Saxe-Coburg-Gotha, the Queen's consort, was a progressive and pioneering figure, a driving force behind the rebuilding of the Houses of Parliament to Charles Barry's Gothic design, and the Great Exhibition of 1851. Although mostly completed after his death, the museum and cultural complex in South Kensington – nicknamed Albertopolis – is perhaps his greatest legacy. Both he and Victoria admired and encouraged scientific invention, and Albert was quick to climb aboard the nascent railway, the Golden Age of which was fast approaching.

George Gilbert Scott's fantastical St Pancras, Edward Middleton Barry's French Renaissance-style Charing Cross Station Hotel, Isambard Kingdom Brunel's Paddington featuring Matthew Digby Wyatt's glorious interior, and the two glass vaulted train sheds of Lewis Cubitt's King's Cross, deriving from the Crystal Palace, are among the surviving monuments to the glory days of steam travel.

Innovation and preservation

Other temples to Victorian engineering include Joseph Bazalgette's stupendous pumping stations, such as that at Crossness. His gift to London of a sewerage system and the resultant Thames Embankments brought incalculable benefits. Bravura feats of engineering, today taken so much for granted, include Tower Bridge and the Blackwall Tunnel. The present northbound tunnel was built in 1897 to allow horse-drawn carts and carriages to pass under the Thames, and now caters for up to 50,000 cars and lorries a day.

In 1958, Anne, Lady Rosse, John Betjeman (later Sir John, poet laureate) and the art and architecture historian Nikolaus Pevsner became founder members of the Victorian Society, which was formed to campaign for the preservation of Victorian buildings under threat of demolition. They did not always succeed, but at times they triumphed. If British Rail had had its way, the glorious edifice of St Pancras would have been reduced to rubble in 1966.

➋➑ Victoria & Albert Museum

The infinite variety of human creativity is revealed in this repository of decorative arts. Sculpture, ceramics, glass, furniture, photographs, costume and ironwork are here to surprise and instruct. Items range from the sublime, such as a tiny blue glass vase from 3,500 BC Egypt, to the massive – the whole of Sir Paul Pindar's wooden three-storey house front from Bishopsgate. The museum was one of the main beneficiaries of the Great Exhibition, for which Prince Albert and the tireless Henry Cole had striven in order to educate the people. The museum's sculpture halls display brilliant copies of Michelangelo's David and Trajan's Column, which attract students of every age, while the costume department is the place to go for any

period reference. The Arts & Crafts era in which the building was born is best evoked in the glorious Morris, Gamble & Poynter Room, now the museum's restaurant, where notes from a piano sometimes float between the tiled pillars and the Burne-Jones windows.
Cromwell Road, SW7 2RL. South Kensington tube. Free admission.

➋➒ Natural History Museum

'The animals' Westminster Abbey' opened its doors in 1881 – and has been opening eyes ever since. The museum traces its origins to Sir Hans Sloane, who left his extensive specimen collection to the nation in 1753. It was housed in the British Museum, but as other collections were added, the museum's

NATURAL HISTORY MUSEUM

fossilised ammonite, perhaps 400 million years old. Some 55 million animals and 28 million insects are represented here, with 9 million fossils, including one of just six known examples of the earliest-known flying bird. The 6 million plant specimens include algae, ferns, mosses and seeds; there are more than half a million rocks and minerals, and 3,200 meteorites.
Cromwell Road and Exhibition Road, SW7 5BD. South Kensington tube. Free admission.

㉚ Darwin Centre

The Natural History Museum enters the 21st century with this research centre and repository for 22 million zoological specimens. In stark but not unpleasing contrast to the main museum building, the award-winning, climate-controlled Darwin Centre, opened in 2002, is strictly utilitarian. From connecting walkways, visitors can watch scientists at work in their laboratories, and in the giant Cocoon, wander through graphic displays. This is world-class science in action!
Cromwell Road and Exhibition Road, SW7 5BD. South Kensington tube. Free admission.

㉛ Science Museum

Like science itself, this museum has been a continuous work in progress. Its origins can be traced to the Great Exhibition of 1851 and the opening of the South Kensington Museum in 1857, which included among other miscellanea an exhibition of machinery, featuring an early Boulton & Watt beam engine, Symington's marine steam engine of 1788, the locomotive Puffing Billy of 1814, and Stephenson's Rocket of 1829. As the scientific exhibits multiplied, so the argument grew for a separate institution dedicated to science. When the Kensington Museum was renamed the Victoria & Albert and designated an art museum, as the late queen had intended, that argument became incontrovertible.

The science museum's exhibits range from the microchip and the world's first airmail stamp (for mail sent by the balloon Buffalo at Nashville, Tennessee, in 1877) to full-sized aircraft, via timekeeping, computing and the science and art of medicine in different worlds. James Watt's workshop is just as he left it. Recently restored, it includes such odd ideas as a machine for copying sculpture. There is a re-creation of Charles Babbage's 19th-century Difference Engine No. 2, which is a vast mechanical calculator, and a 1956 Ferranti Pegasus – the world's oldest working computer.
Exhibition Road, SW7 2DD. South Kensington tube.

superintendent, Sir Richard Owen, pressed for a dedicated new building – and what a building this is! It was to be the work of Captain Francis Fowke, who had also begun the Royal Albert Hall, but with his sudden death in 1865, it passed to Alfred Waterhouse, who altered the design from Renaissance to German Romanesque. Visitors, pausing outside, should look up at the huge façade, the high, spired columns and rounded arches that recall a cathedral. Inside they are confronted by a 26m (85ft) cast of a diplodocus – and a glorious gallery with painted ceiling and grand staircase. The museum houses the largest and most important natural history collection in the world, with 70 million specimens collected over 400 years, from microscopic spores to the bones of a woolly mammoth and the ineffable mystery of a

KENSINGTON

North

From the verdant surroundings of Primrose Hill and Hampstead Heath, the vast city opens out in spectacular views. In the streets below, the cheerful bustle of Portobello Road and Camden markets contrasts with the serenity of the magnificent Victorian cemetery at Highgate, while curious museums, galleries and theatres wait to be discovered.

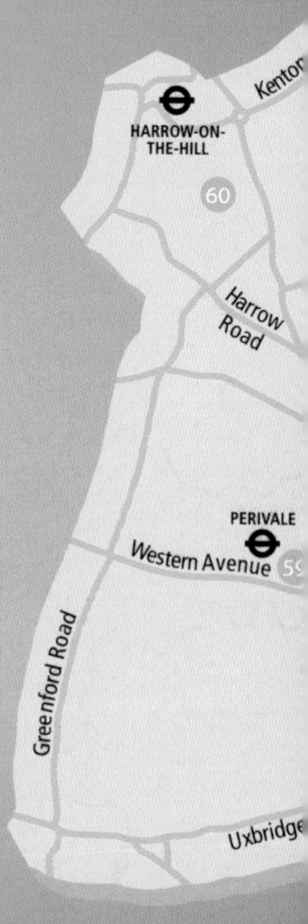

HARROW-ON-THE-HILL

Kenton

60

Harrow Road

PERIVALE

Western Avenue 59

Greenford Road

Uxbridge

ARNOS GROVE 39

North Circular Road

WOOD GREEN

Lordship Lane

MUSWELL HILL 38

North Circular Road

EAST FINCHLEY 40

STAMFORD HILL

Finchley Road

GOLDERS GREEN

Archway Road

MANOR HOUSE

45

46

43

42

41

ARCHWAY

36

35

37

Hendon Way

Edgware Road

47

48 49

44

FINSBURY PARK

Stoke Newington Road

Fryent Way

WEMBLEY PARK

61

55 53

50

ARSENAL

WEMBLEY STADIUM

57

NEASDEN

HAMPSTEAD

54

51

HAMPSTEAD HEATH

34

HOLLOWAY ROAD

Kingsland Road

56

FINCHLEY ROAD

52

CHALK FARM

18

HIGHBURY & ISLINGTON

32 31

33

STONEBRIDGE PARK

58

North Circular Road

17

20

19

CAMDEN TOWN

28 29

30

27

KENSAL GREEN

St John's Wood

16

21 22

26 25

24

ANGEL

7

Harrow Road

15

23

13

St Pancras

King's Cross

Maida Vale

11 10

12

14

EUSTON

WARWICK AVENUE

6

1

8 9

BAKER ST

GT PORTLAND STREET

LADBROKE GROVE

2

EDGWARE ROAD

REGENT'S PARK

4 3

Westway

5

PADDINGTON

NOTTING HILL GATE

QUEENSWAY

KEY

● Bayswater
● Regent's Park
● Camden
● King's Cross
● Islington
● North of Islington
● Hampstead & Highgate
● Northwest

KENSAL GREEN CEMETERY

BAYSWATER

❶ Little Venice

It is said that the poet Robert Browning gave the name of Little Venice to this picturesque and surprising place, where the Regent's Canal meets the Grand Union Canal. Browning had a house in the area from 1862 to 1887, and Browning's Pool and Browning's Island are named after him. Seeing the brightly painted houseboats, trailing willows, ducks and swans, the visitor would not be struck by any great similarity to the 'Queen of the Adriatic', or the 'City of Light', but there is a picture-postcard charm about it on a sunny day, which is quite unexpected in a location just minutes from Paddington Station and the streaming traffic on the Westway. One particular delight is the Puppet Theatre Barge, which has been presenting marionette and rod puppet spectacles in a 50 seater barge theatre since 1982. The puppets are beautifully crafted and the productions as beguiling to adults as to children.
Opposite 35 Blomfield Road, W9 2PF. Warwick Avenue tube.

❷ Porchester Spa

One step inside the Porchester Spa and a visitor knows this is something special. With potted plants, tiled floors and walls, high ceilings and wide arches round the icy plunge pool, this is not the ersatz spa of the pampered rich, but the real, basic thing. Built in 1929 in Art Deco style, it is the best surviving Turkish bath from the era. There are two Russian steam rooms, three Turkish hot rooms, whirlpool spa and sauna, and a 30m (98ft) swimming pool; and various rubs, wraps, massages and shaves are on offer. Men's and women's sessions are separate.
Queensway, W2 5HS. Queensway tube.

❸ Museum of Brands, Packaging and Advertising

Tucked away in a Notting Hill mews, and far more fun than its rather dull name suggests, this is a place to make people smile. Some 12,000 cartons, bottles, cans, posters, periodicals, toys and games make up the Robert Opie collection of advertising, which totals some 500,000 items and charts a history of the British consumer society over the past 200 years. Among them are 'wind pills' for sea sickness, Servants' Friend stove polish and many household names going back to Victorian times. Opie has been a lifelong collector, starting with a wrapper from a packet of Munchies in 1963, when he was 16. The museum, which shows just a part of his hoard, promotes traditional brand names and sells items ranging from baskets and bicycles to Victorian tiles and wooden sledges.

2 Colville Mews, Lonsdale Road, W11 2AR. Notting Hill Gate tube.

❹ Electric Cinema

A great place to watch independent and art-house films, the Electric, Portobello Road, has large leather armchairs with plenty of leg room, footstools and two-seater sofas for back-row canoodlers. Built in 1920 to the design of Gerald Seymour Valantin, it opened with a 20 minute silent film from Herbert Beerbohm Tree's acclaimed performance in *Henry VIII*. It has been in use ever since and its present luxury is the result of an expensive restoration in 2001. The auditorium has a bar, and each of the 98 seats has a table by the arm rest with a place for drinks. The café-brasserie is a fashionable place to meet, and upstairs is a club, The Electric House.

191 Portobello Road, W11 2ED. Notting Hill Gate, Ladbroke Grove tube.

❺ Portobello Road

Saturdays are busy days on this street of antique shops and stalls, because that is when the street market operates, and there is always something to stop and look at between around ten in the morning and four in the afternoon. The original road was a lane that led to the 69ha (170 acre) Porto Bello Farm, named after the Spanish silver port in modern Panama that, in 1739, had just been captured. In the late 19th century, gypsy horse trading took place here and there were fruit and vegetable stalls, which still dominate the heart of the market between Elgin Terrace and Talbot Road. Proper antiques are at the southern, Notting Hill end of the street and some of the stalls are open during the week. The market stretches for about 2 miles and other items on offer range from street fashion, around the Westway flyover, to secondhand goods. There are pubs and cafés along the way, and shops along the street are open six days a week.

W11. Notting Hill Gate, Ladbroke Grove tube.

❻ Trellick Tower

For years Ernö Goldfinger's 1973 residential tower block was reviled, but today its flats are at a premium. For a time, it was the tallest building of its kind in England, with 317 duplex flats distributed over 31 floors. They have windows on both sides, showing the influence of Le Corbusier's Unite d'Habitation in Marseilles. Each one has a balcony, and views from the upper floors extend to the South Downs.

The Tower was built with a nursery, old people's club, launderette, hobby rooms, doctor's surgery and shops. The boiler house, located high on the lift tower, was made redundant shortly after completion, because oil prices made it uneconomical, and a recent application to turn it into a penthouse flat was rejected. The man with the Midas touch himself had his office here for the last five years that he practised. Trellick Tower is open during the London Open House weekend. (See also Goldfinger's home, No 2 Willow Road, page 143).

Maida Hill, W10 5PA. Paddington rail and tube.

❼ Kensal Green Cemetery

A neoclassical triumphal arch flanked by lodges leads to this peaceful and beautiful resting place. 'Many would regard Kensal Green Cemetery as the most distinguished of London cemeteries,' writes Hugh Meller in *London Cemeteries*, although it is not as well-known as Highgate (see page 140). It was founded by barrister George Frederick Carden, and its design was inspired by Père-Lachaise in Paris. Its 29ha (72 acres) are enclosed on two sides by high walls, while the southern side looks towards the Grand Union Canal through neoclassical railings. Walls, railings, gateways, chapels and numerous tombs, memorials and mausoleums have been variously listed, including the Grade I All Souls Chapel. Among its many distinguished 'residents' are the Brunels, Emile Blondin, Charles Babbage, Wilkie Collins, Thomas Hood and James Leigh Hunt. Tours of this, the largest of the 'Magnificent Seven' burial parks built around London in the early to mid 1800s, are conducted by the Friends of the Cemetery twice a month, and visitors are led down into the arched brick catacombs lined with decaying coffins. There is a hydraulic catafalque by which coffins were spirited to the underworld from the chapel above, its mechanism concealed by drapery. Most of London's catacombs are sealed off, so this provides a rare opportunity to visit such a place.

Harrow Road, W10 4RA. Kensal Green tube.

REGENT'S PARK

❽ Alfie's Antiques Market

The astonished visitor to one of the world's largest antiques arcades might ~~sooner think~~ Aladdin than Alfie. Since it opened more than 35 years ago behind the Egyptian-style Art Deco façade of the Edwardian Jordan's department store, the emporium has become home to 100 specialist dealers in 20th-century antiques. Within a labyrinth of stalls, nooks and alcoves, they sell furniture and furnishings, glassware, jewellery, vintage fashion, textiles, accessories and much else. This is no dusty flea market, but a place of true fascination. The best fun is to be had on the first floor, where Nina's Hair Parlour specialises in vintage and retro hair and beauty. For sale are period hats from the 1930s to the 1960s, hair accessories and snoods. Church Street these days is devoted to chic antique shops, but when Benny Gray launched Alfie's in 1976, the old store was dilapidated and half the shops were boarded up and vandalised. Gray named the market after his father, a jazz musician. There's a nice rooftop café and terrace.
13–25 Church Street, NW8 8DT. Marylebone, Edgware Road tube. Tuesday–Saturday 10am–6pm.

❾ Rudolf Steiner House

The visitor to this house, dedicated to the father of Anthroposophy, beats a spiritual path to freedom. The Austrian-born Dr Rudolf Steiner (1861–1925) was a writer, philosopher, architect and social thinker, who urged spiritual renewal of western culture in the face of global challenges. Schools, clinics and farms around the country today put his beliefs to practical purpose, and the Anthroposophical Society in Great Britain continues to explore his teachings. Steiner described Anthroposophy as 'a path of knowledge, to guide the spiritual in the human being to the spiritual in the universe'. The centre welcomes visitors to workshops, talks and exhibitions. The sole example of Expressionist architecture in London, the Society's building, by Montague Wheeler (begun in 1924, with a second phase in 1937), explores Steiner's preference for curves over angles, and uses distorted shapes to convey a sense of movement and metamorphosis. The curious student is not alone in finding Steiner's ideas somewhat opaque. His friend Albert Schweitzer, no intellectual slouch himself, said: 'To take part in Rudolf Steiner's high flight of thought of spiritual science was not given to me. I know, however, that in this he lifted up and renewed many people, and his disciples attained exceptional accomplishments in many realms. I have rejoiced at the achievement which his great personality and his profound humanity have brought about in the world.'

A distinctive café in an irregularly shaped courtyard to the rear, inspired by the Chapter House at Wells Cathedral, is a new attraction, and serves food produced according to Steiner's biodynamic principles.
35 Park Road, NW1 6XT. Baker Street tube.

❿ Lord's Cricket Ground

The visitor entering the world's most active cricket club through the Grace Gates – a memorial to cricket hero W.G. Grace – gains an immediate sense of the site's heritage. In the 1700s, cricket was an élitist game for noblemen, who played on White Conduit Fields in Islington. The entrepreneurial Thomas Lord, a bowler for the White Conduit team, leased land in Marylebone, on what is now Dorset Square, to stage his first match. On May 31, 1787, Middlesex played Essex and thus came into being the Marylebone Cricket Club, the MCC. The following year, the club set down a 'Code of Laws' by which the game should be played.

After a spell in Regent's Park from 1811–13, Lord's club moved to an idyllic rural site in St John's Wood. In 1805, the tradition of the Eton-versus-Harrow match began. Among the Harrow players was Lord Byron, who later wrote to his publishers that he was 'once a good cricketer, particularly in batting', and that at the match he had gained more 'than any except Ld Ipswich and Brookman on our side'.

In the same letter he revealed the howling snobbery of the game, writing of the vicar and sonneteer William Bowles: 'Bowles must be *bowled* down – 'tis a sad matter at Cricket – if the

A FUTURISTIC, CURVING, ALUMINIUM MEDIA CENTRE
LORD'S CRICKET GROUND

fellow can get any Notches … If he once gets into "Lord's Ground" … I think I could beat him in one Innings.'

In 1825, aged 70, Lord sold the ground to William Ward, a director of the Bank of England, for £5,000. The grass was cropped by sheep until the first mowing machine arrived in 1864. Emigrants to Australia, meanwhile, took cricket with them and in 1877 an England team set off by steamer for the first Test match. In 1889 the foundation stone was laid for a new Pavilion – the original had burnt down – but most of the club's facilities today are far more avant-garde, with a vast steel-and-concrete stand dating from 1987, a grandstand for 2,000 spectators built in 1998, and a futuristic, curving, aluminium media centre prefabricated by superyacht builders Pendennis and welded together *in situ*. It has space for more than 200 journalists and was described by the Stirling Prize judges as 'a breath of architectural fresh air … a wacky solution to a singular problem.' Howzat! *St John's Wood, NW8 8QN. St John's Wood tube.*

⑪ Lord's Tour and the MCC Museum

Fans can go behind the scenes with an expert guide to explore the spiritual home of cricket. Tours start with a visit to the MCC Museum and a sight of the legendary Ashes urn borne home by Ivo Bligh from Australia in 1883 (see The Oval, page 103, to find out why such a tiny trophy meant so much). An unfortunate sparrow, knocked out by Jehangir Khan in 1936, is there, and kit used by such great players as Jack Hobbs, Don Bradman and Shane Warne, plus an exploration of the life of that greatest of cricketers, Dr W.G. Grace. In the Brian Johnston Memorial Theatre, footage of past games is available to see. Onward then through the Pavilion to the Long Room, with its panoramic views and cricketing portraits, the players' dressing rooms, a court for the old game of real tennis, and the media centre, acclaimed in 2001 as one of the 50 best buildings in Britain. *St John's Wood, NW8 8QN. St John's Wood tube.*

⑫ Islamic Cultural Centre and London Central Mosque

Against a blue sky, the burnished copper dome and soaring white minaret of this spectacular mosque are stunning and exotic additions to the London skyline. In October 1940, with the Blitz under way, Churchill's War Cabinet drummed up £100,000 for a site on which to build a mosque in London. This was, as *The Times* reported, a gesture of gratitude: 'The gift is the more welcome since in the struggle in which Great Britain and the British Empire are engaged the Moslem communities of the Empire have clearly shown where their sympathies lie.' In 1944 George VI made an unconditional gift to British Muslims of this prime site, nearly a hectare (2.3 acres) in size, by Hanover Gate in Regent's Park, as a tribute to the thousands of Indian Muslim soldiers who had died in defence of Empire. A Mosque Committee was set up and the cultural centre was officially opened by the king, but it was not until 1978 that Sir Frederick Gibberd's mosque opened its doors. Visitors with an interest in Islamic architecture and faith, having removed their shoes before entering, find themselves in a vast, carpeted hall with a beautiful chandelier, ornate tiling and space for around 2,000 worshippers. There is a separate gallery for women, who must cover their heads.
146 Park Road, NW8 7RG. Baker Street, Marylebone, St John's Wood tube.

⑬ Regent's Park

Tamed and landscaped, a former royal hunting chase in the Forest of Middlesex is a place of beauty, recreation and entertainment. Henry VIII was a man with great appetites – for women, food and hunting. In 1538, as was his divine right, he seized from the Abbess of Barking 224ha (554 acres) of thickly wooded land, a trot and gallop from Whitehall Palace, on which to chase deer. It became known as Marylebone Park and, later, was turned over to farming until, in 1811, the Prince Regent chose John Nash to create 'the Regent's Park' – a circular pleasure garden with a lake, canal and a new royal residence – to be linked to St James's Palace by a grand processional route (hence Regent's Street).

Eight villas were built on the park, of which two still stand, and grand Regency terraces rose up around it, but plans for a princely home were abandoned. The park was closed to all but royalty and the 'carriage set' who lived by it. Then, in 1835, the east side was opened to the public, and

the Royal Zoological Society engaged Decimus Burton to build new headquarters there. The Royal Botanic Society laid out the Inner Circle.

Known as 'the jewel in the crown', the park is rich in wildlife. There are bandstands, puppet shows, deckchairs and boats for hire, and the largest grassed area for sports in central London. Where better to watch *A Midsummer Night's Dream* than in the open-air theatre? There are cafés and restaurants, too, but visitors approaching through York Gate to the south can pick up a perfect picnic on Marylebone High Street on their way. Decimus Burton's Clarence Terrace on the Outer Circle has been home to the novelists Wilkie Collins and Elizabeth Bowen, and the poet Louis McNeice. Collins wrote *The Woman in White* while living there, and the park is a palpable presence in Bowen's novel *The Death of the Heart* – but the heart can only lift in such surroundings.

Regent's Park, Great Portland Street, Baker Street, St John's Wood, Camden Town tube.

⑭ Queen Mary's Garden

It's roses, roses, roses all the way in Queen Mary's Garden, especially during the summer months, when the air is laden with the mingled scents of 400 rose varieties. When the Royal Botanic Society decided not to renew its lease in the 1930s, in its place in the Inner Circle formal rose beds were laid out. Some 30,000 rose plants grow in mixed beds around a small lake with ornamental wildfowl and carp. Where else in London would the visitor find Gertrude Jekyll mixing with William Shakespeare and Othello, Wild Edric and A Shropshire Lad? The Garden Café opened in 1964 as The Little Chef, and close by, a recent planting of old damasks and perennials by rose specialists David Austin is especially lovely. Here, too, is the national delphinium collection. For her story *Among the Roses*, Doris Lessing chose Queen Mary's Garden as a setting for a meeting between an estranged mother and daughter. A park within a park.

Regent's Park, Great Portland Street tube.

⑮ London Zoo

The world's first scientific zoo is one of the best-loved, home to more than 650 species of animals. Founded by Sir Stamford Raffles in 1826, the zoo's grounds and buildings were laid out by Decimus Burton, including the Grade II listed classical roman Giraffe House. Among the many world beaters to be found here are the first reptile house, constructed in 1849, and the first

aquarium, in 1853. The term 'aquarium', derived from aquatic vivarium, was coined here. The zoo acquired the first hippo to be seen in Europe since the Roman Empire, and in 1880 the largest known elephant, Jumbo, lived here, but was later sold to Barnum and Bailey's circus. A resident Canadian black bear named Winnipeg inspired A.A. Milne's *Winnie the Pooh*. The zoo's oldest building, Burton's 1828 Clock Tower, based on Tudor design, was originally for the llamas.

Berthold Lubetkin's Round House was one of Britain's first modernist buildings. Lubetkin famously said that nothing was too good for ordinary people, and the same held good for ordinary penguins. His penguin pool, designed in 1934, was based on an egg shape with two spiralling intertwining ramps. Its occupants have now marched off to their new home within the zoo, Penguin Beach, and today the structure is a water feature.

Conservation is a key part of the zoo's work; 112 species kept here are listed as endangered. Many of the expected inmates are here, too, from the magnificent Asian lion and Sumatran tiger to the komodo dragon and giant Galapagos tortoise, via monkeys, gorillas and giraffes, but what truly astonishes is the range and diversity of the animal kingdom. In London's only living rainforest, golden-headed lion tamarins and tamandua are to be found. On a roll call that runs from long-nosed potaroo to Black Sea cucumber, appear the panay cloudrunner, the aye aye and brown-nosed coati (mammals), the red-tailed Amazon and tawny frogmouth (birds), the Parson's chameleon, green-crested basilisk and eyelash palm pitviper (reptiles), and a piscine marbled headstander and a lipstick leporinus (fish).

Regent's Park. Chalk Farm, Camden Town tube.

⑯ Primrose Hill

Once a part of Henry VIII's great chase, and rising 73m (256ft) to the north of Regent's Park, this popular green space offers two spectacular, protected views from the summit. From there, it's possible to gaze out over central London to the southeast, and Hampstead and Belsize Park to the north.

A plaque marks the site of the first meeting of the Gorsedd of the Bards of the Island of Britain in 1792, and commemorates its founder, Iolo Morganwg. Poet and political radical, Morganwg was also one of the founders of the Unitarian movement in Wales. The Gorsedd lives on in Wales as part of the annual cultural festival, the National Eisteddfod.

Primrose Hill. St John's Wood, Chalk Farm tube.

CAMDEN

⑰ The Roundhouse

A former steam-engine repair shed, built in 1846, and later a bonded warehouse for Gilbey's Gin, this is an important performing art space, mainly devoted to youth. In 1964 the playwright Arnold Wesker launched Centre 42 in this building – taking the name from Article 42 of the trades union movement, which states that art should be for everyone. Today this Grade II listed building – an outstanding example of mid-19th-century architecture – revolves, as it were, around the young, with a lively programme of music, theatre, dance, circus, installations and new media. There is a continuous schedule of creative projects for 11 to 25-year-olds in studios with broadcast and production facilities, media suites and rehearsal rooms. Young audiences are able to interact with artists on stage – an exciting feature of an unusual enterprise.
Chalk Farm Road, NW1 8EH. Chalk Farm tube.

⑱ Marine Ices

Buonissimo! **Delicious homemade ice cream has been sold by an Italian family on this site since 1947,** but the business traces its roots back much further, to the opening of a grocer's shop on Drummond Street in Euston, in 1928, by Gaetano Mansi. At the age of 12 Mansi had been sent to London by his father from his native Ravello in southern Italy, to make his way in the world. He lodged with relatives in Bermondsey and worked hard as his father had wished. After opening his grocer's shop, he was soon able to open a second shop, on Euston Road, and because he couldn't bear to throw away surplus fruit, he started to make fresh sorbets. They were such a big hit with customers that he began to order fruit especially to make more of them. It was a natural progression, then, for him to open Mansi's Café on Haverstock Hill in 1931, where he made ice cream and sorbets.

War intervened, and the man who had given Londoners so much pleasure found himself suddenly categorised as an undesirable alien and was interned on the Isle of Man. After the war, in 1947, the café was rebuilt by Gaetano's son, Aldo, with the bridge of a ship as its theme, and the family was back in business. When the first Pizza Express opened on Wardour Street in 1963, it was to Marine Ices that the owner came. Today, in numerous restaurants the ice cream served is from here, but it somehow tastes extra special at this original *gelateria*, where the 'porthole' of Aldo Mansi's ship-bridge design can still be seen.
8 Haverstock Hill, NW3 2BL. Chalk Farm tube.

THE ROUNDHOUSE

⑲ Camden Lock

Goths, punks, romantics, psychobillies and silly billies rock up to Camden Lock for the fun on 364 days of the year. Arts, crafts, jewellery, vintage and new fashion all vie for space amid a youthful party atmosphere. This is the original craft market, which opened by the canal in 1974. The canal itself has been in use since 1820 and visitors to the market can arrive via the bridge that was once used by horses. Warehouses appeared along the canal banks over the ensuing years, but with the rise of road freight and canal transport in decline, from the 1950s some of these buildings became obsolete. In 1971 a number of them were sold to three enterprising young men who sublet a few as craft workshops, and within a few years a market was established on cobbled yards close by. The market was fruitful and multiplied, determining the character of downtown Camden. Not just Londoners but tourists poured in. Restaurants, cafés and takeaway shops proliferated. In 1990 many of the old buildings were overhauled, and a new three-storey Market Hall was built over one of the open areas. This is *the* place to come for Doc Martens, plague crosses, fetish chokers, platform shoes, pixie boots, bowling shirts, bondage trousers, body pierces, plastic hair, Fifties frocks, hippy smocks, holographic T-shirts, baubles, bangles and beads.
NW1. Camden Town, Chalk Farm tube.

⑳ Camden Stables Market

The former warren of stables that accommodated the barge horses has had a makeover and is now home to 450 outlets, attracting 35 million visitors a year. As well as acres of alternative fashion, household goods are on offer – ethnic, secondhand, antique – Asian carpets, beanbags, mirrors, African drums, lighting, hand-blown glass and much more. Grazers can take their pick of foods from bagels to Thai via Chinese, Cuban, Italian, Japanese and Mexican. Massive bronze sculptures recall the role of the horses that once hit the hay here. A cobbled ramp leads to the Grade II listed horse hospital, now known as Proud Camden, a place to relax by day, watching flat-screen TV, and to hear live music at night. Seven stables have been given a radical makeover while retaining original features. Where injured horses once convalesced, Dizzee Rascal and the Kooks, among many others, perform, while celebrities such as Amy Winehouse and Sadie Frost frequent the bar.
NW1. Camden Town, Chalk Farm tube.

129

ST PANCRAS INTERNATIONAL

KING'S CROSS

㉑ Camley Street Natural Park

In an old coal yard behind ornate wrought-iron gates, in the middle of King's Cross, lies nearly a hectare (2 acres) of lush, unspoilt countryside, right on the canal. Created in 1984, and under the stewardship of the London Wildlife Trust, this little natural space brims with wild flowers, songbirds and restful glades. Kingfishers, reed warblers, ducks, geese, buntings, frogs, toads, bats and butterflies are all perfectly at home hard by the Eurostar terminal. The soothing sound of water comes from a nearby lock. Seats are made from recycled materials. This is a world away from immaculate Regent's Park and the shiny new cultural centre of Kings Place, close by. It revels in dishevelment, encompassing a pond, meadow, marshes, woodland – and to think it would have been a coach park if the local authorities had had their way!

12 Camley Street, NW1 0PW. King's Cross St Pancras tube.

㉒ London Canal Museum

The visitor to this old ice warehouse will discover a fascinating history of the canal age. Here, on Battlebridge Basin, Carlo Gatti, from Italian-speaking Switzerland, established his business in the 1850s, taking delivery of his first cargo of 400 tonnes of ice from Norway, to be stored in ice wells. He was one of the first people to sell ice cream in London, and the museum also explores the history of the ice-cream trade.

A large wall map shows the canal network of Greater London. In the cramped confines of a reconstructed narrow boat, a boatman and his family, sitting around the dining table, can be heard to discuss their life on the waterways – courtesy of the Keeper's Lock Theatre Company. A film, *Barging Through London*, made in 1924, is played on video. Especially charming is the exposition of traditional folk art known as 'roses and castles', with which barges are still adorned. Here also, 12m (40ft) deep, is the only commercial ice well to be preserved in Britain. The horses that used to pull the barges are remembered; the towpaths were laid down for them. There is even an ice-cream vendor's bicycle of the kind first introduced by Wall's, who coined the slogan 'Stop me and buy one'. The view from the rear is of the basin, filled with narrowboats, where once were timber wharves, a flour mill and jam factory.

12–13 New Wharf Road, N1 9RT. King's Cross St Pancras tube.

㉓ St Pancras International

The old terminus of the Midland Railway, one of the engineering wonders of the Victorian age, is now home to Eurostar, providing a fast connection to Paris. William Barlow's famous train-shed arch spans 73m (240ft), soaring to 30.5m (100ft) at its apex. On its completion in 1868 it formed the largest enclosed space in the world.

George Gilbert Scott's neo-Gothic former Midland Grand Hotel, built between 1868 and 1876, formed part of the station and, its frontage now restored, retains a magnificent street presence. The building consumed 60 million bricks and 9,000 tonnes of ironwork and was the first to have a smoking room where ladies could enjoy tobacco. When it opened, it had just eight baths – guests would ring for water to be brought to their rooms to wash. It closed as a hotel in 1935 and was used as railway offices. In 1966, in the demolition craze of that decade, it came under threat of the bulldozer. John Betjeman – not yet Poet Laureate or a 'Sir' – stepped in to lead the fight to save it. London had already suffered what was deemed one of the greatest acts of post-war vandalism in Britain when nearby Euston Station had been flattened in 1962, and public opinion was galvanised. One of the greatest Victorian buildings in the city was spared and received Grade I listing. Even so, when the offices were vacated in the late 1980s, it stood empty, falling into decay. In the mid 1990s the exterior, with its polished granite and limestone columns, was restored, and after a £150 million makeover, this is now the St Pancras Renaissance Hotel. Martin Jennings's affectionate bronze statue of Sir John Betjeman in the station pays tribute to what he achieved here. The visitor may wish to raise a glass to him at Europe's longest champagne bar.

Euston Road, NW1 2AR. King's Cross St Pancras tube.

㉔ Model Railway Club

Perennial schoolboys steam along here to Thursday meetings. The club, founded in 2010, takes its hobby seriously, with an extensive library and a lower hall in which modelling projects are always in progress. Layouts are built on a variety of scales. One of two touring layouts, Copenhagen Fields, is based on the lines out of King's Cross. There are occasional lectures and presentations, and project leaders welcome enthusiastic newcomers.

Keen House, 4 Calshot Street, N1 9DA. King's Cross St Pancras tube.

ISLINGTON

㉕ Camden Passage

This famous 'antiques village' is renowned for its range of enchanting shops and arcades. Since the first antiques shop opened here in 1960, 199 more dealers have arrived. The visitor can browse displays of Art Deco and Art Nouveau jewellery and ornaments, clocks and watches, ceramics, silverware, glassware, oriental treasures, militaria, music boxes, singing birds and automata, and all forms of mechanical music. At the African Waistcoat Company, Africa meets Savile Row. Paul A. Young Fine Chocolates sells confections hand-made by a professional patissier and chocolatier.

N1 8ED. Angel tube. Wednesday and Saturday.

㉖ Culpeper Community Garden

In the inner city, on a once derelict site, this tranquil spot provides an infusion of hope and peace of mind. Despite being ringed by busy roads, the garden is calm and beautiful, and what is even more special is the spirit behind it. The garden began life 30 years ago as a joint project between the Free School on White Lion Street – a local alternative school for excluded children – and neighbouring Penton Primary School (both now closed). In 1982 the plot was literally a wasteland dumping ground. Then Islington Council made available a small grant, a landscape architect drew up a design, and volunteers got to work. Managed by and for local people, the garden has helped to transform lives as surely as it has transfigured a blighted inner-city patch, because the organisers have always sought to involve sometimes-troubled youngsters.

It was named after Nicholas Culpeper, the great 17th-century herbalist, physician and astrologer, who had been apprenticed to an apothecary on Threadneedle Street. At 24 he married Alice Field, aged 15, after treating her father for gout, and used her dowry to build a house on Red Lion Street, next to the Red Lion inn by Spital Field. Among his observations, Culpeper noted: 'Many a times I find my patients disturbed by troubles of Conscience or Sorrow, and I have to act the Divine before I can be the Physician. In fact our greatest skill lies in the infusion of Hopes, to induce confidence and peace of mind.' For those beset by 'Conscience or Sorrow', the opportunity to learn to grow and care for plants, and to help to create this green oasis, with its drifts of wild flowers, cascading roses, pond, pergola and picnic area, has been as therapeutic as any herbal remedy.

2 Cloudesley Road, N1 0EG. Angel tube.

㉗ S&M Café

S&M stands for sausage and mash and the mission of the company, since 2002, has been to reclaim old-style greasy spoon caffs and to celebrate great British grub. Sausages and mashed potato are not the only items on offer in this 'designer greasy spoon', which has Formica-topped tables and red leatherette chairs. There's pie and mash, too, with mushy peas, and all-day breakfast and meaty mixed grill. The menu does stray over frontiers into three-bean chilli and blackened salmon with rice, but it's all fun, and cleverly done. There is another branch in Spitalfields.

6 Essex Road, N1 8LN. Angel tube.

㉘ King's Head Theatre

The first pub theatre in England since Shakespeare's time, and one of London's smallest, has nurtured the careers of some of the biggest names of British acting. It was a young American, Dan Crawford, who in 1970 spotted the potential of a down-on-its-luck north-London pub. He had worked in the US as an actor and stage manager, and arrived in Britain in 1969 with a clear plan to run London's first contemporary pub theatre. The King's Head was an unloved and neglected boozer that didn't even have a landlord. Crawford set about realising his dream here, even building the stage himself, just 3.5m (12ft) wide and 2.5m (8ft) deep. The first play was not a success, but the second, a dramatisation of John Fowles's *The Collector*, was an instant hit, and the place was on its way.

Crawford brought such great flair and verve to creating a groundbreaking venue for new drama and revivals, musicals and revues, that for the next 35 years, until his death in 2005, actors who could have trod the boards on Shaftesbury Avenue and Drury Lane, commanding star dressing rooms, would play at the King's Head, sharing cramped backstage 'facilities', for a flat £120, for the love of it and the cachet. The careers of Alan Rickman, Ben Kingsley and Rupert Graves were launched here. Among many young hopefuls, Tom Conti, Hugh Grant and Joanna Lumley all appeared at the King's Head.

In the words of Tom Stoppard, the man was 'stark, raving sane' and he is terribly missed. Today, the pub's walls are hung with portraits of the greats who have performed here, and stage performances continue to thrive, the place having been 'rebranded' as London's Little Opera House at the King's Head Theatre.

115 Upper Street, N1 1QN. Angel tube.

ENCHANTING SHOPS AND ARCADES
CAMDEN PASSAGE

Dancing in the street

The pageantry and high spirits of London's street festivals and parades make any one of them an occasion not to be missed on a trip to the capital city.

Benjamin Zephaniah's poem *The London Breed* perfectly encapsulates the spirit in which Londoners turn out on the street to party, celebrating diversity and harmony. The year begins with a New Year's Day Parade through the West End. Even as the last of the night's revellers are staggering home, people are leaping out of bed to practise their baton twirls and paradiddles, to grease their slide trombones and don the motley. Today it attracts 10,000 participants and hundreds of thousands of spectators. Dancers, musicians, marching bands, choirs, ensembles, cheerleaders, clowns and acrobats make up the biggest event of its kind in the world.

The Chinese New Year, determined by the positions of the sun and moon, falls in January or February. The festivities centre around Soho's lantern-bedecked Chinatown, with processions and symbolic dance. Traditional lion dancing scares away evil spirits. The long and snaking dragon, a work of art in red, green and gold, represents good fortune and power. Half a million people come to the party each year, making it, they say, the biggest Chinese New Year get-together outside Southeast Asia.

Irish hooley

In March, the colour green predominates as the St Patrick's Day Parade of floats and marching bands, stilt-walkers and costumed characters processes from Green Park to Trafalgar Square.

Baishaki Mela, the Bengali New Year, kicks off in April with a procession to Brick Lane. Marchers wear colourful costumes and garlands, and the parade includes patchwork elephants and Bengal tigers trundled on wheels.

In June or July, it's the turn of the exuberant Pride Parade. Since the first London Gay Pride Rally was staged on July 1, 1972, when some 2,000 people gathered in a mood of protest, the event has taken on the air of a fiesta. A million people join in, wearing outlandish costumes and waving rainbow flags.

NOTTING HILL CARNIVAL

The most joyful annual event, the Notting Hill Carnival, has been held on the streets of west London every August Bank Holiday since 1966. This is Europe's largest street festival. People wearing outlandish costumes cavort around a district rocking with music and redolent of Caribbean food.

Unsuspecting visitors would not 'Adam 'n' Eve' (believe) it. Of all the London spectacles under the 'currant bun' (sun), the Pearly Kings' and Queens' Harvest Festival is one of the oddest, their rhyming slang language baffling to the uninitiated. Every London borough has its own 'King' and 'Queen', and in September, they all turn out, wearing suits adorned

> The music of the world is here
> Dis city can play any song
> They come to here from everywhere
> Tis they that made dis city strong.
>
> BENJAMIN ZEPHANIAH

with tens of thousands of opalescent buttons. From Guildhall Yard, the Pearlies parade to St Mary-le-Bow for a service attended by mayors, donkeys and carts and marching bands. In October, they hold another harvest festival in St Paul's Church, Covent Garden.

Under the eye of Nelson

The epicentre of the city, Trafalgar Square, hosts numerous celebrations. For the Eid Islamic Festival, when Muslims break their month-long fast, it takes on the aspect of a bustling souk with market stalls, music and dance. The festival is held on varying dates, depending on the Islamic lunar calendar.

Music and dance are also a feature of Diwali, the 'Festival of Lights', solemnised by Hindus, Sikhs and Jains. For a day between mid October and mid November, the square becomes a sea of swirling saris.

By midnight on December 31, the square is full of people eager to see the old year out and the new year in. As Big Ben's familiar chimes ring out, fireworks streak, cascade, incandesce and blossom over the Thames. The crowd erupts in a delirious chorus of the universally adopted Scottish anthem 'Auld Lang Syne'. Strangers embrace. Hot-blooded youths jump into the fountains. The cry goes up, 'Happy New Year!' And the next day it all begins again.

NORTH

㉙ Little Angel Theatre

For more than 50 years the puppeteers at this modest 100 seat theatre have been delighting young and old in one of only three building-based puppet theatres in England. The theatre was established in a derelict former temperance hall, complete with pews, behind busy Upper Street back in 1961. Its purpose was to stage marionette shows for children, but since then it has grown in its aspiration and endeavours. Productions are no mere end-of-the-pier shows but explorations of the art form, employing puppets of every kind. In Paper Cinema shows, hand-drawn cut-outs are projected onto screens. In its first half-century the company created and performed more than 50 shows, including such Little Angel classics as *Sleeping Beauty* and *The Secret Garden*, taking them on tour around the country. In a joint venture with the Royal Shakespeare Company on a production of *The Tempest*, live performers interacted with puppets. Oh, brave new world that has such creatures in it! *14 Dagmar Passage, N1 2DN. Angel tube.*

㉚ Table Tennis at Rosemary Gardens

Enthusiasts who arrive here with bat and balls and an opponent will have the opportunity to play a game. As part of their Park Ping Pong initiative in 2010, the Table Tennis Association installed 47 tables around London public spaces. Most have a single table, but here there are four. *Southgate Road, NI 3JP (no tube nearby).*

㉛ New River Walk

A little waterway, which is neither new nor remotely a river, runs by the houses of Canonbury Grove, hidden by shrubbery and draped with fronds of willow. This is Hugh Myddelton's New River aqueduct, which was built in 1613 to bring drinking water to London from Hertfordshire. It still supplies some 8 per cent of London's water, and the path along this stretch has been preserved as a nature trail, with native flora. The water is pumped to create the impression of a flowing river. Canonbury developed as a suburb in the early 19th century, with grand villas and beautifully proportioned houses, many in Italianate style and themselves something to see. The walker, strolling as far as Newington Green, will see the oldest surviving terrace of houses in England. *Canonbury Grove, N1. Highbury & Islington tube.*

CANONBURY TOWER

㉜ Canonbury Tower

One of Islington's oldest buildings, a relic of the Manor of Chanonbury, is dedicated to the study of western esoteric traditions. What the passer-by sees is the remnant of a building commissioned for his canons by Prior Bolton of St Bartholomew in Smithfield, Henry VIII's master of works for the chapel in Westminster Abbey. It dates from the early 1500s, is steeped in history, and since December 1998 has been a home for the Canonbury Masonic Research Centre.

In 1535, Thomas Cromwell moved into the Manor, from where he organised the Dissolution of the Monasteries on behalf of Henry VIII, and their transfer to royal ownership. So grateful was the king that he made a gift of the building to Cromwell in 1539 – only to have him executed a year later. In 1770–80, the south side of Bolton's building was knocked down and replaced by the elegant Nos 1–5 Canonbury Place. Guided tours are available on request. A pistol bullet buried above the door of the Compton Room was allegedly fired at Sir Walter Raleigh.
Canonbury Place, N1 2NQ. Highbury & Islington tube.

㉝ Estorick Collection of Modern Italian Art

One of the finest collections of early 20th-century art anywhere in the world has a splendid home in a Grade II Georgian house. The collection is named after the American sociologist Eric Estorick. As a student at New York University in the early 1930s, he came upon the Gallery of Living Art in Washington Square College, with paintings by Picasso, Miró and Matisse, and was smitten. In 1947 he married Salome Dessau and while on honeymoon, at the studio of Mario Sironi in Milan, he bought 'hundreds and hundreds of drawings' and as many paintings as he could pack into his car. After that, he and Salome would visit Italy often, befriending artists, and their collection took shape.

Six months before his death in 1993, Estorick set up a foundation, donating all his Italian works. Today, 120 paintings, drawings, prints and sculptures are displayed in a light and airy house. Here are works by the great Italian exponents of Futurism – Giacomo Balla, Umberto Boccioni, Carlo Carrà, Gino Severini, Luigi Russolo and Ardengo Soffici, as well as works by Giorgio de Chirico, Amedeo Modigliani, Giorgio Morandi, Mario Sironi and Marino Marini. There is also a library and a café with seating in a walled garden.
39a Canonbury Square, NI 2A. Highbury & Islington tube.

NORTH OF ISLINGTON

❸❹ Emirates Stadium

Arsenal FC has come a long way since it was formed in 1886 by workers at the Woolwich Arsenal Armament Factory.
The club moved around between pitches before finding a permanent base in Highbury in 1913, where it stayed until 2006. For some fans, the transfer to the Emirates was a wrench. They feared they would miss the warmth, the Art Deco elegance, and the sense of 'home' and belonging, not to mention the North Bank and Clock End at 38,000 seat Highbury. How could a £390 million stadium seating nearly 65,000 have the atmosphere that was so much a part of the experience? How would swanky new facilities make up for the loss of 93 years of history?

Quite easily, it seems. It took little time to win them over. Far from being clinical and corporate, the new four-tiered stadium of concrete and curved glass is not only magnificent – a match for Milan's San Siro or Munich's Allianz – but it feels to the faithful that the best-supported club in the capital has at last got its due. A beautiful pitch, huge, comfortable seats and brilliant acoustics add to the pleasure, and a party atmosphere prevails as the crowds – encouraged to arrive early and stay on after the game, to ease pressure on the gates – freely mix and mingle, exchanging gossip, banter and speculation. The Armoury club shop on the concourse is the size of a big supermarket.
75 Drayton Park, N5 1BU. Arsenal, Holloway Road tube.

❸❺ Finsbury Park

A listed Victorian park is now home to baseball and American football. Finsbury Park opened in 1869 in the grounds of demolished Hornsey Wood House, through which the 17th-century New River ran (see page 136). The house had an American garden of the sort that became popular in the late 18th century as botanists returned from America with new plant species. More recent imports are facilities for American sports. Finsbury Park is home to the London Blitz football team and London Mets baseball side, and this is where in Britain the baseball anthem can be heard, 'Take

me out to the ball game, take me out with the crowd'. The song, by Jack Norworth and Albert von Tilzer, was published in 1908 and in a revised version in 1927.
N4 2DE. Manor House, Finsbury Park tube.

❸❻ Parkland Walk

A planned extension of the Northern Line from Finsbury Park to Alexandra Palace via Highgate was disrupted by the Second World War and was never completed. Known as Northern Heights, it was finally abandoned in 1971 and has now been transformed into the Parkland Walk. Many species of wildlife live here. Foxes, squirrels and hedgehogs are quite at home where goods trains and underground stock once rattled up on tracks now long since lifted. Charles Holden's Highgate Station, closed in 1954, remains untouched since that date. The Parkland Walk, some 4 miles long, was officially opened in 1984, and is divided into two sections – Finsbury Park to Highgate, and Cranley Gardens to Muswell Hill. It is London's longest, but not its biggest, nature reserve.
N4, N6, N8, N10.

❸❼ Stamford Hill

London is an intriguing patchwork of areas to which ethnic communities lend their own distinctive colour and texture, as can be seen from a trip to this 'square mile of piety'. The shop signs tell the tale – Moses supermarket, Sharon's bakery, J. Grodzinski and Daughters. Delicatessens sell matzah ball soup, pickled herrings and kneidlach dumplings.

The borough of Hackney has been home to the Jewish community since the early 18th century, and the one-time 'Sandford Hill' has the largest community of Haredi Jews in Europe. They began to settle here at around the time of the Second World War. The Haredis follow the most conservative interpretation of Orthodox Judaism. Their appearance is distinctive. The men dress in long black coats and hats, wear their hair in ringlets and have beards. Women favour long dresses, and cover their hair with wigs or headscarves.
N16. Stamford Hill rail.

FOXES AND HEDGEHOGS ARE QUITE AT HOME HERE
PARKLAND WALK

38 Alexandra Palace

For a phoenix to rise once from its ashes is pretty impressive – but 'The People's Palace' and 'birthplace of television' has had to do it twice. The original 'Ally Pally' opened its doors in 1873, and 120,000 people passed through them before it was destroyed by fire just 16 days later. In May 1875 a new building, by John Johnson, was in business. It was centred on the Great Hall with a Willis Organ driven by two stream engines and giant bellows. The first public television transmissions were made by the BBC from a part of the building in 1936 – famously introduced with the words, 'This is direct television from Alexandra Palace' – for those who could afford the 60 guineas (£63) for a TV set. The venue remained the BBC's main transmission centre until 1956. From here was beamed out coverage of George VI's coronation procession in 1937, the London Olympics of 1948, and the Queen's coronation in 1953. In July 1980, the building caught fire again, and large parts of it were destroyed, although the Palm Court was spared. After development and restoration it re-reopened. Alexandra Palace sits in 79ha (196 acres) of parkland, with great views over London, and attractions include concerts, exhibitions, theatre, an ice rink, boating lake and animal enclosures.
Alexandra Palace Way, N22 7AY. Wood Green tube.

39 Arnos Grove Station

A glazed and corniced brick, steel and glass drum of a station building rises confidently from the street, a modernist triumph, opened in September 1932. Famous around the world as an emblem of what the London Passenger Transport Board (LPTB) represented, this modern metro stop, with its circular booking hall and high windows, was subject to thorough restoration in 2005. It was commissioned by the visionary Frank Pick, head of the LPTB, and designed by Charles Holden. Pick and Holden had made a summer tour of new Scandinavian, Low Country and German architecture in 1930, so they were aware of the rising influence of Le Corbusier and Gropius's Bauhaus movement. But the two teetotal Arts & Crafts enthusiasts had in mind for the London Underground something that, although new and distinctive, would be rooted in architectural history. They had been much impressed by Stockholm City Library, designed by the modern classicist Gunnar Apslund, and by a new city hall in Hilversum by Willem Marinus Dudok, and returned inspired by both. The result was this building, unlike anything before seen in London. A disused ticket office (or 'passimeter') at the centre of the ticket hall houses an exhibition on the station's, and the underground's, history.
325 Bowes Road, N11 1AN. Arnos Grove tube.

ARNOS GROVE STATION

HAMPSTEAD & HIGHGATE

40 Phoenix Cinema

The country's oldest purpose-built cinema, a survivor from the days of silent film, narrowly escaped demolition, and is now owned in trust for the community. The East Finchley Picturedrome opened its doors in May 1912, the year the first Keystone Kops movie, *Hoffmeyer's Legacy,* was released. Stars of the day included Charlie Chaplin, Fatty Arbuckle and Mabel Normand. Mickey Mouse was not born for another 16 years. The building actually dates from 1910, but its owners, Premier Electric Theatres, went the way of the *Titanic* – sunk in April 1912. The natural fall of the land was used for the raked seating and 428 seats were installed in rows of 16. In 1924 the name was changed to the Coliseum, and in 1938 new owners rechristened the cinema the Rex, and redesigned the auditorium, reversing the layout and adding extra seating. The barrel-vaulted ceiling was retained, the interior was done in rich red, bronze and gold, and Art Deco panels around the walls concealed strip lighting. The exterior was given a whole new look, with glazed black tiles, cream plaster, a broad canopy and neon sign. From the 1970s, the cinema moved away from trite and glitzy double bills, gaining a reputation for showing art-house and global cinema. The works

of Fassbinder and Fellini, Truffaut and Chabrol flickered across the screen. The name change to the Phoenix came in 1975, but by the 1980s it began to look as if that mythical bird would perish in the ashes of the moving-picture industry as it went into decline. Permission was granted by the council to flatten the building and erect an office block and lock-up garages on the site. However, local opposition prevailed, and the Phoenix is today owned by the Phoenix Cinema Trust. North Londoners do not take things lying down!

52 High Street, East Finchley, N2 9PJ. East Finchley tube.

41 Highgate Cemetery

'But least of all he liked that place/Which hangs on Highgate Hill/Of Soaked Carrara-covered earth/For Londoner's to fill.' John Betjeman's gloomy ruminations on a portrait of a deaf man evoke a very different picture from the one familiar to the Friends of Highgate Cemetery, who wholly own this beautiful and historic burial ground. The Victorians were very keen on monumental masonry, and the well-to-do marked their passing in style. The London Cemetery Company, created in 1836 by Act of Parliament, spent three years landscaping nearly 7ha (17 acres)

HAMPSTEAD HEATH

of what had been the grounds of Ashurst Estate, on the steep hillside from Highgate Village, to accommodate them. Stephen Geary, the company founder (who also designed gin palaces) appointed James Bunstone Bunning as surveyor and David Ramsay as landscape artist. The imposing entrance on Swain's Lane was part of an ambitious building project to encourage the wealthy to book their spaces. There were exotic plantings, two Tudor-style chapels and, at the heart of the grounds, a most improbable structure, an avenue of vaults entered via an Egyptian-style arch and leading to the Circle of Lebanon around an ancient cedar of Lebanon. The cemetery opened on May 20, 1839, and first in, on May 26, was Elizabeth Jackson of Little Windmill Street, Soho. Building continued with catacombs constructed above the Circle of Lebanon in the Gothic style, with a 73m (80-yd) frontage and space for 825. So fashionable was this airy upland necropolis that an extension of 8ha (20 acres) was created. Known now as the East Cemetery, it was connected by a consecrated tunnel beneath Swain's Lane to the Anglican chapel on the old west side.

From their heyday, London's great Victorian cemeteries went into decades-long decline. Highgate was going to rack and ruin when the Friends organisation was formed to save and restore it. The air of decay and long desuetude add palpably to the mystery of the place. Numbers of the oldest mausoleums have been listed by English Heritage. Slumbering lions, urns and wall-eyed angels bear silent witness. Of the 52,000 graves, the best known is probably that of Karl Marx, but here, too, lie Michael Faraday and George Eliot, Sir Ralph Richardson and Malcolm McClaren, Christina Rossetti, Beryl Bainbridge, Douglas Adams and Max Wall. The overgrown West Cemetery, open for tours only, has to be seen in all its eerie loveliness.
Swain's Lane, N6 6PJ. Archway tube.

㊷ Lauderdale House and Waterlow Park

This lovely park, bordered on two sides by Highgate cemetery, was bequeathed to the public by Sir Sidney Waterlow in 1889, who saw it as 'a garden for the gardenless'. Within its 8ha (20 acres) stands gorgeous Lauderdale House, which dates from 1582. The original house was built by Sir Richard Martin, Master of the Mint and three times Lord Mayor, and its name comes from the Scottish Royalist Earl of Lauderdale, since it was bequeathed to his wife, Anne. Its most famous resident, albeit for a short time, was Nell Gwynn, the Restoration actress and mistress

of Charles II. The exterior is late Georgian and, behind it, little survives of the Tudor building.

Sir Sidney Waterlow was the last private owner. He gave the house and grounds to the London County Council 'for the enjoyment of Londoners' – and both are very much enjoyed today, not least for a programme of jazz, cabaret, classical concerts, poetry and open-air theatre. However, it was not always so. Lauderdale House served as a park tearoom and keepers' flats for 70 years, until a fire in 1963 destroyed the roof and much of the interior. After that it lay derelict until, in 1978, after 15 years of fundraising, lobbying and petitioning, it was reopened by the late Yehudi Menuhin, the virtuoso violinist, as a centre for arts and education. Today, it is once again one of the nicest places in London to have tea.
Highgate Hill, N6 5HG. Archway tube.

㊸ Hampstead Heath

'The wind on my face was lovely and when I did go back inside to live I found it very hard to sleep,' said author Colin Wilson. In 1956, Wilson wrote his first book, *The Outsider*, in the British Museum by day, and at night slept on the Heath. The same breeze tugs at, chivvies and buoys up the kites flown on Parliament Hill (popularly known as Kite Hill), from where a great sweep of the City, St Paul's Cathedral and Canary Wharf may be seen. One story has it that a supporter of Guy Fawkes and his co-conspirators watched from here in 1605, waiting in vain for the seat of government to go up in smoke. John Constable lived nearby on Well Walk, and loved to paint the Heath and its skyscape. C.S. Lewis, walking here, was inspired to write *The Lion, the Witch and the Wardrobe,* and Victorian popular novelist Wilkie Collins used it as a backdrop to the opening of *The Woman in White.*

There are 324ha (800 acres) of hills and valleys, glades and meadows to explore – and a curiosity. Near the top of one of the meadows can be seen 'the Tumulus', which a Professor Hales, resident in Hampstead, claimed must contain 'the dust of the slain' from a battle between tribes based in London and St Albans. When archaeologist Sir Hercules Read excavated it in 1894, he found no trace of burial, just a top layer of recent materials, but he nonetheless concluded that it was 'very probably an ancient burial mound from the Bronze Age period'. Local folklore has it that this is the grave of Boudica, Queen of the Iceni, but she is also said to be buried under a platform at King's Cross.
N6. Hampstead tube, Hampstead Heath rail.

NORTH

㊹ Hampstead Heath Ponds

Among the Heath's greatest attractions are its many ponds. The bigger ones were dug as reservoirs for London in the 17th and 18th centuries and fed by the River Fleet. There are more than 30 of them, with six major ponds in two different valleys. One is designated for mixed bathing, one for men's bathing, one for women's. The men's pond is a kind of naturists' club within a fenced enclosure. The murky waters of the bathing ponds, in sylvan settings and sequestered glades under open sky, provide a very different swimming experience from the wavering, chlorinated waters of enclosed swimming pools. Children under eight and less-than-competent swimmers are excluded, but for them there is the distraction of the model boating pond.
N6. Hampstead tube, Hampstead Heath rail.

㊺ Kenwood House

From its hilltop vantage amid landscaped parkland on the Heath, this beautiful neoclassical house has London at its feet. It was built by John Bill in 1616 and remodelled for the Earl of Mansfield by Robert Adam in 1764–9. A portico and a library were added at this time, with beautiful friezes and grand colonnades. George Saunders built the wings that house the music and dining rooms, in 1793–6. Art treasures include the Iveagh Bequest of important paintings by such great artists as Rembrandt, Vermeer, Turner, Reynolds and Gainsborough, and one of Constable's Hampstead Heath pictures, a sketch in oils, is here, too.

The Suffolk Collection on the first floor comprises mainly family portraits passed down from the 1580s and presented to the nation in 1974 by the Hon. Mrs Greville Howard, as was the wish of her late mother-in-law, the 11th Countess of Suffolk. There are fine depictions of Stuart ladies and noblemen by William Larkin, Van Dyck and Lely. English Heritage hold picnic concerts in the grounds, the design of which was influenced by the work of Humphry Repton, the influential 18th-century landscape gardener.
Hampstead Lane, NW3 7JR.

㊻ Spaniards Inn

Surrounded by the Heath, this weather-boarded inn has the genuine feel of a country pub, but it is located just ten tube stops from London's centre. It stands on a narrow bend in the road, behind a white picket fence, and dates in parts from around 1585, although it was extended in the Edwardian era. Myths about the place abound. Was it the birthplace of the highwayman Dick Turpin? Does he haunt the place even now? Some swear that he does. His father was the landlord here in the 18th century, and, apparently, the upstairs Dick Turpin Bar sometimes turns spookily cold. Then how to explain the phantom tugs at the sleeve felt by drinkers in the downstairs bar? Is there truth in the tales of a ghostly horse in the car park, or a woman in white in the garden? Does the pub's name derive from the fact that this was a country retreat for the Spanish Ambassador to the Court of King James – or does it refer to the Spanish brothers, and proprietors, who fought a duel to the death over a woman? Keats may have written his 'Ode to a Nightingale' here – or it may have been under a plum tree in his garden, depending on whether one accepts the popular version or the account of his friend Charles Armitage Brown. Dickens certainly knew the place, and mentioned it in *The Pickwick Papers*.
Spaniards Road, NW3 7JJ.

㊼ The Hill Garden and Pergola Walk

The Hill Garden and Pergola Walk are an Edwardian dream come true. They were commissioned by William H. Lever, later Lord Leverhulme, a wealthy patron of the arts, and designed by the leading landscape architect Thomas Mawson. In 1904, Lever bought a substantial house, called The Hill, which faced North End Way, then a lane. He also acquired adjoining land with the intention of building a pergola, where he would hold garden parties. The plans for this required raising the large gardens of The Hill. As luck would have it, the Northern Line of the tube was being built at the time, and the soil that was dug out was brought here. The first phase was completed in 1906, and the grounds were extended in 1911, the extension being reached by a stone bridge over a public path. The final phase – a Summer Pavilion and viewing terrace – was completed in 1925. When Lord Leverhulme died shortly afterwards, The Hill was bought by Baron Inverforth and renamed after him. Although it has suffered wear and tear, the Grade II pergola remains true to its creator's vision. The 244m (800ft) terrace and pergola were described by Nikolaus Pevsner, the historian of art and architecture, as 'amongst the most impressive of their date in London'.
The Hill Garden, Inverforth Close, North End Way, Hampstead, NW3 7EX. Hampstead tube.

④⑧ Jack Straw's Castle

An Englishman's home is his castle, and the Englishman after whom this one is named was a comrade of Wat Tyler, the leader of the peasant's revolt. This unmissable north London landmark smites the eye with its extraordinary presence. It is not just its prominent position – a former pub, it was said to be the highest above sea level of any in London – but also its stand-out appearance as a timber-frame mock castle complete with castellation. Despite local opposition, it has been turned into flats, providing a very quaint address for a lucky few. It was originally a coaching inn, built in 1721, and commemorates Jack Straw, who addressed groups of peasants on Hampstead Heath from a hay wagon ('Jack Straw's Castle'). A landmine caused extensive damage in the Second World War and the pub was rebuilt in 1962 by Raymond Erith and Quinlan Terry. The castle frontage was prefabricated and assembled on site. Dickens, Thackeray and Wilkie Collins knew the place in its first incarnation.
12 North End Way, NW3 7ES. Golders Green, Hampstead tube.

④⑨ Hampstead Museum

A fine Queen Anne mansion now houses a small museum devoted to Hampstead life. The house was built for the Sewells, a Quaker family, in 1703 and is one of Hampstead's oldest. It takes its present name from Reverend Allatson Burgh, who bought it in 1822. The house has served as a militia headquarters and officers' mess in wartime. Rudyard Kipling's daughter lived here in the 1930s before it passed into the hands of the council in 1946. Threatened with demolition, it was rescued and is run by a trust.

There are now more than 3,000 objects in the museum's collection, relating to art and life in Hampstead, including many old photographs, various documents and a rather odd mix of objects – a matchstick model and a knitted picture of Burgh House, a mayoral throne, a scout's whistle and an Air Raid Warden sign among them. A small book, *25 Ways of Serving Oatmeal*, recalls the days of rationing, and *Blossom the Brave Balloon* was written for children at a time when barrage balloons were stationed over the city. The High Hill Penguin, a sculpture commissioned by the Penguin publishing company in 1960, was signed by local authors at the High Hill Bookshop on the High Street. There is a programme of events and talks, many of them free.
New End Square, NW3 1LT. Hampstead tube.

⑤⓪ No 2 Willow Road

This is the family home of a modernist from Budapest, that so incensed James Bond's creator that he named an arch villain after the architect. The unique development of three houses was built on Willow Road in 1939 by Ernö Goldfinger, in place of four old cottages, at a cost of £3,885. Goldfinger saw it as an opportunity to explore his talents and to create a functional home for a growing family. His Hampstead neighbour, author and spy Ian Fleming, viewed it as an eyesore and created the character of Auric Goldfinger, an avaricious psychopath, in revenge. The real Goldfinger, his wife, Elizabeth, and their three children lived very happily in the middle house, which is now run by the National Trust and contains an impressive collection of modern art.
NW3 1TH. Hampstead tube.

⑤① Keats House

'I think I shall be among the English poets after my death,' John Keats wrote to his brother George in the spring of 1818. He had been stung by bad reviews of his four-book poem 'Endymion', described by author and critic John Gibson Lockhart as 'calm, settled, imperturbable, driveling idiocy', but in September of that year began an *annus mirabilis* for Keats. His friend Charles Armitage Brown invited him to live in the smaller of two new two-storey stucco houses. In a whirlwind 12 months, he fell in love and became engaged to Fanny Brawne, the girl next door. He began an early version of 'Hyperion', and wrote 'The Eve of St Agnes', 'The Eve of St Mark', 'Ode to Psyche', 'La Belle Dame sans Merci', 'Ode to a Nightingale', and around the same time the 'Ode on a Grecian Urn', 'Ode on Melancholy', 'Ode on Indolence', 'Lamia Part I', 'Otho the Great' (with Brown), 'The Fall of Hyperion', the 'Ode to Autumn' and 'Lamia Part II'. By winter of 1819, the creative fires had burnt out. He contracted tuberculosis, and in 1820 moved to Italy for his health, dying there the following February, aged 25.

The two houses were later knocked into one, and there has been a museum here since 1825. It contains a number of touching personal possessions, such as a plaited lock of Fanny's hair, the gold engagement ring she wore until her death in 1865, and personal letters. Entry to the garden is free. Here grew the plum tree under which Keats wrote his paean to that 'immortal bird' that is so fraught with premonitions of his own end. He was right, though – he is among the English poets, immortal, too.
Keats Grove, NW3 2RR. Hampstead tube.

52 Freud's House

Sigmund Freud and his family lived in this house after they fled Austria and Nazi annexation in 1938. Anna Freud, the great man's youngest daughter, lived here until her death in 1982, and the big old house has the authentic feel of a cherished family home. It was Anna's wish that it should be a museum dedicated to her father, and his study is preserved as it was in his lifetime, with the psychoanalyst's couch, draped with a Persian rug and piled with chenille cushions. This is where patients would lie while describing their dreams. On the shelf behind Freud's desks are works by Goethe and Shakespeare, Heine and Anatole France. In the library hangs a painting of *Oedipus and the Riddle of the Sphinx.*

Paintings, Bedermeier chests, tables and cupboards were brought here, lock, stock and barrel from Vienna. Here, too, are fine antiquities from Egypt, Greece, Rome and the Orient. Freud's passion for collecting was second only to his taste for cigars (and yes, as he said, sometimes a cigar is just a cigar). On the landing is a portrait of Freud by Salvador Dali. The garden was designed by Freud's architect son, Ernst – a cluster of six brick houses on Frognal Close are by him. The Anna Freud Room contains her analyst's couch and a loom. She was an enthusiastic weaver and knitter and would often click away as patients unburdened themselves. *20 Maresfield Gardens, NW3 5SX. Finchley Road tube.*

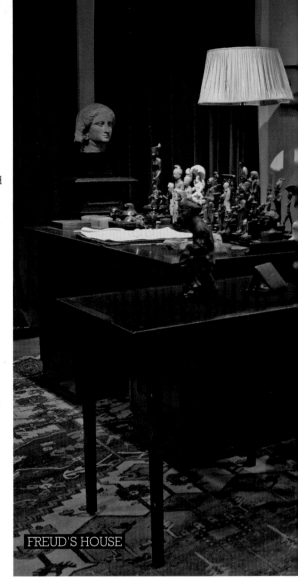

FREUD'S HOUSE

53 New End Theatre

Stage fright is an occupational hazard at a theatre in a former mortuary said to be haunted. Built in 1890, the mortuary served New End Hospital, to which it was linked by a tunnel so that bodies could be transported under the road. It was converted to a theatre by Buddy Dalton in 1974 and quickly gained a reputation for discovering new writers. Pluto Productions took over in 1997 with a continued commitment to great new writing and some classic revivals. *27 New End, NW3 1JD. Hampstead tube.*

54 Everyman Cinema

A night at the cinema doesn't get much more glamorous than at this former 19th-century drill hall and assembly rooms, opened as a picture house on Boxing Day 1933. The building dates from the 1880s and served as a theatre from 1920. Refurbishment in 2004 and 2006 spared all the period features in the screening rooms, set over three floors, while creating a venue of unmatched luxury. The filmgoer can watch a choice of mainstream and art-house movies from the comfort of an armchair or cushion-strewn sofa, while snacking on olives and honey-roasted cashews and sipping chilled champagne. *5 Hollybush Vale, NW3 6TX. Hampstead tube.*

55 Fenton House

This brownish redbrick merchant's house was built in around 1686 by William Eades, and is one of the earliest, largest and finest in Hampstead. It was home to Joshua Gee, a trader in silk and iron and a member of the Society of Friends, who bought the place from the widow of the first owner, Thomas Sympson, in 1706.

THE STUDY IS AS IT WAS, COMPLETE WITH COUCH

Together with George Washington's father, Gee was a founding partner in the Principio Company, which produced pig iron in Maryland for sale to England. He was a friend of William Penn, after whom Pennsylvania is named. Gee's initials and those of his wife are intertwined in the ironwork over the front gate, which was made by the French master blacksmith Jean Tijou's craftsmen. The house was renamed by Philip Fenton, who moved here in 1793, and was gifted to the National Trust in 1952 by Lady Binning.

The visitor can admire collections of early keyboard instruments, porcelain, needlework and paintings, including works by Constable and Breughel the Elder. Among the musical instruments is a 1612 harpsichord, which was played by Handel.

The garden is much as it was three centuries ago. More than 30 old varieties of apples are still grown in the orchard, and in September, on Apple Day, visitors are welcome to taste them. *Hampstead Grove, NW3 6SP. Hampstead tube.*

SHRI SWAMINARAYAN MANDIR

NORTHWEST

56 Shri Swaminarayan Mandir

One of the biggest, most ambitious and beautiful Hindu temples ever assembled is to be seen on a suburban street in north London. For the building popularly known as the Neasden Temple, 2,820 tonnes of Bulgarian limestone and 2,000 tonnes of Italian Carrara marble were shipped to India and carved by 1,500 craftsmen. The resulting 26,300 pieces were sent to London and the Mandir, or sacred Hindu place of worship, was put together on site. Its gleaming white pinnacles and soaring pillars have been attracting Hindu devotees from all over the world since it opened its doors in August 1995. *105–119 Brentfield Road, NW10 8LD. Neasden, Stonebridge Park tube.*

57 Wembley Stadium

On a summer's night in June 2004, a giant arc of light appeared in the sky over London. The England football team had just scored a victory against Croatia, and the Football Association, in a mood of celebration, had ordered the nascent new Wembley Stadium to announce itself in spectacular fashion.

Football was played at Wembley Park way back in the 1880s, but it was not until after the Great War that a national sports ground was built as a centrepiece to the British Empire Exhibition. The 'Empire Stadium' – built by Sir John Simpson and Maxwell Averton – went up in just 300 days and cost £750,000. It went through many adaptations over the decades, but in 2000 the

world's most famous football stadium was no longer fit for purpose, and closed. At £757 million its replacement cost a little over ten times as much as the original. Behind schedule and way over budget, it was described as a 'fiasco' as a work in progress, but all that is forgotten. The futuristic arena, designed by Norman Foster, has a sliding roof and seating for 90,000. Its 1,333m (4,373ft) arc is a landmark. As well as hosting football's flagship events and international games, including providing a superb venue for the 2012 Olympic and Paralympic Games, Wembley accommodates truly sensational concerts.
Wembley Park, Wembley Central tube. Wembley Stadium rail.

58 Ace Café

The Ace Café opened on the North Circular Road in 1938 to serve enormous fry-ups and steaming mugs of tea to hungry lorry drivers. By the late 1950s it had become the haunt of the 'ton up' boys, motorbikers who liked to race their Triumph 500s, Bonnevilles and BSA Gold Stars at 100mph (sadly for these tearaways, the 70mph speed limit was introduced in 1967). The café was also frequented by rock 'n' roll stars, such as Gene Vincent, Billy Fury and Johnny Kidd (also known as Vincent Eugene Craddock, Ron Wycherley and Frederick Heath). It closed in 1969 but reopened in 2001 after a refit, and is now rocking again.
Ace Corner, North Circular Road, Stonebridge, NW10 7UD. Stonebridge Park rail and tube.

59 Hoover Building

'Sensitively preserved as a Tesco supermarket' sounds an unlikely tale, but to give the global grocer's its due, the company ensured the survival of Britain's greatest Art Deco palace, adding a touch of class to the shopping experience. The store behind the factory frontage has an entrance decorated with fan windows similar to those on the main building. A landmark on the A40, the distinctive façade of coloured glazed tiles and angular windows, lit up at night like a Hollywood extravaganza, seems as fresh now as the day it opened in 1933. The three storeys, undetectable from the outside, were once busy with 600 staff. The ground floor was the production centre for vacuum cleaners, and soon the Hoover was collecting dust in thousands of British homes. The building was designed by Wallis, Gilbert and Partners, whose other London buildings include Victoria Coach Station.
Hoover Building, Western Avenue, UB6 8DW. Perivale tube.

60 Harrow's Old Speech Room Gallery and Museum

Harrow school, dating from 1572, was granted a Royal Charter by Elizabeth I. Since then, it has produced eight future British prime ministers, including Winston Churchill. The Speech Room, built in 1819–21, was intended to encourage the art of public speaking. Here Churchill could hone the skills that made him one of the greatest orators of the 20th century.

In 1976, it was converted into a gallery to house the school's collection of fine art and antiquities. One highlight is Churchill's *A Distant View of Venice* (1929). Not all of the collection can be shown at one time, but the visitor will usually see the portraits and busts of such Old Harrovians as Lord Byron and the playwright and politician Richard Sheridan, as well as Egyptian and Greek antiquities. There are English watercolours, modern British paintings, and a set of gilt Easter eggs by Stuart Devlin, in the tradition of Fabergé, each revealing a surprise when opened.
5 High Street, Harrow-on-the-Hill, HA1 3HP. Harrow-on-the-Hill tube. Open most afternoons but check before visiting.

61 Brent Reservoir

London's largest lake is popularly known as the 'Welsh Harp', after a tavern that stood nearby until the 1970s. Built in the mid 19th century to fill the baths and kettles of London, the reservoir is fed by the evocatively named Silk Stream, and flows into the River Brent. It is a Site of Special Scientific Interest and an important breeding ground for waterfowl. A great white egret, Hume's warbler and Montague's Harrier are rarities among the 250 bird species seen here.

In the latter half of the 19th century, it was people who came flocking for an evening's entertainment, laid on by W.P. Warner, landlord of the Welsh Harp Tavern and a Crimea veteran. The first greyhound races with mechanical hares took place by the lake, and there were always bank holiday fairs, but the crowds attracted were mixed to say the least, causing one commentator to describe an event as 'a carnival of vice'. In 1921 nude sunbathing on reservoir land, modelled on practice in Germany, sparked public opposition and led to the naturists being attacked in what was dubbed 'the Sun-Bathing Riots'. There are no riots today. This is preserved as a place of peaceful recreation and a haven for ornithologists, thanks to the Welsh Harp Conservation Group.
Birchen Grove, Kingsbury, NW9 8RY.

EALING
BROADWAY

Uxbridge Road

WHITE CITY

Westway

Boston Road

Uxbridge Road

ACTON TOWN

Goldhawk Road

TURNHAM
GREEN

M4

OSTERLEY

HAMMERSMITH

Great West Road

SYON
LANE

BARONS
COURT

Fulham Palace Road

London Road

KEW
GARDENS

Castelnau

ISLEWORTH

Hanworth Road

MORTLAKE

PUTNEY
BRIDGE

CLAPHAM
JUNCTION

BAT

RICHMOND

WANDSWORTH
TOWN

Roehampton Lane

Chertsey Road

ST MARGARETS

West Hill

Trinity Road

TWICKENHAM

Kingston Road

SOUTHFIELDS

Merton Road

BAL

TOOTING
BEC

Staines Road

Kingston Hill

Robin Hood Way

Wimbledon Park Side

TOOTING
BROADWAY

STRAWBERRY
HILL

WIMBLEDON

Hampton Court Road

Kingston Road

Western Road

MORDEN

KEY

Battersea

Wandsworth

Tooting

Wimbledon

Fulham

Hammersmith

Chiswick & Beyond

Southwest

1 2 8 9 10 13 14 15 16 17 18 19 20 21 22 23 24 25 26 27 28 29 30 31 32 33 34 35 36 37 38 39 40 41 42 43 44 45 46 47 48 49 50 51 52 53

VAUXHALL

Brixton Road

Brixton Hill

West & Southwest

Historic houses and palaces are found in abundance south of the river while, interspersed throughout the leafy suburbs, parks and commons, gardens and nature reserves breathe life into the busy city.

BATTERSEA

❶ Couper Collection

Between Battersea Bridge and Albert Bridge, a flotilla of Thames barges at their 18th-century moorings provides an unlikely home for a museum of art and events. On show are installations by London artist and performance composer Max Couper, all made onboard, and there is also a permanent gallery of first works by London artists under the age of 18. Couper has worked here for 20 years. Among the archive is *Fleeting Opera*, composed by Couper for the Thames in 2000, performed by members of the Royal Opera, the Royal Ballet and Dame Judi Dench, who found the opportunity to be part of this waterborne artwork 'irresistible'. 'The last time any such serious artistic statement was created and performed for the river,' she said, 'was Handel's Water Music in 1717. I passionately believe the Thames is underused. This is so valuable because it draws attention to it in a spirited way.'
Hester Road, SW11 4AN.

❷ Battersea Park

'I saw that I must mix my flower colours, plant in wide pools and drifts, let pale pinks overlap into clear lemon yellow, interplant orange with red-purple,' wrote the great landscape artist Russell Page of creating the now-restored Festival Garden in one of London's most interesting parks, beside the Thames. The garden was designed as part of the 1951 Festival of Britain, to bring some colour back into the lives of Londoners, who were still subject to rationing in their bomb-battered city. Page's scheme called for 20,000 yellow tulips, and raised beds of crimson and pink floribunda roses.

Sadly, meanwhile, the subtropical garden in the park had fallen into neglect. This garden was planted in 1863 by the park's first superintendent, John Gibson, a plant-finder who had travelled to India and South Africa on a hunt for orchids for the Duke of Devonshire. The first public subtropical garden in Britain, it had attracted intense interest, but in the Second World War, with the gardeners called up to fight, much of the park was turned over to allotments as the populace was urged to 'Dig for Victory.' The planting of a palm tree in 1992 was the first move towards the restoration of this garden, to its original plan.

Page's Festival Garden included a children's zoo, and still today the Battersea Park Zoo is a tremendous draw. Around the lake, the visitor can see waterfowl, herons and cormorants, and great crested grebes, while in this intimate little menagerie, meerkats and mynah birds are on view, along with Kune Kune pigs and pygmy goats, giant monkeys, miniature ponies, donkeys, chipmunks and ring-tailed lemurs.
SW11 4NJ. Battersea Park rail.

❸ Peace Pagoda

As the sun rises over Battersea Park, a Buddhist monk, wearing a saffron robe, beats softly on a drum as he makes his way from his temple to a Peace Pagoda. The war that raged around the park more than 60 years ago, here commemorated by a number of memorials, was to end with the bombings of Hiroshima and Nagasaki in Japan. Some years later, the Most Venerable Nichidatsu Fujii sent monks and nuns of the Nipponzan Myhoji Order into the world to build such pagodas as part of a campaign for peace and social and moral justice. The first in Britain, incorporated into the new town of Milton Keynes, was begun in 1978, and opened in September 1980. Battersea's was completed in 1985. The pagoda is a spiritual beacon and a place for quiet reflection for Buddhist and non-Buddhist alike – and wholly unexpected in a Victorian pleasure garden, laid out for the benefit of public health and for its civilising effect on the denizens of the surrounding slums.
SW11 4NJ. Battersea Park rail.

NEW COVENT GARDEN FLOWER MARKET

④ Pump House Gallery

This unique gallery has an idyllic lakeside location in Battersea Park, in a converted pump house. The tower was built in 1861 by Simpson & Son to house a coal-fired steam engine and pump that would circulate the lake water, irrigate the plants and drive cascades at the lake's north end. Restoration between 1988 and 1992 returned it to its Victorian glory, and in 1999 it was turned into an art gallery. Works of contemporary visual art are displayed over four floors, and up to half a dozen exhibitions are staged each year. *309 Battersea Park Road, SW11 4NJ. Battersea Park rail.*

⑤ Battersea Power Station

What is to become of London's most conspicuous ruin? This coal-fired power station, with its four big chimneys, has generated great controversy but not a spark of electricity since 1983. Giles Gilbert Scott, designer of London's red telephone boxes, is described as 'architect of the exterior', although it was the work of a team of architects and engineers. In its day it met a fifth of the capital's electricity needs. On Lupus Street the Churchill Gardens Estate was heated by hot waste water pumped under the river from the station. Redevelopment plans for the largest brick building in Europe, which still has its original Art Deco interior décor and fittings, have serially failed to come to fruition. To some it is an eyesore, but to most Londoners it is an important landmark. It appeared in The Beatles' film *Help!* in 1961, on the cover of Pink Floyd's *Animals* album, and in 2007 it provided a location for the Batman film *The Dark Knight*. A slumbering giant, it continues to fire passions. *188 Kirtling Street, SW8 5BN. Battersea Park rail.*

⑥ New Covent Garden Flower Market

At five o'clock in the morning, the sleepy visitor is confronted with an abundance of exotic and home-grown blooms in the purpose-built market in Nine Elms. This is a wholesale market, so not the place to buy a posy, a *boutonnière* or one perfect English rose, but anyone wanting to deck the halls can do no better than to come here where, as fresh as daisies, the traders have been on the go since 3am in their temperature-controlled Eden. Plants are available, too, and olive trees and sculptured bushes, all destined to brighten lives and gladden hearts. Britain's biggest fruit, vegetable and flower market opened on this 23ha (57 acre) site in 1974, so strictly speaking, it is no longer 'new' and there are plans for major redevelopment. *Nine Elms, SW8 5EE. Vauxhall rail and tube.*

151

WANDSWORTH

❼ Battersea Arts Centre

There is a terrific sense of fun about the Battersea Arts Centre. All around the wide arches and deep terracotta walls are places to sit and things to look at. Some corners, tucked behind furniture screens, are set as scenes in a play, items dangle from the ceiling, notes and projects are pinned to walls. Mothers take their children to the indoor playground, people chat at the café's motley tables, music rehearsals are heard down corridors. A lot seems to be going on.

Built in 1893 as Battersea's Town Hall, it has a welcoming entrance hall with a marble staircase beneath a glass roof encircled by plump cherubs. Upstairs is the half-panelled council chamber, still with 'Ayes' and 'Nos' inscribed over its doors. Theatre is sometimes put on in this room. At other times, plays are performed at the back of the building, in the Grand Hall, a magnificent space with a sprung maple dance floor, balcony and bar. Performances always push back the boundaries. *Jerry Springer – The Opera* premiered here. Expect to be engaged.

Lavender Hill, SW11 5TN. Clapham Junction rail.

❽ The Fish Club

A turquoise blip among the shops on the shady south side of St John's Hill turns out to be a restaurant serving terrific fish and chips, either to eat in or take away. Inside, the décor is modern, with bar stools and simple wooden tables. It is a business with a mission: 'to educate and inform people about the beauty of good, sustainably caught fresh fish, and chips'. Fresh fish is delivered daily and displayed on a slab, and the blackboard menu lists more options – oysters, shrimps, squid, prawn and chorizo kebabs, and pies. It is licensed, and home-made ice cream and puddings are available, too. This is the original Fish Club; there is another in Clapham High Street.

189 St John's Hill, SW11 1TH. Clapham Junction rail.

❾ The Hive Honey Shop

Among the market stalls, boutiques and bijou stores of Northcote Road, the Hive Honey Shop has found a niche. From teapots to tinctures, via honey mead, beeswax and cakes, everything in these small premises is bee-oriented. There's even a hive with a glass front where thousands of live bees can be seen setting about their melifluous work. Honey comes from Wandsworth and surrounding boroughs, as well as North London, and can account for between 25 and 89 per cent of produce sold, depending on the harvest.

'Most years are good,' says James Hamill, the shop's head beekeeper. 'City environments tend to have a denser population of flowers, so the bees are spoiled for choice, and Londoners' love of gardens means bees here have millions of flowers to collect nectar from. Exotic annual flowers are planted each year, so the honey from half a mile apart will taste completely different.' Hives are on sale, and help, tips and courses for budding apiarists are also available.

93 Northcote Road, SW11 6PL. Clapham Junction rail.

❿ Royal Victoria Patriotic Building

Originally the Royal Victoria Patriotic Asylum, the building, like the name, reeks of patronage. It is an institutional colossus, high Gothic with corner towers and the obligatory St George and Dragon sculpture above the main door. It was built by public subscription for 300 girls orphaned by the Crimean War, and opened by Queen Victoria in 1857. The girls were trained to go into service, for which there was a high demand in booming south London, and after passing through a fairly brutish regime, each would leave equipped for the world with a Bible and a trunk full of clothes from nearby Arding & Hobbs department store.

During the First World War the building became a military hospital. In the Second World War it was a clearing centre for aliens, run by MI6 under chief interrogator Colonel Oreste Pinto, a Dutch counterintelligence officer, played by Bernard Archer in a popular TV series, *Spycatcher* (1959–61). Today the tranquil building, which is set out around three courtyards, has studios and workshops on the ground floor, and flats above. A small bar and restaurant, Le Gothique, uses the north courtyard.

The main occupant of the building is the Academy of Live and Recorded Arts (ALRA), which has around 120 pupils. Their theatre is on the south side of the building, and regular performances are open to the public. ALRA also uses the Great Hall, which was the orphans' dining room, as a rehearsal space, but they are not allowed to perform there. The ceiling, two storeys high, is painted with the shields of the municipalities and counties that contributed to the foundation of the orphanage. It could be damaged by bright lights.

John Archer Way, SW18 3SX. Clapham Junction rail.

ROYAL VICTORIA
PATRIOTIC BUILDING

TOOTING

11 The London Sewing Machine Museum

The sewing machine is, along with the bicycle, one of the last pieces of technology the ordinary person has been able to comprehend fully. The two rooms of this museum show how it can be beautiful as well as functional. Starting it all is a Singer No 1 from 1850, the first to be made by Isaac Merrit Singer. Display cases, treadle tables and cabinets sparkle with the gold and lacquer of domestic and industrial machines produced over the following 100 years, including a model given by Queen Victoria to Princess Victoria, her oldest child.

More than 600 machines were amassed by Thomas Albert Rushton, who started the collection in 1946. His original shop front is displayed, and the business has moved several times, hence the name of the sales and repair shop next door – Wimbledon Sewing Machine Shop, which has migrated here from SW20. The business is run by Rushton's son Ray and his family, selling antique machines and machine parts to enthusiasts. The museum is free and opens on the first Saturday of each month from 2 to 4.30pm.

308 Balham High Road, SW17 7AA. Balham tube.

12 Tooting Bec Lido

Britain's biggest outdoor pool is a bracing place. The water is unheated and the lido is fully exposed to the elements on Tooting Common, although the surrounding banks, planted with trees, act as windbreaks, as well as giving shelter to a multitude of songbirds. The coloured cubicles that run along the side of the pool are also unheated.

The baths measure 100 x 33m (328 x 108ft), hold a million gallons of water and were opened in 1906 for the benefit of the great unwashed. This is where those without baths at home would come for a necessary douching. It was called Tooting Bathing Lake then, and didn't get its fancy Italian title until the 1930s, when even the well scrubbed started to go swimming. A

filter and fountain were added to clean it up, and mixed bathing was allowed for the first time. The pool opens to the public from the end of May to the end of September, and is used in winter by the South London Swimming Club, a hardy set of people who hold races on Christmas day when the water can be 1°C (34°F). The UK Cold Water Swimming Championships in January have a carnival air.
Tooting Bec Road, SW16 1RU. Tooting Bec, Balham tube.

13 The Gala Bingo Hall

The Tooting Granada was the first cinema to be given Grade I listing, and even from the outside it looks impressive. The architect was Cecil Masey and the 1931 façade, with four Corinthian columns, is in grand Art Deco style. But it's the interior that is so astonishing. The Gothic fantasy is the work of the multi-talented Russian Theodore Komisarjevsky, who, with Masey, had just completed the Phoenix Theatre in Charing Cross Road (see page 59). For glorious exuberance, it outclasses many theatres in the West End. Chartres Cathedral was its inspiration, and the plaster arcading and extraordinary Gothic detailing make it look more suitable for religious purposes than for a game of Housie Housie. The foyer, grand staircase and cloister-like hall of mirrors are all decorated.

The cinema seated 3,000 and was built to be used for both film and theatre. There was a 20 piece house orchestra and a Wurlitzer organ, which is still in place. In the early days, an evening's double bill might include a musical act as well as a film, and there was a seasonal pantomime. Frank Sinatra, the Andrews Sisters, the Beatles and the Rolling Stones have all played here. It closed in the 1970s and was converted for use as a bingo hall. The building can be fully explored on Open House weekends.
50–60 Mitcham Road, SW17 9NA. Tooting Broadway tube.

14 Morden Hall

A metal weathervane in the shape of a trout over the clockhouse gate at Morden Hall is a sign of things past – and, with luck and perseverance, things to come. The National Trust property lies alongside a rural stretch of the River Wandle, which rises in the chalky North Downs, and follows a 14 mile trail from Croydon to the Thames at Wandsworth. On its way, it flowed through Lord Nelson's moated Merton Place.

At Morden Hall, mills ground snuff, while water power at Merton Abbey Mills was harnessed by Huguenot weavers and by William Morris's print works factory, which also used the river for dying and rinsing fabrics. Morris stocked the river with perch from the Thames at Kelmscott, but before industry and around 100 mills polluted it, the Wandle was best known for brown trout. In 1868, Frederick Halford, the 'father of modern dry fly fishing', began his lifetime passion on an estate owned by a family friend, where he first cast a line alongside Wandle fishermen already skilled in using flies. It was then 'a beautifully clear stream in which every stone could be seen in four or five feet of water'. Today it is not as clean as that, but attempts have been made to rid it of pollution, and brown trout have been reintroduced. Anglers can also hope for barbel, carp, chub, dace and roach.
21 Morden Hall Road, SM4 5JD. Morden tube.

TOOTING BEC LIDO

WIMBLEDON

15 Southside House

The wonderful home of the Pennington Mellor Munthes draws the visitor right into the past lives of an intriguing family. It is mainly thanks to Major Malcolm Munthe, who retreated to a quiet life here after a highly adventurous time in the Second World War, that the house has been so well maintained. Major Munthe was the son of Axel Munthe, a Swedish doctor and author of *The Story of San Michele*, ostensibly a book about a house he bought and restored in Capri. He produced such a vivid account of so many encounters that, at one time, it outsold the Bible. But the story of Southside really belongs to the family of Axel's wife, Hilda

Pennington Mellor. She was descended from its founder, Robert Pennington, who had commissioned the house from a Dutch builder following his return from exile in Holland on the Restoration of Charles II. Topped with a clock tower and flanked by statues of the Penningtons, the house remains essentially as it was in the 17th century. Inside, it is full of portraits, family photos, mementoes and items that have stories to tell. Admiral Nelson and Sir William and Emma, Lady Hamilton passed through its grand entrance hall, which rises two storeys through a gallery, and Emma performed her 'Attitudes' in the elegant music room. A garden of nearly a hectare (2 acres) has elaborate pathways, corners, follies and water features. Lord Byron met with his publisher,

A TOUR ENCOMPASSES
THE MILLENNIUM BUILDING

WIMBLEDON TENNIS CLUB

John Murray II, in the garden, in the same spot that Axel Munthe met with his publisher, John Murray VI. The house, along with the family's manor, Hellens, in Much Marcle, Herefordshire, is run as a trust by Malcolm's son, Adam.
3–4 Woodhayes Road, SW19 4RJ. Wimbledon rail and tube.

⑯ Caesar's Camp and Caesar's Well

Julius Caesar never came this way, but that hasn't stopped two ancient sites on Wimbledon Common being named after him. Among these 445ha (1,100 acres), the ponds of Rushmere and Queensmere have wildlife interest, as does Beverley Brook, and although the windmill no longer turns, its museum is a focus for walks. Wimbledon Common Golf Course is open to all; the Royal Wimbledon Golf Club is not, although it occupies much of Caesar's Camp, a hillfort dating from around the 6th century BC. Covering some 5ha (12 acres), it had a ditch 9m (30ft) wide and 4m (12ft) deep with a wooden palisade 6m (20ft) tall. Elizabethans knew it as Bensbury, and Julius Caesar's name was not invoked until the 19th century when most of the camp was levelled. Parts can still be seen down Camp Road and there is a footpath that crosses it.

Some 457m (500 yd) to the north is Caesar's Well, named at the same time as the Camp on a map of 1824. Water can no longer be drawn from its depths, which are encircled by granite blocks, but a nearby standpipe brings spring water up from 5.5m (18ft) below ground. At the centre of a copse of pine trees that whistle in the wind, it seems a magical place.
Camp Road, SW19 4UW. Wimbledon rail and tube.

⑰ Cannizaro Park

The Italian name adds a touch of the exotic to the well-kept estate beside Wimbledon Common. A sunny aspect and paved garden areas certainly give it an Italian feel. It is easy to imagine Countess Cannizaro on the terrace, singing snatches of Verdi as she goes about her flower arranging, not caring that her husband has run off with some floozy in Milan. The Countess was Sophia Johnstone, a Scottish heiress who rented the house with her Italian husband in 1817. Described by diarist Charles Greville as 'uneducated but full of humour and vivacity', she collected musical scores, held Sunday concerts and, said Greville after her husband had bolted, 'consoled herself with her music and a strapping young Italian singer, who plundered her without

shame'. The house is now a hotel, and visitors can take tea on the terrace. The grounds are a public park, with rhododendrons, azaleas, camellias, maples and beeches. The parkland falls away towards woods, a pond and a walled garden.
West Side Common, SW19 4UE. Wimbledon rail and tube.

⑱ Wat Buddhapadipa

The first Buddhist temple in Britain, and the only Thai temple in Europe, looks quite out of place under grey London skies. The brilliant white building, Uposotha Hall, has red-and-gold doors and windows, and a Caturamuk, a four-gabled roof with finials of golden mystic figures. There are three Buddhas in the Shrine Room – the main black bronze was a gift from the Thai royal family, patrons of the temple. Colourful murals depict the life of Buddha and other figures, including the blessed Margaret Thatcher. The monastery was built for teaching Theravada Buddhism, and resident monks and nuns, in saffron-coloured robes, live in a house with a library and dining room. Visitors are welcome to wander the 1.6ha (4 acres) of grounds, where there are flower gardens, a grove, ponds with bridges and wise sayings to contemplate.
14 Calonne Road, SW19 5HJ. Wimbledon rail and tube.

⑲ Wimbledon Tennis Club

A highlight of a tour of Wimbledon tennis club is CentreCourt360, a viewing platform from where visitors can look out across the whole of the club's grounds and beyond. To many people, Centre Court looks much smaller than imagined, although it holds 11,000 spectators. The tour encompasses the players' entrance and café in the Millennium Building, television studios and interview room where visitors can sit in the hot seat for a photo. Outside are the picnic terraces (Henman Hill or Murray Mount) and water gardens from where there is a view over London. Before or after a tour, visitors are left to their own devices in the museum, which tells the story of the All England Tennis and Croquet Club, from its beginnings in 1887. On display are some of the 15,000 items in the collection, dating from 1555. These include paintings, toys, trophies and the cast-off kit of former champions. Instructive analyses are offered with video replays of great games on a 200 degree screen, while on another screen John McEnroe explains what it's like to be a player on these hallowed grounds.
Church Road, SW19 5EA. Southfields tube.

FULHAM

⑳ Bishops Park

Part of the attraction of Bishops Park is the view across the Thames to Putney Hard, and there are convenient seats from which to contemplate it. The park that surrounds Fulham Palace stretches for about half a mile from Putney Bridge to Fulham football ground, and was given to the public by the Bishops of London in 1888. A large injection of funds in 2010 enabled much of the central area around the boating lake to be totally revamped, and part of the lost moat in front of the Palace Lodge has been dug out. A walk follows the course of the mile-long waterway, which might have been a Roman earthwork. The park also has football pitches and tennis courts. By Putney Bridge are formal gardens and a commemorative stone to some 40 volunteers from the borough who fought in the Spanish Civil War. A clutch of London bishops are buried in All Saints Church by the bridge.
Putney Bridge Approach, SW6 3LA. Putney Bridge tube.

㉑ Fulham Palace

A few small windows high up in the redbrick outer wall, and the heavy, dark gate doors give Fulham Palace the look of a typical Tudor farm manor. Chickens should be scratching beneath the clocktower beside the courtyard fountain. The Bishop of London, based at St Paul's Cathedral, gave up his riverside palace in 1975 and for some years it continued to be a quiet backwater. But after recent refurbishments, the airy Drawing Room Café has opened, as well as a museum in the Georgian dining room and library. An art gallery has been added and the extensive walled garden revitalised. The Palace and gardens are now looked after jointly by the council and a trust, and entrance is free. However, there is a charge for the monthly guided tours. The museum and gallery are open from Sunday to Wednesday in the afternoon; access to the Great Hall and highly decorated 19th-century Tait Chapel is by guided tour only.
Bishops Avenue, SW6 6EA. Putney Bridge tube.

㉒ Craven Cottage and Fulham FC

'It was a dark and stormy night ...' The classic opening lines of the 1830 novel *Paul Clifford* were written by Edward Bulwer-Lytton, who lived in Craven Cottage. This phrase is not generally one to fly from the lips of fans of London's oldest football club as they head along the Green Mile of Bishops Park towards the riverside stadium any time the Cottagers are playing at home.

The original cottage was built by William Craven, 6th Baron Craven, in 1780, and it stood beside the Thames somewhere around the centre circle of the current pitch. Ninety-nine years later, football-playing members of the congregation at St Andrew's Church, a mile away, formed the fledgling Fulham FC team, and after the cottage had been destroyed by fire and abandoned, the club moved in. The first shaky tiers of seating were replaced under the direction of Scottish architect Archibald Leitch, who built the redbrick stand in Stevenage Road in 1896, and later added the Pavilion, the current cottage. A specialist in football stadia, he had recently completed the Ibrox stadium in Glasgow, but Craven Cottage is considered his masterpiece. The small grilled ticket windows and black turnstile doors give the brick façade the appearance of a bullring.

Now named the Johnny Haynes Stand after the former England captain, who died in a car accident in 2005, Leitch's stand still serves as the main entrance. It has a shop at one end and, at the other, the Café at the Cottage is open until 4 o'clock every day. The stand, which is the oldest in the football league, still has some of the original wooden seats. The 25,700 capacity stadium is one of the smallest in the premier league, but its choice riverside site makes it a valuable property and one of the most satisfying places to watch a ball being kicked around a park.
Stevenage Road, SW6 6HH. Putney Bridge tube.

㉓ Queen's Club

Tennis, real tennis, squash, rackets – Queen's Club has been a centre of racquet sports since 1886. Its 28 tennis courts have been described by Andy Roddick, former world No 1 tennis professional, as arguably the best grass courts in the world. The annual grass court championships for men, now sponsored by Aegon and formerly by Stella Artois, take place in early June, a few weeks before Wimbledon, and this popular tournament is a good barometer of who will end up dominating Centre Court.

Queen's Club stages national championships in real tennis, squash and rackets. It was the real tennis (*jeu de paume*) venue for the 1908 Olympics. At that time, Queen's Club, which claims to be the world's first sports complex, was also a football ground. In 2011 there was another first: the Women's Open Rackets Championship. Invented in London's debtors prisons, this fast and

furious game, in which balls can travel at 180mph, had until then been a male preserve. Queen's is a private members' club, and the dedans – spectators' small galleries in the walls of the courts – are hired for private functions.
Palliser Road, W14 9EB. Barons Court tube.

㉔ St Paul's Studios and Colet House

Along Talgarth Road, some redbrick buildings with outsized windows were designed by Frederick Wheeler in 1890 as studios for bachelor artists. They faced north so that no direct sunlight should fall through their cheval-glass windows, which were big enough to hand out even the largest canvas. The ceilings are 6m (20ft) tall and the studios measure 9m (30ft) by 7m (22ft). Each has three ground-floor rooms; the basement was for the housekeeper.

Slightly different is No 151, Colet House, built five years earlier by, it is thought, painter Sir Coutts Lindsay. It had two large ground-floor studios with domestic rooms behind, and an upstairs studio the width of the building. Nicolai Legat, the Russian ballet master, held classes here, and counted Dame Margot Fonteyn and Ninette de Valois among his pupils. Fonteyn lived for a while at No. 8 St Paul's Studios, and her practice mirrors are said to be still there. Until 2003, the Royal Ballet School was at No 155, now occupied by the London Academy of Music and Dramatic Art (LAMDA).

In 1938, Russian philosopher P.D. Ouspensky set up his headquarters in Colet House, and it remains the centre of his Study Society, open to the public for events. On the first Friday of the month, at guest ceremonies, whirling dervishes can be seen.
135–51 Talgarth Road, W14 9DA. Barons Court tube.

LONDON'S OLDEST FOOTBALL CLUB
CRAVEN COTTAGE AND FULHAM FC

The great outdoors

Any map of southwest London is generously splashed with green. A full two-thirds of the urban area comprises open space and water. No other comparable city has as much.

Commons, gardens, parks and meadows stretch from Battersea to Putney and Wimbledon, and out to Richmond, Kew and Ham. Richmond and Bushy Parks, where deer still graze, are among the jewels of London's open spaces, royal parks that were once hunting grounds. Royal patronage has ensured they are well looked after, but in the 19th century, as London rapidly expanded, it took some effort to keep developers from encroaching on common land. In 1865 the battle was joined by the Commons Preservation Society (today the Open Spaces Society). John Stuart Mill, the philosopher and Octavia Hill, an instigator of the National Trust, were among its founders, and it counted Wimbledon Common, Hampstead Heath and Epping Forest among its early successes. Wimbledon Common was owned by John, 5th Earl Spencer. He

wanted to turn it into a gated park, but gave in to popular demand, selling it to a public body in 1871 – the same year that Hampstead Heath was taken over by the Metropolitan Board of Works. Hampstead Heath is now owned by the City of London Corporation, which tends around 200 small parks and gardens in the square mile alone. It also owns Epping Forest, a former royal property that stretches 12 miles from Manor Park to Epping. The corporation bought the land in 1876 to stop threatened development.

That was the year the Commons Act was passed, establishing bodies of conservators to manage common land. The Home Secretary, Sir Richard Cross, told parliament that people needed fresh air as much as they needed food, and the Bill established the idea that a landscape could exist for the public good.

In the early Victorian era, the increasingly industrialised and insanitary city of overcrowded slums and heavy traffic cried out for fresh air. This led to the creation of Victoria Park, the first municipal leisure space, in East London. It was laid out in the 1840s, around the time that Greenwich Park was opened to the public. The architect, John Nash's chief assistant, James Pennethorne, was also called upon to enclose a shrinking Kennington Common, turning it into a park with railings and opening hours, to show developers they had gone far enough.

As farms, market gardens and grazing grounds disappeared, it became increasingly important that parks were mapped out. The London County Council, established in 1889, appointed Lt Col J.J. Sexby as its first Superintendent of Parks. He set the standards and so they remain, with regimented flower gardens, fountains, lakes, bandstands, pavilions and sporting areas, conveying a Victorian ideal of health, happiness and civic pride. They were also used to show off new varieties of trees and shrubs imported from all corners of the Empire to add to the ubiquitous London plane, which can thrive for centuries on city grime. These parks formed centrepieces in the new suburbs, created by the railways. South of the river miles of well-planted streets, lined with terraced houses, followed the tracks.

Communal gardens

After the Great Fire, houses built for the rich began to fill the area between the City and Westminster, and beyond. These were not the great palaces of other European cities, but terraces tucked tight around squares, with mews and services nearby, and shared gardens for mutual delight. Bloomsbury Square was the first, establishing the style, soon followed by St James's Square, developed by Henry Jermyn, Earl of St Albans.

Under the Restoration all the royal parks, with the exception of Greenwich, were opened to the populace, and Londoners enjoyed them by right. When Queen Caroline, wife of George II, extended the gardens at Kensington Palace and wanted to enclose the whole of Hyde Park as well as St James's for exclusive royal use, Prime Minister Sir Robert Walpole advised against such an unpopular measure. In reply to her question about what it might cost, he said, 'Only three crowns' – meaning the crowns of England, Scotland and Wales. Nor would Londoners give up one square inch of their parks today. In the changing landscape of the city, their eternal quality, linking the metropolis to the countryside, the present to the past provides reassurance as well as recreation.

After a century and more, London's public parks and greens are little changed, enjoyed as much today as they ever were, and so familiar as to be taken for granted.
CRICKET ON KEW GREEN

THE LYRIC, HAMMERSMITH

HAMMERSMITH

㉕ BBC Television Centre

The famous headquarters of the BBC closes in 2013. Television and radio news moved to Broadcasting House (see page 63) in 2011, but there is still plenty to see here, including memorabilia from *Dr Who* and *EastEnders*. Visitors may also take a peek into luxury dressing rooms and see what it's like both behind and in front of the camera; and there are celebrities to spot, of course. Tours last between an hour and 90 minutes and depend on what is being broadcast. *Wood Lane, W12 7RJ. White City tube.*

㉖ The Lyric, Hammersmith

A beautiful, gilt-and-plush 550 seat Victorian theatre is concealed inside a 1970s concrete box with a roof garden. It was brought here piece by piece from farther down King Street following a public outcry when it was forced to close in 1966.

The Lyric has a chequered history. Its reputation spread far beyond west London after Frank Matcham redesigned an existing opera house in 1895. Lily Langtry was the first on stage and fortunes ebbed and flowed over the next century. Its halcyon days were under Nigel Playfair, who was manager from 1918 to 1933. Ellen Terry made her last appearance at the Lyric and Harold Pinter's *The Birthday Party* premiered here in 1958. A 120 seat studio theatre has been added in the new building, and the Lyric, open every day, has a restaurant and roof garden open to all, part funded by Marks & Spencer's 5p charge on carrier bags. *King Street, W6 0QL. Hammersmith tube.*

㉗ The Dove

Oak settles, stone floors, a tiny bar and a suntrap terrace make the Dove the best known of several inviting pubs along this stretch of the river. Ernest Hemingway is said to have had a drink here. It started as a coffee house some time in the 18th century, and all the artists and literary figures in the neighbourhood would have known it. The Scottish poet James Thompson had lodgings in or near the building, and in 1741 wrote *Rule Britannia*, no doubt inspired by the beefy oarsmen on the river, who still go sculling by. The bar measures 1.3m (4ft 3in) by 2.4m (7ft 10in) and the ceiling is low, making it snug in winter, when there's a fire in the grate. The pub is owned by Fullers, whose nearby Griffin Brewery has been brewing since 1654. *19 Upper Mall, W6 9TA. Hammersmith tube.*

㉘ Kelmscott House Museum

'In this magical house ... everything that was necessary was clean and handsome; everything else was beautiful and beautifully presented.' So said George Bernard Shaw of William Morris's grand, wisteria-swagged riverside home in Hammersmith, named after his manor in Oxfordshire. The three-storey Georgian house, where the key figure of the Arts & Crafts movement lived for 17 years until his death in 1896, is privately owned and open on just one day a year, when there is a garden party and house tour. Visitors must otherwise content themselves with looking at the servants' quarters in the basement, home to the William Morris Society. A hand press is in operation to show how Morris would have worked at his Kelmscott Press, which he set up in rented cottages nearby, making his own paper and designing books with Sir Edward Burne-Jones and other artists. Some examples, and the typefaces he designed, can be seen in the coach house, where the artistic and literary giants gathered. Talks and other events are held here by the Society. *26 Upper Mall, W6 9TA. Hammersmith tube. Open Tuesday and Saturday afternoon.*

㉙ Emery Walker House

Ample compensation for not seeing inside William Morris's place is provided by a visit to nearby Emery Walker House, the best-preserved Arts & Crafts home in Britain. Sir Emery shared with Morris a taste for Santa-sized beards and fine printing, helping him to set up Kelmscott Press. He moved into this tall, narrow, 1750s terraced house in 1903, after spending 25 years a few doors away, at No 3. Preserved by his daughter as he left it on his death in 1933, it remained unseen by the public until 2005.

The house gives a good idea of how Morris's own home would have looked. It is decorated with distinctive William Morris wallpapers and fabrics, hand-made furniture, William de Morgan ceramics, and furniture willed to Sir Emery by Morris's partner, the architect Philip Webb. The top bedroom has far-reaching views, and a four-poster bed. A beautiful crewelwork bedcover was made by Morris's daughter, May, for Sir Emery's invalid wife, Mary. In the conservatory is a vine grown from a cutting taken in Hogarth's house. The garden leads directly to the river and is planted as it was in Sir Emery's time. *No 7 Hammersmith Terrace, W6 9TS. Hammersmith tube.*

CHISWICK & BEYOND

30 Tabard Theatre

An 80 seat theatre above the Tabard pub has a firm local following and can attract top headline names. The relaxed, country atmosphere of the building was intended as an antidote to Victorian gin houses by its architect Robert Norman Shaw, who planned the surrounding area of Bedford Park as London's first garden suburb. The Tabard had an upstairs meeting hall and, on the top floor, the landlord's flat, which is still used. Although, originally, amateur dramatics were occasionally staged in the meeting hall, the main theatre was in the club house, which closed in 1936 and is now a Buddhist temple. The modern Tabard theatre is reached via a staircase in the garden.
2 Bath Road, W4 1LW. Turnham Green tube.

31 Jukebox Showroom

Bal Ami, Rock-Ola, Seeburg and Wurlitzer – these top-name jukeboxes have never gone out of fashion. A modest-looking store, Jukebox Showroom has the most colourful window display on the Parade. On sale are fixed-up classics from the silver age of the 1950s and flash new reproduction Bubblers. Adapted for 45rpm vinyl, compact disc, iPod docking or touch screen, they no longer need a shilling for three plays, and cards can be pre-printed to match the buyer's collection.
9 Park Parade, Gunnersbury Avenue, W3 9BD. Acton tube.

32 PM Gallery and House

A fancy flint and redbrick gateway raises visitors' expectations on approaching West London's largest contemporary art gallery. Pitzhanger Manor, the architect Sir John Soane's country house, stands in the 22ha (55 acre) Walpole Park. The original house was built by Soane's former boss, George Dance the Younger, and when Sir John bought it in 1800, he demolished all but the south wing and set about making a home where he could keep antiquities and paintings. Some of these are now on show in his London house (see Sir John Soane's Museum page 44), with which the manor shares some architectural similarities.

Sir John owned the house for just ten years, and it passed through several hands before serving as Ealing borough's central lending library from 1901 until 1984, when money was pumped in to restore the rooms to how Soane had left them. The intimate, neoclassical style of the Breakfast Room, Library and Drawing Room are particularly successful. A library extension is used as the art gallery, and exhibitions sometimes extend into Soane's rooms.
Walpole Park, Mattock Lane, W5 5EQ. Ealing Broadway tube.

33 Osterley House

Osterley contains one of the best examples of a Robert Adam interior still to be seen. It was Thomas Gresham, the Elizabethan banker after whom the City street is named, who had the three-storey brick palace built around a central courtyard. But the goldsmith and financier Sir Francis Child made it what it is today by employing Adam not only to create the splendid interior, but to design a classical main portico and grand entrance hall.

The house looks now much as it did in the mid 18th century, with Adam's fancy plasterwork and furniture by John Linnell. The 40m (130ft) Long Room, described by the American author Henry James as 'a cheerful upholstered avenue into another century', is lined with 17th and 18th-century Venetian paintings. Richest of all is the Tapestry Room, which has wall hangings designed by François Boucher for the Gobelin manufactory, and a carpet of Adam's creation. The grounds, laid out by Gresham, still have formal plantings, and Adam's beautiful Garden House survives. Much of the 144ha (357 acre) grounds, including three lakes, is pastureland overshadowed by the M4, which has been driven right across it.
Jersey Road, Isleworth, TW7 4RB. Osterley tube.

34 Kew Bridge Steam Museum

Anybody who has ever doubted the power of steam should stand beneath a working 35-tonne beam engine. Cornish beam engines come no larger than this 12m (40ft) tall leviathan, with 229cm (90in) valves, designed to pump water at a rate of 2,146 litres (472 gallons) at a single stroke. From these Victorian buildings, the Grand Junction Waterworks Company brought water to Londoners for almost a century, until 1944.

Most of the machines in the collection, the largest in the world, are Cornish beam engines, developed to keep tin mines dry and perfected by James Watt in his rotative steam engine. An example of that is here, too. These are the machines that powered the industrial revolution, built with pride that shines through their beautiful finishes of iron and brass. At weekends visitors can ride the steam train that was used to bring coal from the barges to fuel the boilers.
Green Dragon Lane, TW8 0EN. Kew tube.

㉟ Strand-on-the-Green

Of all the picturesque stretches of London's waterfront, Strand-on-the-Green wins the prize. In spite of its name and village feel, there is no green here, just a pedestrian path east of Kew Bridge, about half a mile long, ending at Grove Park Road and lined with tidy cottages. When spring tides are high, the Thames floods across the path – residents could not live any closer to the water. Strand-on-the-Green began as a fishing settlement. It was gentrified when the Hanoverian court came to Kew and a bridge replaced the ferry. German painter Johann Zofanny moved here and bought several properties, dying at No 65 in 1810.

By the beginning of the 20th century, many of the buildings had become run down, and in the 1950s some were condemned as unfit for human habitation. But the romantics won the day, preserving them and keeping them shipshape, despite the flooding. Nancy Mitford lived at Rose Cottage. Dylan Thomas stayed with his friend Professor Carstairs in Ship House, probably the oldest building, dating from the 17th century.

Out in the river, small, wooded Oliver's Island, named after a rumour that Oliver Cromwell had once hidden there, was where a barge once moored to take tolls from river traffic. Author Geoffrey Household (No 29) roasted a deer there for the Queen's Coronation in 1953.
Strand-on-the-Green, W4. Kew tube.

㊱ The Bull's Head

One of three historic waterside pubs in Strand-on-the-Green, this is the farthest from Kew Bridge, and the oldest. Its licence was first issued in 1722. It looks like a simple whitewashed country inn, and inside there is a warren of half-panelled rooms with different floor levels, low-beamed ceilings and open fires. Tide heights and times are pinned on a board, which is useful for customers wondering whether to wear Wellington boots when they next visit.
15 Strand-on-the-Green, W4 3PQ. Kew tube.

㊲ Chiswick House

'Too small for a house, too big to hang on a watch chain' was a contemporary comment, and although the house is grand, it is easy to see what the visitor, Lord Hervey, meant. Chiswick House seems like an elaborate folly. At the time it was built, few people had set eyes on an Italian villa, and the white-domed box must have looked strange beside the heavy Jacobean mansion that until then had been the Burlington family's country house – their London home was Burlington House in Picadilly, now the Royal Academy.

The villa was built to be a place for entertaining and to show off the collection of the greatest arts patron of his day, Richard Boyle, the 3rd Earl of Burlington. Inspired by Palladio's Villa Capra near Vicenza and working to his own designs, the earl completed his homage to the Italian Renaissance architect in 1729. A square building with an octagonal central dome, the villa's simple ground floor contrasts with the ornate upper floors, which contain three velvet-lined rooms. The Green Velvet Room has views by Dutch artist Pieter Andreas Rysbrack, showing how the garden was landscapede. The Goddess of Architecture floats on a cloud on the Blue Velvet Room's ceiling, and the Red Velvet Room has stone picture frames dated 1729.
Burlington Lane, W4 2RP. Turnham Green tube.

㊳ Chiswick House Gardens

'One of England's greatest contributions to Western culture' is how the chief executive of English Heritage describes the 26ha (65 acre) gardens of Chiswick House. Laid out by Richard Boyle, the 3rd Earl of Burlington, and William Kent, they marked the first step in a move away from the formal towards the picturesque. The beautiful 91m (300ft) conservatory has been heroically restored following a £12.1 million restoration of the gardens. Hundreds of new trees and formal beds have been planted, and some statues have been replaced since the originals left with former owners, the Devonshires. Important items, such as the arch by Inigo Jones, remain.

There is a café, and the gardens provide plenty of space for strolling, by the lake and cascade, through formal plantings, in a wilderness, or along the *patte foie* – the 'goose foot' of three radiating avenues that once led to garden buildings. There is an original bowling green and a cricket pitch, in use every weekend in summer. A walled garden is occasionally open to visitors.
Burlington Lane, W4 2RP. Turnham Green tube.

㊴ Wetland Centre

Europe's largest wetland-creation project is built on the site of four redundant reservoirs beside the Thames. Five years in the making, the mosaic of lagoons, lakes, ponds, reed beds and wet woodland, which opened in 2000, covers just over 44ha (105 acres). Fourteen habitats – from Australian billabong to Siberian tundra – have been created here. From half a dozen hides, some of them three-storeys tall, and the Bird Airport observation tower, visitors can look out for some of the scores of bird species recorded – as many as 70 in one day, including kingfishers and bittern. There are also eight kinds of bats, slow-worms, newts, toads and varieties of dragonflies and damselflies. A deep-water reef for breeding fish attracts the birds. CCTVs give close-ups on habitats in the Sir Peter Scott Visitor Centre.
Queen Elizabeth's Walk, Barnes, off A306. Hammersmith tube.

㊵ The tomb of Sir Richard Burton.

It seems incongruous to have a Bedouin tent pitched in a graveyard, its canvas rippling in the wind. A second look reveals that the tomb of Sir Richard and Lady Isabel Burton is made of sandstone. The first European to enter Mecca (in disguise) requested that he and his wife, who was from a devout Catholic family, 'lie side by side in a tent' in the churchyard of St Mary Magdalen. Complying with his wishes, Lady Burton afterwards burnt the last manuscripts of the man who had first translated the *Kama Sutra* into English, before joining him in the tent five years later, in 1896. She also paid for a stained-glass memorial window in the Victorian church, in which Burton is depicted as a Christian knight.
St Mary Magdalen, 61 Worple Way, SW14 8PR. Mortlake rail.

WEST & SOUTHWEST

SOUTHWEST

㊶ Royal Botanic Gardens, Kew

The best part of a day can be spent in the incomparable gardens at Kew. Covering 120ha (300 acres) of flowerbeds, glasshouses and hothouses, with a Chinese pagoda and other follies, it is full of delights and surprises. The gardens are a tribute to the energy and curiosity of early explorers and collectors, who brought back specimens for what is now one of the world's foremost botanic institutions. Much of its pre-eminence is owed to botanist Joseph Banks, who in 1776 accompanied James Cook on his five-year voyage around the world, returning to begin the plant collection at Kew and to become president of the Royal Society for more than four decades. Kew now has the biggest collection in the world, with more than 30,000 species.

A Treetop Walkway by the architects of the London Eye gives a bird's-eye view, while John Pawson's Sackler Crossing leads across the lake. Despite the large Temperate House, and the Princess of Wales Conservatory, where ten climatic zones share the same roof, the most thrilling structure in the gardens is still Decimus Burton's Palm House, completed in 1848. In this 110m (363ft) long masterpiece in cast iron and glass, staircases and walkways lead visitors on a steamy walk among tropical plants.
Royal Botanic Gardens, Kew, TW9 3AB. Kew tube.

㊷ Kew Palace

The redbrick four-storey Jacobean mansion is so like a doll's house that from a distance it looks as if it would be possible to reach out and open the whole façade to see cut-away rooms inside. A Dutch merchant built it as a private home in 1631, which explains the curving gables and its original name – the Dutch House.

The smallest of the royal palaces, it was first rented by the crown in 1728. George III spent some of his childhood here and later purchased it from the Levett family. It was to Kew that the king retreated when he became ill, and his wife, Queen Charlotte, died here in 1818. Their granddaughter, Victoria, later to be queen, ordered that her grandmother's bedroom remain just as she left it.

A 10 year programme of restoration has taken the ground and first floors back to glorious Georgian days. The second floor includes the bedrooms of Princesses Augusta and Amelia. The Palace's history is explained in the People's Library, and there are cartoons of the much-caricatured George III. Jigsaw maps used by the governess of his 15 children are on display, and there is an elegant doll's house. The Queen's Garden has been re-created around the Palace. Queen Charlotte's Cottage, an elaborate thatched summerhouse at the southern end of Kew Gardens, was designed by the queen herself.
Royal Botanic Gardens, Kew, TW9 3AB. Kew tube. An additional entrance fee is charged. Open April to September.

㊸ Syon House and Park

London's last surviving ducal residence and country estate is the home of Ralph Percy, 12th Duke of Northumberland, who otherwise resides in northeast England at Alnwick Castle. Syon takes its name from Mount Zion, an abbey founded on the site by the 14th-century Bridgettine order of nuns and dissolved by Henry VIII. When the king's coffin was brought here to rest overnight *en route* for burial at Windsor, it burst open and his huge body was set upon by dogs – retribution, some said, for closing down the monastery.

The first private owner of the property, Edward Seymour, Duke of Somerset, built a Renaissance palace, which passed to the Northumberland family, by marriage, in 1594. In the 1760s, the 1st Duke of Northumberland employed Robert Adam and the Scottish architect pulled out all the stops, laying down what has become known as the Adam style, integrating decoration with furniture, fixtures and fittings. Imperial Rome is evoked in the Great Hall, Ante Room and Dining Room, while the Red Drawing Room has silk-hung walls, and 293 medallions painted on the ceiling by Giovanni Battista Cipriani. Paintings of the Stuart royal family recall the time when Charles I's children were looked after in the house while the king was confined to Hampton Court Palace. The beautiful, book-lined Long Gallery, designed as a

ENGLISH ARCHITECTURE AT ITS MOST ECCENTRIC
STRAWBERRY HILL HOUSE

withdrawing room for women to escape the rowdy company of men, has a view over the Thames' last tidal water meadow.

At the same time as Adam was at work on the house, Capability Brown was designing 16ha (40 acres) of gardens, with many rare trees and an ornamental lake. But the highlight of the 81ha (200 acre) park is the Conservatory. Built in 1826, it was designed by Charles Fowler, and provided the inspiration for Joseph Paxton's Crystal Palace 25 years later.

London Road, TW8 8JF. Syon Lane rail. The house is open from March to October on Wednesday, Thursday, Sunday and Bank Holiday Monday. The gardens are open daily, weekends only in winter.

44 London Apprentice

A cosy pub at the end of a lane, the London Apprentice has an 18th-century exterior that hides a building going back to the 15th. The carving on the first-floor River Room ceiling may have been by Italian apprentices who were working for Robert Adam at Syon House. But a painting in the pub suggests that others might have given their name to the former inn. It shows colourfully dressed apprentices from City Livery Companies rowing upriver on their days off. The pub also has a cellar connected to the church behind it, inviting tales of smuggling.

Isleworth was an inland port and river-crossing point. The site has been inhabited since Neolithic times, and the inn was used by many river travellers, including Henry VIII, Elizabeth I and Charles I, or so it is said. In front of it is Isleworth Ait, one of the Thames's larger islands, attracting kingfishers and herons.

62 Church Street, TW7 6BG. Isleworth rail.

45 Twickenham Stadium

In Britain, only Wembley is bigger than this stadium, the 80,000 capacity home of English rugby. A good idea of its size can be gained from the top of the stands, a view offered during the daily tours that take in the England dressing room, medical room, players' tunnel and royal box. In the museum, memorabilia and information about the worldwide game include the first England shirt. This is where trophies are displayed, including the William Webb Ellis Cup, named after the game's founder and given to the Rugby World Cup winners. Tours start in the South Stand, the newest part of the stadium, which has added 19,000 seats on three tiers and 11 hospitality suites.

Rugby Road, TW1 1DZ. Twickenham rail.

46 Strawberry Hill House

English architecture is at its most eccentric in this building, which was designed to be a theatrical experience. Its white pinnacled and battlemented exterior gives a flavour of the histrionics to come. Horace Walpole, who coined the word 'serendipity', spared nothing in the use of so many pointed arches and so much fancy vaulting. He was the author of *The Castle of Otranto*, the Gothic novel that began a genre, which he printed here on his own presses in 1764.

In Strawberry Hill, Walpole bucked the classical trend that was invading aristocratic mansions in this part of the country. Using papier-mâché in place of plaster and stone, he was able to create rooms that harked back to old St Paul's Cathedral and to medieval tombs. Dark halls and sinister passageways lead to rooms of brilliant fantasy, which he filled with art treasures long since dispersed. The Tribune Room was built especially for his collection of miniatures. A recent multi-million-pound refurbishment has brought Strawberry Hill back to spectacular life, with new gilding, silks and damasks.

268 Waldegrave Road, Twickenham, TW1 4ST. Strawberry Hill rail.

47 Marble Hill House

There is nothing out of place in this big white box beside the river. Designed in the manner of a Palladian villa of the time, and landscaped to include 27ha (66 acres) of parkland stretching down to the Thames, Marble Hill House was the height of Georgian fashion. It was built for Henrietta Howard, Countess of Suffolk, mistress of the Prince of Wales, later George II. The architect, Roger Morris, was aided by Henry Herbert, Earl of Pembroke, who was Lord of the Bedchamber to the Prince. Horace Walpole, a friend and neighbour of the Countess in Strawberry Hill, said of Pembroke, 'No man has a purer taste in building.' Six years after the house was completed, the Countess married George Berkeley MP, enjoying 11 years of married life before his death. She lived another 32 years here.

After that, the house had various owners, and fell into decay until rescued by the Cunard family at the beginning of the 20th century. Everything the visitor sees of the interior today is reproduced as closely as possible to the original, which English Heritage has gone to great lengths to discover. It includes hand-painted Chinese wallpaper and a chinoiserie collection as well as paintings and furniture of the period.

Richmond Road, TW1 2NL. St Margaret's rail.

48 Hammerton's Ferry

This ferry service, one of the few remaining across the Thames, links Marble Hill House with Ham House. It was started by Walter Hammerton in the early 20th century after both properties were opened to the public. The service operates every day, weekends only in winter.
Orleans Road, Twickenham, TW1 3BL. St Margaret's rail.

49 Ham House

It's one thing to be the king's mistress, and quite another to be his whipping boy. That is how William Murray began his career, receiving punishment for any bad behaviour by the future Charles I. His reward came in 1637, with the manors of Ham and Petersham and a title, Earl of Dysart. He extended the house that had been built by Sir Thomas Vavasour, Knight Marshal to James I. The Great Staircase, Hall Gallery, Long Gallery and North Drawing Room are all his doing, and some of his art collection remains. His daughter, Elizabeth, brought Ham House to a degree of splendour, furnished, according to John Evelyn, 'like a great prince's'.

The house remained in family hands until the National Trust took it over in 1948, and is one of the greatest surviving houses from the 17th century. The riverside gardens, which can be visited separately, are also great survivors from the period, closely following plans made in 1671. Among the variety of interests to be found here are lavender parterres, pomegranate trees, a cherry garden and a wilderness, plus an orangery, ice house and dairy.
Ham Street, TW10 3RS. House closed November to March.

50 Petersham Nurseries

Some places have got it just right. This nursery is a delight to visit, a feast for every taste. Its greenhouses are full not just of flowers but of interesting objects, some antique, some picked up on travels. It was a regular nursery when Gael and Francesco Boglione took it over. They lived in a Queen Anne house, and weren't planning to expand, merely to consolidate what had been part of the Petersham Estate.

Getting it right again, they took on the *Vogue* cookery writer Skye Gyngell to run the restaurant. Reckoning on the close relationship between vegetable plot and plate, the Australian gained a Michelin star and had Madonna and Richard E. Grant turning up for lunch. Motley tables and chairs are scattered around the glasshouses for self service cakes and tea.
Church Lane, Richmond, TW10 7AG. Richmond tube.

51 Richmond Green

Richmond's historic Green is an atmospheric place to watch a game of cricket, although the pitch is just part of the square, which is too grand to be thought of as a 'village' green. The Cricketers and the Prince's Head pubs in the southern corner provide the teams, who turn out on Thursdays and Saturdays during summer. The game is first mentioned as being played here in 1666. By then the monarchy had been restored – too late to save much of the great Tudor Richmond Palace, which had been sold off and dismantled under the Commonwealth. What remains is the castellated corner around Palace Gate House and the Wardrobe and Trumpeters' House beyond, now all privately owned,

extending between Richmond Green and the
River Thames. The Theatre on the Green, built
in the 1760s, was replaced in 1899 by the
Richmond Theatre on the adjacent Little Green.
Designed by Frank Matcham, it is a Victorian
beauty, as a look in at the lobby will reveal.
The Green, TW9 1LX. Richmond tube.

52 Richmond Hill

**'Nothing I had ever seen or ever can see
elsewhere is to be compared to it,' the
German writer Charles P. Moritz** proclaimed
in his 1772 *Travels in England*. 'Whatever is
charming in nature or pleasing in art, is to be
seen here.' However often the view from this
lump of London clay has been lauded in print or
in paintings, the vision is always fresh. Moritz's
book came out just after the completion of
The Terrace, the broad, fashionable promenade
that provides an unprecedented panorama of the
Thames on its way into London. Boats are
moored midstream below Gover's Island, and
meadowlands stretch beside the river, making this
a scene as English as any painting by Sir Joshua
Reynolds, who lived in Wick House at the high
end of The Terrace for the last 20 years of his life.

In Sir Joshua's day, Mrs Fitzherbert, who
married the Prince of Wales, later George IV, was
living by The Terrace. Their marriage could not
be sanctioned in law, and is recalled in the lines
'I'd crowns resign to call thee mine' in the song
'Sweet Lass of Richmond Hill'. More recent
songs were composed next door to Wick House
in the large Georgian mansion called The Wick,
which Ronnie Wood of the Rolling Stones
bought from the actor Sir John Mills, and sold to
the Who's Pete Townshend.
Richmond Hill, TW10 6RN. Richmond tube.

53 Richmond Park

**The deer are the stars of Richmond Park,
London's largest open space. Inured to
cyclists, joggers,** walkers, picnickers and cars,
they stroll about in herds. Sometimes stags lock
their magnificent horns in battle for the does,
their belling echoing across the park on autumn
evenings. Herds of red and fallow deer have
shaped the land since 3,000 of them were
introduced by Charles I, who, in true cavalier
fashion, threw off the peasant farmers and built an
8 mile wall to enclose a royal hunting ground.
They keep down the grass, clip leaves up to head
height and prevent trees from seeding. Bracken,
ponds and woodlands abound, and the whole park
is graded a Site of Special Scientific Interest and a
National Nature Reserve. King Henry's Mound,
named after Henry VIII, who apparently came to
this spot to watch the hunting, is the high point in
the park. From here, the view extends to St Paul's
Cathedral more than 10 miles away.

The 16ha (40 acres) of shaded walks, lawns,
streams and ponds that make up the Isabella
plantation are the park's most colourful corner.
Here, fenced off from the grassland and grazing
deer, lies a leafy wonderland of beech, oak, sweet
chestnut and rowan. Beneath this canopy, spring
erupts in a triumph of colours as the woodland
garden comes into bloom – magnolias,
rhododendrons and azaleas, one after the other. It
has the national collection of Kurume azaleas, and
continuous colour is provided by daffodils and
bluebells through to mahonia and hellebore. This
is the place to see great and lesser spotted
woodpeckers and nuthatches, and to hear seasonal
songsters, such as the chiffchaff and wood warbler.
Richmond Park Office, Holly Lodge, TW10 5HS.

ROTHERHITHE 1 2
BERMONDSEY 3
CANADA WATER 4

Evelyn Street

Old Kent Road

ELEPHANT & CASTLE 6

Camberwell New Road

7

Brixton Road

New Road

PECKHAM RYE

Brixton Hill

BRIXTON 8
9

EAST DULWICH 5

HERNE HILL

10 11 12

NORTH DULWICH

Lordship Lane

13
14
WEST DULWICH 15
16
18

21

CROFTON PARK

20

19 FOREST HILL

WEST NORWOOD 17

Streatham High Road

SYDENHAM

CRYSTAL PALACE 48 49
50
PENGE WEST

Beulah Hill

Croydon Road

Bromley Road

London Road

Bromley Road

CUTTY SARK
24
27 28
26
29
35
22 25
34
23
DEPTFORD BRIDGE
GREENWICH
36 37
33 32
30
31
NORTH GREENWICH
Tunnel Approach
Lewisham Way

39
40 BLACKHEATH

Brownhill Road

CHARLTON
41

Shooter's Hill Road

Shooter's Hill

East Rochester Way

Bexley Road

38

47 MOTTINGHAM

Sidcup Road

Mottingham Road

42

44 WOOLWICH ARSENAL

43

KEY
Rotherhithe
Peckham
Brixton
Dulwich
New Cross & Deptford
Greenwich & Blackheath
Farther East
Farther South

Bronze Age Way

VEDERE ⇄

Erith Road

Erith Road

Southeast

Exuberance and restraint exist side by side southeast of the city, in destinations that revel in the creative imaginings of artists, musicians and dancers. The once powerful maritime centre of Greenwich still draws crowds, lured by its history, architecture and magnificent park.

ROTHERHITHE

❶ St Mary's Rotherhithe

Rotherhithe's maritime past is recalled by its name, Rother (sailor), hythe (haven). It was from Rotherhithe that the *Mayflower* set sail for America in 1620. Christopher Jones, the ship's captain, is buried in an unmarked grave in St Mary's churchyard, and commemorated with a recent statue funded by the Sons and Daughters of the Pilgrims.

Lee Boo, a Pacific Island prince, is also buried here. He lived with the family of a Captain Wilson, and worshipped at St Mary's. Captain Wilson had been shipwrecked in the Pacific in 1783, and having rafted to the islands ruled by Lee Boo's father and built a new ship, agreed to take the boy back with him to become an Englishman. Lee Boo's fate was that of many Englishmen of the day – he died of smallpox, aged 20.

There has been a church here since the 13th century, although the present building, by John James, dates from 1714, and the spire was added by Lancelot Dowbiggin in 1739. It was designed to seat 1,000 people, with galleries, box pews and a three-tiered pulpit. An interior redesign by William Butterfield in 1876 introduced bright colours, a reredos carved by Joseph Wade and an east window with a representation of the Assumption of our Lady. The present pulpit is the former top deck of the original. Another curiosity here is the Bishop's Chair, carved from timbers salvaged from a gunship that had played its part in the Battle of Trafalgar and was painted by J.M.W. Turner as *The Fighting Temeraire*. The organ is a work of art.
St Marychurch Street, SE16 4JE. Rotherhithe tube.

❷ Mayflower pub

This cosy Thameside pub looks on to the river, close to where the *Mayflower* set sail. Its jetty beer garden is a particular attraction. The interior is cosy, with oak beams, settles, a brick fireplace and nautical knick-knacks. Its menus are ambitious, including cream teas, and, uniquely, it is licensed to sell not just alcohol but US postage stamps.
117 Rotherhithe Street, SE16 4NF. Rotherhithe tube.

❸ Nordic London

For a long time, Rotherhithe and Surrey Docks were a port for Scandinavian ships. Greenland Dock is the oldest of London's riverside wet docks – once a trading post for the import of softwoods, with berths for more than 100 ships, today a mix of offices and luxury homes. Anyone homesick for Helsinki can visit the 1950s Finnish church, take a sauna in the basement below the altar, or buy Finnish newspapers and magazines from the shop within the church – frozen reindeer meat, Baltic herrings, rye bread, salt liquorice and cloudberry jam are also on offer, and a cafeteria serves Finnish fare. The present building, opened in 1958 by Cyrill Mardall-Sjöström, is Grade II listed, light and airy.

Close by is the distinctive St Olav's Norwegian Church and Seamen's Mission, its spire topped with a galleon weathervane. There has been a Norwegian church in London since the late 17th century. This building, designed by John Love Seaton Dahl, was consecrated in 1927. A small shop sells Norwegian goods, coffee and cakes, and in November hosts a Christmas fair.
33 Albion Street, SE16 7HZ and St Olav's Square, SE16 7JB. Bermondsey, Canada Water tube.

❹ Stave Hill

Out of the wreckage of once-thriving docks has risen a 9m (30ft) artificial mound, just across the river from Canary Wharf. From the 1860s, Surrey Docks had been a major timber port, but by the 1970s, much of the area had become derelict. The timber ponds – large areas of water where timber was kept to season – were filled with domestic refuse, rubble and subsoil from all over the city. Re-excavation and redevelopment provided the materials to create a 2ha (5¼ acre) nature area. This patchwork of grassland, woods, scrub and wetland sustains a great variety of wildlife. A plaque at the top of Stave Hill shows the area the docks once covered. From here there are great views over Docklands and the Russia Dock woodland. On a clear day, the arch of Wembley Stadium is visible.
Timber Pond Road, Rotherhithe, SE16. Canada Water tube.

PECKHAM HONEY COMES FROM THEIR BUSY BEES
LONDON WILDLIFE GARDEN

PECKHAM

❺ London Wildlife Garden

Quorn Road and Pytchley Road, just up the hill, recall the Quorn and Pytchley Hunt, but sly old foxes are safe here. Established in the late 1980s on the site of an old council depot, this wildlife centre is a great attraction for local families, wildlife watchers and wild-flower growers, offering a summer meadow, woodland copse, stag beetle sanctuary, pond and bog garden. Members of the community tend raised beds and Peckham honey is available from their busy bees.
28 Marsden Road, SE15 4EE. East Dulwich rail. Open Tuesday, Wednesday, Thursday and Sunday.

❻ Chumleigh Gardens

Opened in 1995 as part of Burgess Park, Chumleigh Gardens are designed to reflect different world regions, from Asia, the Mediterranean and the Caribbean, with a lovely Islamic garden. The gates to the vegetable plot, sponsored by the Metropolitan Police, take the form of a map of the world, an acknowledgment of the multicultural diversity of Southwark.

It is hard to see Burgess Park as the act of vandalism it was when workers' cottages were razed and a branch of the Grand Surrey Canal filled in to create it, leaving only a scattering of industrial relics, such as a lime kiln once part of E.R. Burtt & Sons lime works, and some former almshouses. The park is a haven for wildlife, and a place of peace and relaxation.
SE5 0RJ. Elephant & Castle tube.

❼ South London Gallery

In 1995, Tracey Emin pitched her 'tent' at the South London Gallery (SLG), which had been the first to show her unmade bed installation. Two years later it staged a solo show by the 'bad girl of Brit Art', and she cites this exhilarating gallery as the crucible of her success.

The SLG had its beginnings in 1868 in the South London Working Men's Club in Blackfriars Road, under T.H. Huxley, the biologist grandfather of the author Aldous Huxley. After a move to larger premises in Kennington in 1878, it opened the first free library in south London, and the following year staged its first art show. The inaugural president was the prime minister William Gladstone; and gallery manager William Rossiter enlisted the support of leading artists Edward Burne-Jones, G.F. Watts and Sir Frederic Leighton, president of the Royal Academy.

Maurice Bingham Adams's ornate but sturdy building of 1896–8 is the SLG's present home. The interior exhibition space is magnificent, and the gallery is known for its changing programme of contemporary art shows. Along the way it has built up a collection of 6,000 pieces (not on permanent display), including works by such prominent figures in Brit Art as Emin, Antony Gormley, Sarah Lucas and Anish Kapoor. In the terrific, individualistic café, 'live' art is painted directly onto the walls by leading artists of today, and there is also a garden.
65 Peckham Road, SE5 8UH. Peckham Rye rail.

CHUMLEIGH GARDENS

BRIXTON

⑧ Franco Manca

Here is possibly the best pizza in Britain. This brilliant little venture is owned by Neapolitan-born Giuseppe Mascoli and Brixton-based artist Bridget Hugo. The choice runs to just six pizzas, made to exacting standards with sourdough bases that have been left to rise for at least 20 hours, and are fired in wood-burning ovens.

The story goes that the starter culture for the dough was stolen from a bakery on the island of Ischia in the Gulf of Naples, and dates from the 1730s. The flour is sourced from Naples; organic tomatoes are imported from Salerno. A specialist cheesemaker was brought in from Sorrento to advise the Somerset makers of the organic buffalo mozzarella. Queues are long, turnover fast. There are organic wines, organic lemonade – and now, in the same street, the owners have opened a delicatessen and catering business, Wild Caper. *4 Market Row, SW9 8LD. Brixton tube.*

⑨ Brixton Market

'Cheap and cheerful' would fairly describe Britain's biggest Afro-Caribbean market. The atmosphere under the 1920s and 1930s covered arcades, which were given Grade II listing in March 2010, is friendly and upbeat. The market has social significance beyond offering cut-price DVDs, yams and plantains, cho cho and callaloo, parrot fish and patties, dread caps and nylon wigs. It is a vibrant meeting place. In 1983, in 'Electric Avenue', musician Eddie Grant was moved to write of violence but the tinderbox atmosphere is no more. The visitor who rocks down this way should not miss Rosie's Deli in Market Row; Rosie Lovell, the enthusiastic young author of *Spooning with Rosie*, runs the show. Not to be missed either is the Edwardian baroque town hall, built in 1908 to a winning design by Septimus Warwick and Herbert Hall. *Electric Avenue, SW9 8JX. Brixton tube. The market is open daily 8am–6pm.*

BRIXTON MARKET

⑪ Olley's

One of the best fish-fry joints in London takes its name from a passage in *Oliver Twist* in which Dickens makes reference to fish and chips. The quaint décor is designed to evoke the atmosphere of the Dickensian age, although the pine, brick, trailing plants and tones of blue and terracotta are more reminiscent of the 1970s than Victorian London. Celebrity customers such as James Nesbit and Lord Archer have dishes named after them – 'Cilla Black's Experience' is a hearty haddock, chips, three prawns, three scampi and two onions.
Olley's Fish Experience, 65–69 Norwood Road, Herne Hill, SE24 9AA. Herne Hill rail.

⑫ The Velodrome, Herne Hill

Bradley Wiggins, three-time Olympic gold medallist, began his competitive cycling career here at the last remaining venue of the 1948 London Olympics still in active use. World records have been established at old Herne Hill. Passers-by on Dulwich's Burbage Road and Village Way might have no inkling that, behind the houses, cyclists are going hell for leather around this thrilling, steeply banked, 450m (492yd) track, but commuters aboard the trains that pass between Tulse Hill and North Dulwich briefly get ringside seats.

In 1890, the amateur racing cyclist George Lacey Hillier conceived the idea of a cycle track for south London and, with the help of local clubs, founded the London County Athletics Ground Ltd, to build the first track in 1891. At the time, the bicycle was seen largely as a toy for young men of means with a yen for danger. But John Dunlop had just invented the pneumatic tyre for a smoother ride and the 'freedom machine' became a popular means of transport and recreation. So dawned the golden age of the bicycle. Inside the cycle track was a cinder running track and, at the heart of the ground, a rugby pitch. For the 1948 Olympics the cycle track was brought up to scratch with stands and the installation of 12 telephone boxes for journalists to file their reports.

The track has fallen into some decay, but it would be very sad if this fine old facility were to close for want of funding for repairs. Local residents have launched a campaign to save it, and it is hoped that pedal power will prevail. In its glory days the 'drome attracted crowds of 10,000 to its annual Good Friday highlight, and the Good Friday tradition continues today.
Burbage Road. Herne Hill, SE24 9HE. North Dulwich rail.

⑩ Brockwell Park

Brockwell Estate was opened as a public park in 1888. The estate had been owned by John Blades, a Ludgate Hill glassmaker, for whom the late-Georgian Brockwell Hall was built by D.R. Roper, architect of the classical Grecian St Mark's in Kennington. The Hall crowns but does not dominate the park. The stone portico is part of Roper's original plan; the south-facing cast-iron verandah and bell turret are Victorian add-ons. A popular, if slightly scruffy, café in the Hall has unmatched chairs and cheery boho clientele.

Probably the most famous attraction of the park is the Art Deco lido, recently extended to incorporate modern fitness facilities. Less well known is the scheme, set up in 1997, to keep the greenhouses open. The site includes two large glasshouses, part of a walled garden, a small forest garden, vegetable plots and beehives. The beds are tended by volunteers who are rewarded with a lunch of bread and cheese and freshly picked salad, and the project is partly funded by the sale of herb seedlings, apple juice and seasonal vegetables.
Dulwich Road, SE24 0PA. Herne Hill rail.

SOUTHEAST

DULWICH

⑬ Dulwich Picture Gallery and Mausoleum

England's oldest purpose-built picture gallery owes its existence to two London art dealers and their acquisition of one of the world's most important collections of European Old Masters from the 1600s and 1700s. Noël Desferans died in 1807, followed in 1811 by his partner Sir Francis Bourgeois, who bequeathed the collection to Dulwich College on condition that it should be available for 'the inspection of the public', and that a new gallery be designed for it by Sir John Soane. Soane's classical building is a work of art itself. Its pioneering roof lanterns bathe the galleries below in a subtle wash of natural light. The gallery mounts terrific exhibitions.

The gallery founders rest in Soane's specially designed mausoleum, which is possibly based on Alexandrian catacombs. Soane took a great interest in monumental architecture. In 1815 he erected a similar but smaller version, dedicated to his wife, in St Pancras churchyard.

Close by the picture gallery is the original Dulwich College building, including a lovely chapel and almshouses.
Gallery Road, SE21 7AD. North Dulwich, West Dulwich rail.

⑭ Dulwich Village

Just 5 miles from Trafalgar Square, this epitome of a well-to-do English village could be in deepest Surrey. Charles Dickens had Mr Pickwick retire here, to 'one of the most pleasant spots near London', and is remembered in the name Pickwick Road.

Dulwich Park, opened in 1890, was a favourite with Queen Mary, who loved the American garden, which is a mass of rhododendron blooms in May. In the smaller, Grade II listed Belair Park stands a mansion in the style of – if not, indeed, by – Robert Adam. Within it is an artificial lake, created by damming the River Effra.

On the main street, grand houses stand next to tiny cottages, opposite the much-loved, Grade II listed Crown and Greyhound, affectionately dubbed 'the Dog'. Weatherboarded Bell Cottage on College Road has blue-painted shutters and

Doric door casing, and dates from 1741. The bell in the tower of its neighbour, Bell House, used to be rung to summon help to pump water into the fire engine. Georgian Pond Cottages, built for workers at a tile kiln, stand by a millpond. In the early 1800s, the artist David Cox lived here; numbers of his paintings, including *Houses at Dulwich*, are in the Tate Britain collection.
SE21. North Dulwich rail.

⑮ Dulwich College

'The College of God's Gift' was founded in 1619 by Edward Alleyn, the most famous of Elizabethan actors. Apparently, the vision of the devil that he conjured for the role of Dr Faustus so terrified him that he gave up his rakish ways and devoted his life to helping the poor. Retiring at just 31, he used his fortune to buy land south of the Thames.

Alleyn had dreamt of providing a classical education for 'poor scholars', but no Greek or Latin was taught at his college, and the Master and Warden were not required to be academic, only to be bachelors and to share the name of Alleyn – or Allen, as Alleyn is pronounced. Just before he died, Alleyn laid down stipulations that included the wearing of a uniform with 'a coat of good cloth and sad colours', and a diet of 'loaves, boiled beef, cheese, fish, apple and pear pies' and three times a week 'beere without stint'.

The present building dates from 1866–70 and is by Charles Barry, son of Sir Charles Barry (best known for his part in rebuilding the Houses of Parliament). It combines ornate Palladian, Italian Renaissance and Gothic styles in redbrick and terracotta – a palazzo amid the greensward of playing fields. Among the best-known 'Old Alleynians' are the explorer Ernest Shackleton and authors P.G. Wodehouse and Raymond Chandler.
Dulwich Common, SE21 7LD. West Dulwich rail.

⑯ London's last turnpike

Motorists who drive along College Road towards Crystal Palace find their way barred by London's last survivor of the turnpike legislation of the late 1700s. The pretty little toll booth dates from 1789, and Tollgate Cottage, no

GRAND HOUSES LOOK ACROSS AT TINY COTTAGES
DULWICH VILLAGE

longer home to the gatekeeper, was built in 1862–3. The Estate Governors' notice of charges beside the cottage is misleading. It costs rather more these days than three pre-decimal pennies to pass through with horse or mule, 10 pennies for 'beasts per score', or sixpence for motor car or motorcycle combination. The way is a shortcut, and a novelty, but at £1 the charge is steeper than the road itself.
College Road, SE21.

⑰ West Norwood Catacombs

'It will be enquired, where then shall be the Burials? I answer, in Cemeteries seated in the Out-skirts of the Town ...' As early as 1711, Sir Christopher Wren foresaw the need for burial grounds to be sited around London. But the golden age of London cemetery-building did not dawn for another 100 years or so, with the creation of the 'Magnificent Seven', of which this one, built in 1837, was the second after Kensal Green (see page 123).

It was designed by William Tite (later to be Sir William, the architect of the rebuilding of the Royal Exchange), and planted in what J.C. Loudon noted in his *On the Laying Out, Planting and Managing of Cemeteries* as the 'Pleasure Ground' style. Spacious lawns lead up to the buildings, and clumps of trees are juxtaposed with groups of tombs. West Norwood is judged to hold the finest collection of sepulchral monuments in London, with 69 Grade II and Grade II★ listed structures, including a dedicated Greek Orthodox burial ground that has 18 listed mausoleums and monuments. The cemetery is the last resting place of the 19th-century domestic goddess Mrs Beeton, who died aged just 29.

The original two chapels were damaged in the Second World War, and the Episcopal chapel was demolished in 1955, to be replaced by a rose garden. The catacombs are intact and have long been a place of fascination. Although they are not usually open to the public because of their dilapidated state, occasional visits may be arranged.
Norwood Road, SE27 9JU. West Norwood rail.

⑱ Sydenham Hill Wood

In this ancient woodland, the last remaining tract of the Great North Wood, grow 200 species of trees and wild plants, some of them survivors from the gardens of Victorian mansions that once stood in this sylvan setting. In a curious mix, old oaks and hornbeams keep company with a cedar of Lebanon, a monkey puzzle and a mulberry tree, rhododendron and bamboo. A folly in the shape of a sculptural ruined arch fronts what might have been a water feature. A disused trackbed and rail tunnel are remnants of the old Nunhead–Crystal Palace line, closed in 1954. The tunnel is home to woolly long-eared bats, one of at least five species of bats that live in the woods. A pond is fed by the mainly underground Ambrook, and an avenue of oak trees is known as Cox's Walk. The wood is is a designated Site of Metropolitan Interest, imaginatively managed by the London Wildlife Trust.

A house on Crescent Wood Road was once lived in by John Logie Baird. The transmitter mast on Crystal Palace Parade stands as a fitting tribute to the inventor of television. Nicknamed 'London's Eiffel Tower', it thrusts skyward where the Crystal Palace Aquarium once stood. The mast was erected in the mid 1950s and, at a height of 219m (719ft), it remained the tallest structure in London until 1991, when No 1 Canada Square, Canary Wharf, knocked it into second place.
Entrances are on Crescent Wood Road, and at the Lordship Lane junction with Dulwich Common for Cox's Walk. Forest Hill, Sydenham rail.

⑲ Horniman's Museum

This striking Art Nouveau building was designed by the architect C.H. Townsend to house an eclectic collection started by the Quaker tea merchant E.J. Horniman. A quarter of a million specimens – from fossils to stuffed animals – are kept in the balconied natural history gallery, and the aquarium, founded in 1903, is one of London's most enduring. In 2006, a new, modernised aquarium opened in the museum's basement with 15 displays ranging from a Fijian reef to a tropical rainforest via a British rock pool. In the ethnography displays, tribal masks stare out from among the textiles, jewellery, art, puppets and other items in the 60,000-strong collection. But the musical instruments, one of the finest sets in the world, are the museum's particular glory – 6,500 music-related objects are on display. Magically, by touching a screen, the curious can listen to the sound produced by any one of them.

Townsend's Arts & Crafts building has a tall clock tower, and a large mosaic façade, *Humanity in the House of Circumstance*, by Robert Anning Bell. It rises up on a hilltop among 6.5ha (16 acres) of gardens, with drifts of wild flowers, rare sundials, a strikingly beautiful Grade II listed Victorian conservatory of iron lace, a jolly little bandstand, and a Dutch barn brought from Holland in 1895.
100 London Road, SE23 3PQ. Forest Hill rail.

SOUTHEAST

NEW CROSS & DEPTFORD

⑳ Rivoli Ballroom

Red velvet, gilt-framed wall panels and crystal chandeliers distinguish London's only unspoilt 1950s ballroom. The Rivoli began life as the Crofton Picture Palace in 1913, and was converted by a local businessman, Leonard Tomlin, in 1957. In January 2008, in response to local fears that redevelopment would signal the last dance for the Rivoli, it received Grade II listing from English Heritage. The White Stripes have performed here. Elton John made a video. It has hosted the BBC's *Strictly Come Dancing*. The first Sunday of every month is ballroom night, when amateurs and experts whirl around the sprung Canadian maple floor, caught up in the sheer theatricality of the place.
350 Brockley Road, SE4 2BY. Crofton Park rail.

㉑ The Cemetery of All Saints, Nunhead

Here is a wonderfully atmospheric, dreamy place, with mossy slabs and toppled angels roped down by bindweed, awash with bluebells in spring, hauntingly beautiful in frost or snow. The cemetery was conceived as a smart out-of-town burial park, and consecrated in 1840, at a time when London's overcrowded graveyards were a scandal, and prey to body snatchers. The work of the London Cemetery Company, it was created by James Bunstone Bunning, who had worked with Stephen Geary at Highgate, and occupies 20.6ha (51 acres) of wooded hillside. The names of the departed toll the knell of passing day – Burton Clement Ravenscroft (wig and robe maker), Sydney Prestige Amice (civil engineer), William Lucas Distant (naturalist), Sir Polydore de Keyser (first Roman Catholic Lord Mayor of London since the Reformation), Jenny Hill (music-hall performer, 'the vital spark' extinguished in 1896). Some inscriptions raise more questions than they answer – 'Deborah Elizabeth Bryant, schoolmistress to the Cameron Highlanders, 1st Life Guards and 10th Royal Hussars', 'Dear Jack', 'Dad, don't blame the driver'.

Years of neglect have been benign. This Gothic woodland is overrun by wildlife. The ruined chapel stands out white against a blue sky, roofless, open to the elements. When the bodies of nine boy scouts drowned at Leysdown in 1912 were brought here, a million Londoners lined the streets in sympathy. Had the older ones lived, they might have been sent to the trenches of the Somme. A memorial statue to the Scouts was stolen in 1969 and probably melted down for scrap. A brass plaque reads 'This base is all that remains of the original memorial'.
Linden Grove, SE15 3LP. Two-hour tours on last Sunday of the month.

㉒ Creekside Walks

At low tide every day at Deptford Creek, walkers can enjoy a glimpse of the secret life of the river. The Ravensbourne rises 11 miles away in Keston, and here is where it flows into the Thames. Visitors to the Creekside Centre, which is built on 'green' principles, are equipped with waders and taken on one of London's most unusual guided walks, along a mile of riverbed. It's not the easiest terrain to yomp over, but when the waters ebb, they leave behind not just wildlife – the enthusiast might see redstart and cormorant, Chinese mitten crabs and freshwater shrimps – but all manner of curiosities. Some 600 wrecks litter the Thames riverbed, including that of HMS *London*, part of the fleet that brought Charles II back from exile in 1660. Five years later, as it sailed upriver with 300 men on board, and 14 tonnes of gunpowder, it was blown apart in an explosion that shook the city.

Across the creek is the distinctive Italianate Crossness Pumping Station (see page 191).
14 Creekside, SE8 4SA. Greenwich, Deptford Bridge DLR.

A brightly painted 1960s South East Trains commuter carriage houses a lively café bistro, the first stage of a project to reanimate Deptford's disused railyard. Designed by Morag Myerscough, it has a tiny kitchen, one long table and stools printed with cheeky slogans. Its fame has spread abroad, through articles published in the *The New York Times* and *South China Post*.

The project also shelters, in formerly disused railway arches, a group of 'creatives-in-residence', who have put together a unique outdoor cinema, with hand-built screen and chairs designed and built from wooden palettes.

121–3 Deptford High Street, SE8 4NS. Deptford Bridge DLR.

After dark, Europe's largest contemporary dance centre glows in shades of lime, turquoise and magenta. The building has a sweeping, semi-translucent polycarbonate façade. Designed by the Swiss architects Jacques Herzog and Pierre Meuron, who are also responsible for Tate Modern, it won the Stirling Prize for Architecture in 2003. The centre includes a pilates studio, 13 dance studios, a library, café and 300 seat theatre.

Its origins lie in the northeast, with Rudolf Laban, an Austro-Hungarian refugee and the 'father of modern dance'. In 1938 he fled the Nazis and opened the Art of Movement Studio in Manchester, raising the status of dance as an art form and exploring dance theory and practice. He established 'choreology', a system of dance analysis, and invented a method of notation known as Labanotation or kinetography Laban. The studio was renamed the Laban Centre for Movement and Dance in 1975, 17 years after its founder's death. The school arrived in southeast London in 1977 where it merged with Greenwich's Trinity College of Music to form Trinity Laban, a conservatorium for music and dance. The café and some performances are open to the public. The garden has been sculpted into an amphitheatre, and, like the Creekside centre, the building is topped off with a biodiverse 'brown roof'.

Creekside, SE8 3DZ. Deptford Bridge DLR.

LABAN CENTRE

First-city firsts

The needs of a rapidly expanding population provided scientists, artists and entrepreneurs with opportunities to revolutionise the city. Growth sparked many new ideas.

As one of the world's great cities, London has, not surprisingly, witnessed a number of 'firsts'. Best known, perhaps, is the pioneering underground railway. The Metropolitan Line from Paddington to Farringdon opened in 1863 in the absence of the ageing prime minister, Lord Palmerston, who declined an invitation, saying that he hoped to remain above ground for a little while longer. The noise and smoke of the steam locomotives made any journey a form of mild torture, according to *The Times*.

Today, the underground has 270 stations and 250 miles of railway line. It is run from 55 Broadway above St James's Park station. The building was designed in cruciform shape by Charles Holden, and its integration into the station and shopping mall was also a world's first. It was the tallest secular building in London when completed in 1929. Decorating the façades are statues by Joseph Epstein, Eric Gill and Henry Moore. The storm that followed their unveiling did not abate until Epstein had removed 1½ inches from the penis of his

figure of *Day*. In 2011, the building was upgraded to Grade I listed, and included in the Open House weekend initiative, whereby private buildings of architectural significance are opened to the public, free of charge, for one weekend every September.

Engineering feat

The first tunnel in the world to be dug beneath a tidal river was the 396m (1,300ft) Thames Tunnel, linking Rotherhithe to Wapping. Plagued with floods, fire and fatal accidents, it eventually opened as a novelty, rather than for carriages. The tunnel was designed by Marc Brunel and his famous son, Isambard Kingdom Brunel, and a model of their innovative tunnelling shield, which was devised for the excavation, can be seen in the Brunel Museum in Rotherhithe.

When it finally opened in 1862, people paid a penny to descend into twin tunnels and browse souvenir stalls. Now the London Overground railway rattles through.

THAMES TUNNEL

Before trains came the horse and carriage. Marylebone's Shilibeer Street is where George Shilibeer stabled his horses for the first horse-drawn buses, which ran from Paddington to the Bank of England. The service started in 1829 and the route took the buses along Marylebone Road, outside the zone in which Handsom cabs had a monopoly.

Traffic lights were a 20th-century invention, but in 1868 a traffic signal was set up outside Parliament at a junction that needed four policemen – who belonged to the oldest police force in the world – to direct horse-drawn traffic. It lasted until the following year when it exploded. Drivers had taken little notice of it anyway.

Building works

A grey, tumbledown house in Lordship Lane, Dulwich, is the only surviving 19th-century concrete house in Britain. Designed by Charles Barry Jr, son of the architect for the Houses of Parliament, in 1873, it was built by Charles Drake, using a technique that he had patented. The house finally received recognition in 2009, with a Grade II listing.

More obviously deserving of its Grade II listing is the façade of Marconi House, opposite Somerset House in the Strand. Here, on the seventh floor, in 1922, the world's first national broadcasting organisation, the BBC, began transmitting radio programmes. The transmitter, 2LO, is now in the Science Museum. Three years later, the world's first public demonstration of a television set was staged at Selfridge's in Oxford Street. John Logie Baird showed off the device he had been perfecting in his Soho home. Gordon Selfridge was a great showman – he displayed Louis Blériot's monoplane, the first to fly across the English Channel. In 2011, a 12-inch Marconi type 702 TV set from 1936, said to be the world's oldest still in working order, having had just two careful owners, changed hands at a London auction for £16,800.

London's first department store was Whiteley's in Westbourne Grove, which started life as a single drapery store in 1863 and by 1867 had grown to encompass several shops and 17 departments. Yorkshireman William Whiteley was the 'universal provider' who boasted he could supply anything from a pin to an elephant. He had 6,000 staff, many of them living-in and working 96 hours a week. He came unstuck when a man turned up claiming to be his illegitimate son and demanding his inheritance. Whiteley, aged 76, was shot dead. After a fire, Whiteley's reopened in Queensway in 1911 as the largest store in the world. Adolf Hitler loved it and ordered it not to be bombed; he planned to make it his headquarters when he reached London.

SOUTHEAST

GREENWICH & BLACKHEATH

25 St Alfege

Alfege, Archbishop of Canterbury, was captured by Danish raiders and held in Greenwich before being bludgeoned to death in 1012. Nicholas Hawksmoor's fine English baroque church is the third on this site to commemorate his martyrdom. It was dedicated in 1718, and in 1730 the tower was reinforced and refurbished by John James.

The first Astronomer Royal, John Flamsteed, worshipped here. General Wolfe, the hero of Quebec, was buried here in 1759 – his statue stands on the park by the Observatory. Hawksmoor, for 40 years clerk of the works at Greenwich hospital, was given free rein by Queen Anne's commissioners to impose his style, with columns and pediments surmounted by urns.

In March 1941, an incendiary device lodged in the roof causing a fire, and molten lead collapsed into the nave, but the walls and tower were undamaged and complete restoration was finished by 1953. The wrought-iron altar and gallery rails are believed to be by Jean Tijou, the Huguenot craftsman and refugee whose main work is in St Paul's Cathedral. A window commemorates the composer Thomas Tallis, buried here in 1581. *Greenwich Church Street, SE10 9BJ. Cutty Sark DLR.*

26 Greenwich Hospital Chapel

The stunning hospital chapel that the visitor sees today is the result of a catastrophic fire in 1779. The original chapel of the hospital for retired seamen (see Royal Naval College, right) was a relatively plain affair designed by Thomas Ripley. When it was gutted by flames, James 'Athenian' Stuart rolled up his sleeves and went to town on the interior, adopting a mix of ancient Greek and naval imagery. The glorious neoclassical ceiling has a design of squares and octagons with ornate central ornaments, carved by the master plasterer John Papworth. The acoustics are excellent, and musicians from the resident Trinity College of Music often perform here. The great altarpiece of *St Paul Preserved after a Shipwreck* is by Benjamin West – his only major work still to be seen *in situ*. High-level portraits of saints *en grisaille* were designed by him but executed by Biaggio di Rebecca. Stuart's splendid gold altar stands on a marble key pattern, recently rediscovered under the blue naval carpet.

Whether the fire was started from malice, or accidentally by an old seadog enjoying an illicit pipe of tobacco on the ward, was never established. *Old Royal Naval College, SE10 9LW. Cutty Sark DLR.*

27 *Cutty Sark*

'This vessel, just launched, is from her fine lines, expected to be one of the fastest afloat.' So read the advertisement for the maiden voyage of the *Cutty Sark* on February 15, 1870, and it was. From her first trip to China, this elegant little tea clipper went on to speed around the world. She took cargoes to India, Japan, Singapore, the Philippines and Australia, travelling home from Sydney to London in a record 73 days in 1885. Sold to a Portuguese company and renamed the *Ferreira*, she docked in Europe, East Africa and the Americas.

In 1922 she was acquired by Captain Wilfred Dowman and her original name was restored. *Cutty Sark* is an archaic Scottish term for a skimpy slip or shift, and was perhaps suggested to her original owner, Jock Willis, by the ship's designer, Hercules Linton. The figurehead, Nannie, represents the scantily clad witch in Robert Burns's poem 'Tam O' Shanter', gripping Tam's horse's tail, as she pursues him.

From 1954 Greenwich has been the ship's home. In May 2007, she was gutted by fire. Now she has been rebuilt and is the centre of a museum. Ships' figureheads are displayed around her hull inside the dry dock where she is berthed. What astonishes the visitor is that so small and fragile a vessel should have travelled so far. *2 Greenwich Church Street, SE10 9BG. Cutty Sark DLR.*

28 Greenwich Foot Tunnel

For this shortcut under the Thames between Cutty Sark Gardens and Island Gardens, Londoners are indebted to Alexander Binnie, chief engineer of the London County Council, who was also responsible for the Blackwall Tunnel (1897) and Vauxhall Bridge (1906). The tunnel was built so that workers living south of the river could walk to the thriving docks, and it came about largely thanks to the urgings of Will Crooks, a trade unionist, Fabian and Progressive Party candidate. It opened on August 4, 1902, and cost £127,000 to build. In 1904, there were 4 million transits of the tunnel – rising to 6 million by 1915. In the First World War, dockers' families used it as a shelter from Zeppelin raids.

The tunnel is accessed at either end through round, redbrick entrance buildings under glazed cupola, and by a spiral staircase or lift to a depth of 15m (50ft). The lifts don't operate at night, so then 88 steps at the northern end, and 100 at the southern, must be negotiated. *Cutty Sark, Island Gardens DLR.*

OLD ROYAL NAVAL COLLEGE

㉙ Old Royal Naval College

When Queen Mary commissioned Sir Christopher Wren to build a retirement home for seamen on the site of the old Greenwich Palace, she insisted on her view of the river being maintained. So he designed Greenwich Hospital in two distinct wings and, viewed from across the river, with the Queen's House (page 187) the two parts of his baroque masterpiece form a single symmetrical sweep. The hospital took 55 years to complete. Wren worked on it with Nicholas Hawksmoor, and they were succeeded by John Vanbrugh. The Royal Naval College supplanted the hospital in 1869, and decamped in 1998. The buildings now house the University of Greenwich and parts of it are open to the public. Tours include the Painted Hall. So spectacular was the work of James Thornhill here that the pensioners, for whom the hall was intended as a dining room, were not allowed inside. In Nelson's Room, the Admiral's coffin was kept for more than a week before lying in state for three days in the Painted Hall where 100,000 mourners paid their respects before a state funeral in St Paul's Cathedral. The pensioners' brewery is now a café. The building has served as a backdrop in a number of films, including *The Madness of King George* and *Four Weddings and a Funeral*, and stood in for the White House in *Patriot Games*, and for the Pentagon in *Shining Through*. *SE10 9LW. Cutty Sark DLR.*

㉚ 'Slice of Reality'

On the foreshore of the Thames by the Millenium Dome stands what the visitor, idly glancing, might take for an ocean-going vessel. In fact, it is a vertically sliced section of a sand dredger, revealing the ship's living quarters, bridge, poop and engine room, and mischievously flying a skull and crossbones. Commissioned to create a major public work for the millennium site, the sculptor Richard Wilson produced this look-and-look-again piece. It is supposed to follow the line of the Meridian, as though time itself had sliced through it. The piece is starting to show signs of exposure, so time is indeed taking a toll, but that is part of the charm.
Greenwich Peninsula, SE10. North Greenwich tube.

㉛ The O2 Arena

Where better to erect the world's largest dome than where the third millennium would officially dawn, bang on the Prime Meridian? Built to a design by Richard Rogers, the Millennium Dome (as it then was) has the capacity of 13 Albert Halls. If the 8ha (20 acre) continuous-membrane roof – the world's largest – were inverted under Niagara Falls, it would take 15 minutes to fill. Nelson's Column could stand upright within it. Its appearance is nothing if not distinctive, resembling a giant white umbrella supported by 12 yellow masts, symbolising the hours on a clock dial.

For the first year the Dome housed an exhibition, but then it stood empty. All that changed in 2007 when it reopened as the O2 Arena. An enclosed dome within the Dome, the 23,000 seater music and sports arena pulls in the biggest names in entertainment and has become an established music venue. As well as the main arena, the Dome houses a smaller concert hall, an 11-screen cinema and exhibition space. Access is along a virtual street of bars, restaurants and coffee shops. In November 2008 the structure had the distinction of being named by CNN as 'The World's Ugliest Building'. It is hosting the 2012 Olympic gymnastics and basketball events. But perhaps the most amazing aspect of it is the way that a former barren wasteland, home to defunct gasworks, has become a vibrant place of work and community, and a recreational destination.
Drawdock Road, SE10 0BB. North Greenwich tube.

㉜ Cutty Sark Tavern

When the owners took over this Georgian tavern 40 years ago, the view across the river was of dereliction. Now it's of Canary Wharf and the O2 Arena. Located in a cobbled street of 16th and 17th-century houses, the pub has a distinctive bow window over two upper floors, and was built in around 1810, in the reign of George III. It was named the Union Tavern in celebration of the Union of England and Ireland by Act of Parliament in 1801, but the name was changed with the arrival of the famous tea

TRAFALGAR TAVERN

clipper at Greenwich in 1954. Inside, the pub has beams, barrel seats, nooks and crannies and a dominant wooden staircase.
4–6 Ballast Quay, SE10 9PD. Cutty Sark DLR.

33 Trafalgar Tavern

Charles Dickens used to eat at this Grade I listed, Regency-style public house, which stands right on the riverside with all flags flying. So much must he have enjoyed himself that he chose this as the setting for the wedding feast for John Harman and Bella Wilfer in *Our Mutual Friend*. The place is still popular as a wedding venue. The Trafalgar was famous for its whitebait suppers – small fry, straight from the Thames – which it continues to serve. Prime Minister William Gladstone was a customer, as were the writers William Thackeray and Wilkie Collins.

The building, dating from 1837, is by Joseph Kay, who was the surveyor for Greenwich Hospital (see Old Royal Naval College, page 185). Bow windows look out across the water. It was used for some years as a seamen's mission, then a working-men's club, before award-winning restoration in 1965 of its grand ballroom, saloons, oak panelling, plasterwork, open fireplaces and main bar lined with naval prints. Outside is a statue of Lord Nelson, whose famous victory the pub's name celebrates, and the Nelson theme continues within.
Park Row, SE10 9NW. Cutty Sark DLR.

34 National Maritime Museum

A trickle of water seeps out of the earth in rural Gloucestershire and, gathers itself over 215 meandering miles to the sea. By the time it reaches Greenwich, the Thames feels purposefully ocean-going, subject to the push and pull of the tides. This museum, dedicated to the country's nautical history – the largest of its kind in the world – opened to the public in 1937, within Greenwich Park. The original, bow-windowed, 17th-century shop front of Lloyd's Coffee House, the meeting place for shipping brokers, on loan from the insurers Lloyd's of London, leads the visitor to a fascinating exploration of the history of maritime London and the importance of the hard-working river in shaping national life and destiny. Shipping and shipbuilding, cargoes, commerce, conflict, community, pomp and pageantry all play their part.

A display dedicated to Horatio Nelson includes the vice-admiral's naval undress coat that he wore at the Battle of Trafalgar. It bears the hole where a musket ball, fired from the rigging of the French ship *Redoubtable*, entered close to his left shoulder and felled him. The coat, which is embroidered with four orders of chivalry, was conveyed to Emma Hamilton at their home in Merton, in accordance with Nelson's wishes. An original model for his memorial, Nelson's Column, by William Railton, can be seen to include details that do not appear on the monument in Trafalgar Square.

Among state barges on show are a beautifully carved and decorated shallop that was built for Queen Mary in 1689, and William III's barge from 1691. The Sammy Ofer wing, built with a £20 million donation from the billionaire shipping magnate, provides new exhibition space.
Romney Road, SE10 9NF. Greenwich, Cutty Sark DLR.

35 The Queen's House

The queen is Anne of Denmark, wife of James I. He is said to have given her the manor of Greenwich by way of apology for having publicly sworn at her for shooting one of his hunting dogs. As apologies go, it was handsome. Handsome, too, is this showpiece of the National Maritime Museum (left). Inigo Jones designed it for Anne in 1616, but the queen did not live to see the building's completion in 1638. The house was the first major commission for Jones, who had recently returned from three years in Italy, and it was England's first fully classical building, modelled on the Medici villa at Poggia a Caiano between Florence and Pistoia.

In 1805, George III bestowed it upon the Royal Naval Asylum, for the education of the orphaned children of seamen. Daniel Asher Alexander added colonnades and flanking wings for dormitories. Little survives of Jones's interior except the ironwork of the 'Tulip Stairs' – the first geometric self-supporting spiral staircase in Britain – and the painted woodwork and marble floors of the Great Hall, which retains its uplifting sense of proportion and harmony.

The house is now home to the museum's collection of fine art, which includes paintings by William Hodges, who accompanied Captain Cook on his exploration of the South Seas; people queued to see Hodges' images when they were first displayed. Here too is Turner's painting the *Battle of Trafalgar*, showing Nelson's flagship, the *Victory*, defeating the French *Redoubtable*. The artist designed the painting to be hung high, so that the viewer would be confronted with a foreground depiction of the horrors of war and the high cost of victory.
SE10 9NF. Greenwich, Cutty Sark DLR.

36 Royal Observatory

In 1674, Charles II commissioned an observatory in Greenwich, 'in order to the finding out of longitude of places for perfecting navigation and astronomy'. In 1714, by Act of Parliament, a prize of £20,000 was offered to anyone who could provide a means of finding longitude (east-west position) at sea. This would entail a study of the night sky and certain knowledge of the time at a fixed terrestrial point. Accurate timekeeping on land was possible, but at sea the rolling of ships and changes in temperature and humidity upset clock mechanisms. John Harrison, a working-class joiner, found the answer but it took him more than half a lifetime to convince the Board of Longitude that he was right. Once a successor to Harrison's clocks became standard issue, a notional 'home port' had to be established for all the world's shipping, and Greenwich Meridian was chosen as the Prime Meridian of the world at a conference in Washington DC in 1884.

At the Observatory, it is possible to straddle the line at longitude 0°, planting a foot in both east and west hemispheres. Galleries are devoted to horology, astronomy and the sea. Harrison's seminal timepieces are among the collection, together with the pendulum clocks that generated the BBC's famous six-pip signal. The time to visit is 1pm, when a time ball, produced by the engineer Henry Maudslay, plummets down its mast on the roof, as it has done since 1833. *Greenwich Park, SE10. Greenwich, Cutty Sark DLR.*

37 Greenwich Park

Great views open out across the river from high on the hill in the oldest of the royal parks. Henry VIII, a keen horseman, loved it and may well have hunted here. Deer still roam in the Wilderness area, and a 17th-century orchard of native fruit trees is under restoration. This is where the Olympic and Paralympic equestrian events and pentathlon are to be held.

Among Greenwich's many grand and important buildings, it would be easy to miss the Ranger's House, a Georgian villa that in less exalted company would make quite an architectural statement. It houses the Wernher Collection, which was acquired by the diamond magnate Sir Julius Wernher (1850–1912), one of the founders of De Beers, and includes Old Masters and tapestries, and England's largest collection of medieval and Renaissance jewellery, *Ranger's House, Chesterfield Walk, SE10 8QX. Blackheath rail.*

38 Severndroog Castle

For centuries, Shooter's Hill, the highest point in south London, was a lawless place, topped with a gibbet for highwaymen. The gibbet may be gone but an extraordinary folly remains, standing in a clearing, amid ancient woodland – a Gothic tower built by Richard Jupp in 1784 to commemorate William James. As commander-in-chief of the East India Company's Bombay Fleet, James had led a band of men to

capture the stronghold of Severn Droog on the coast of Malabar from the pirate king Tology Angrier. In bluebell time and at sunset it is a magical place. A building trust has been set up to oversee restoration, with the aim of reopening the café and viewing platform.
Castle Wood, Shooter's Hill, SE18 3RT.

39 Blackheath

Wat Tyler, a Dartford blacksmith, led the peasants' revolt from the heath in 1381, when 100,000 men from Kent and Essex marched on London. Tradition has it that golf was introduced to England on Blackheath in 1608. In May 1660, Charles II came here on his way from Rochester to London to reclaim the throne, amid scenes of great rejoicing. More wine and ale flowed at the annual May fair. The diarist John Evelyn recorded on May Day 1683: 'I went to Blackheath to see the new faire … This was the first day, pretended for the sale of cattle, but I think, in truth, to enrich the new tavern at the bowlinggreene, erected by Snape, his Majesty's farrier, a man full of projects. There appeared nothing but an innumerable assembly of drinking people from London, pedlars, &c …' Evelyn was a royal adviser on building in Greenwich, and as treasurer of the hospital building project dug deep into his own pockets to keep the underfunded project afloat.

This wide open space with long views over Kent and Surrey no longer has a May fair, but hosts an annual kite and bikes festival. On any breezy Sunday the sky is filled with soaring, swooping diamonds, deltas, exotic birds, flying fish and winged boxes. Benjamin Ferrey's 19th-century Gothic All Saints Church, right on the heath, makes a pretty sight. *SE3. Blackheath rail.*

40 Blackheath Village

The wealthy suburb that grew up around the heath from the 17th century contains some architectural gems. On South Row is the detached Georgian Colonnade House by the Regency architect Michael Searles, dating from 1802. Here, too, is his masterpiece, The Paragon (1795–1806), a perfect crescent of 14 houses linked by colonnades, with a lodge house at each end. No resident of The Paragon was to practise 'art, mystery or trade' or occupations that included school teaching and fishmongery.

An early occupant, Miss Eliza Robertson, moved into number 3 with Charlotte Sharpe in 1800, falling in love with the 'sweet situation' of her new home, although noting that young ladies liked to 'range the park, and flirt about to be talked of and envied by their competitors when they think an advantageous offer is on the way.' Much like today, really. Eliza, passing herself off as an heiress, ran up huge debts to tradesmen and was sent to Fleet Prison. Unrepentant, she complained that the builders had 'all greatly exceeded their time and orders', and that tradesmen had 'continually persuaded her that something was wanted'. Again, much like today, really. *SE3. Blackheath rail.*

FARTHER EAST

④1 Charlton House Peace Garden

Formerly known as the Rose Garden, the Peace Garden was opened in the grounds of Charlton House in the summer of 2006 in collaboration with Amnesty International as part of a campaign against domestic violence.

Charlton House is one of the finest remaining examples of domestic architecture from the time of James I, and was built between 1607 and 1612. The house is not open to the public, but the building's fine redbrick exterior and mullioned windows can be enjoyed from the Peace Garden or the Mulberry Tea Room. Also in the grounds is a mulberry tree reputed to be the oldest in Britain, planted in 1608 by order of King James. A summerhouse, which now overlooks the road, is attributed to Inigo Jones. It was built around 1630, and for a few years was used as a public convenience.
The Valley, Floyd Road, SE7 8RE. Charlton rail.

④2 Thames Barrier

Since 1982, the barrier, which straddles the Thames between Woolwich and Silvertown, has been the capital's defence against a surge tide – when a high wind gets behind a rising spring tide. It resembles a row of upended boats, and inside are the hydraulics needed to raise the five-storey, 3,700 tonne gates. The barrier has been used more than 100 times to hold back the water and prevent London from being inundated.

The best way to see the 520m (567yd) wide barrier, the second-largest movable flood barrier in the world, is from the river, although it can also be viewed from Thames Barrier Park on the north bank. This is London's first major new park for more than half a century. The monthly test, when the gates are raised, can be watched from the visitor centre on the south bank.
1 Unity Way, SE18 5NJ. Charlton rail.

④3 Royal Artillery Barracks

The Master General of the Ordnance was equipping British fighting men from here as far back as 1671, although this building, overlooking Woolwich Common, was constructed between 1775 and 1802. At 323m (1,060ft), the façade is the longest single piece of architecture in the country. In essence, it comprises six barracks, and at the centre is a three-storey arch, flanked by smaller side arches. On the attic storey is a swagged portrait panel of Queen Victoria dated 1858, and on the parapet above are trophies of arms and a gilded royal coat of arms. Its military style makes it a fitting venue for the 2012 Olympic shooting and Paralympic shooting and archery events. Some 7,500 spectators will be able to watch from temporary grandstands.
Artillery Place, Woolwich, SE18 5DP. Woolwich Arsenal DLR.

④4 Royal Arsenal, Artillery Museum

Shock and awe are appropriate responses to the weaponry amassed here. The Gunnery Hall is filled with anti-aircraft, anti-tank, coastal defence, light and medium artillery, self-propelled guns and missile launchers. Interactive screens allow those so minded to shoot down a bomber and to destroy a tank. The Field of Fire experience, by means of four giant screens, gives the visitor the opportunity to witness desert and jungle warfare, to watch anti-aircraft guns picking off the Luftwaffe in the Blitz, and to see the bombardment of the Normandy beaches on D-Day. As well as the action on-screen, smoke fills the air, searchlight beams swoop and the floor shakes as bombs explode. Here, too, are the guns that have supplied the bronze for 800 Victoria Crosses, the highest military honour, awarded for acts of exceptional valour in the face of the enemy.

The Royal Military Repository, forerunner of the museum, was established on the site by a Royal Warrant issued by George III. The museum in its present form opened to the public in 2001, in buildings that were once part of the Royal Laboratory Department.

Sir John Vanbrugh, architect of Castle Howard and Blenheim Palace, was responsible for the original, splendid 'Great Pile' in 1717, of which the main gateway survives. Square piers have moulded caps and pyramids of cannonballs. Anyone exploring the area might enjoy a sight of Vanbrugh Castle, the house that Vanbrugh built for himself on Westcombe Park Road, Blackheath, when he succeeded Wren as surveyor to the Royal Naval Hospital in 1719. This was England's first mock medieval folly, with narrow windows and turrets. Vanbrugh modelled it on the Bastille, where he had been imprisoned in 1690–2 on charges of spying.

Woolwich Arsenal is also the birthplace of Arsenal football club, 'the Gunners', to whom the museum loaned two 14.5kg (32lb) smooth-bore, muzzle-loading cast-iron guns on garrison carriages, for display, on the team's move to the Emirates Stadium (see page 138).
SE18 6ST. Woolwich Arsenal DLR.

CROSSNESS PUMPING STATION

45 Crossness Pumping Station

In the 'Great Stink' of 1858, the Houses of Parliament became so foetid that MPs demanded action. Step forward Joseph Bazalgette, chief engineer of the Metropolitan Board of Works, previously employed by the Metropolitan Commission of Sewers. One of the most distinguished civil engineers of the day, he oversaw the building of 83 miles of 'interceptory' sewers to prevent raw sewage from pouring into the Thames, thereby making a major contribution to the health and well-being of Londoners.

The system relied on three major pumping stations – Abbey Mills in the Lee Valley, another at Deptford, and the spectacular Crossness, designed with the architect Charles Henry Driver. Among Bazalgette's other achievements were the Thames Embankments and Battersea, Hammersmith and Putney bridges.

The Beam Engine House at Crossness is a Grade I listed industrial building in the Romanesque style. The four original pumping engines are among the largest surviving rotative beam engines in the world, with 52-tonne flywheels and 47-tonne beams. 'A masterpiece of engineering,' said art and architecture historian Nikolaus Pevsner, 'a Victorian cathedral of ironwork.' *Belvedere Road, SE2 9AQ. Belvedere rail.*

46 Red House

Created and commissioned by William Morris, the Red House was built by Philip Webb in 1859–60 in a Kentish orchard as a romantic home for Morris and his new bride, Jane Burden. Morris and Webb were founding fathers of the Arts & Crafts movement, much influenced by Augustus Pugin and his argument that the plan of a building should reflect its function and that Gothic architecture was the only true style for a Christian society, since it was the only true style of the God-given church. This, then, is a spiritual building, a handsome, avuncular house of studied Englishness, built in an L shape, making play with corbelled red brickwork, overhanging clay roof tiles, hooded windows, portholes, arches, a well and dovecotes, at once 'historical' and belonging to no discernible era. The difficulty in finding ready-made furnishings for the house led Morris, aged just 26, to found Morris & Co. to produce wallpapers and textiles.

The house is now managed by the National Trust. The interior is not fully furnished but contains features and furniture designed by Webb and Morris, and glass and paintings by fellow artist and designer Edward Burne-Jones. The garden, designed to 'clothe the house', is a joy. *Red House Lane, Bexleyheath, Kent DA6 8JF.*

SOUTHEAST

FARTHER SOUTH

④⑦ Eltham Palace

A palace had stood in Eltham since the time of Edward the Confessor, and been a royal favourite through the ages, but eventually it was allowed to fall into disrepair. Then, in 1933, Sir Stephen Courtauld of the wealthy textile family and his wife, Virginia, acquired the lease, with the idea that this would once more be a place of lavish entertainment. Paul Paget and John Seely were commissioned to create an Art Deco masterpiece.

The Great Hall, with its soaring hammerbeam roof, was restored, and a minstrels' gallery added. In the dramatic entrance hall, the work of the Swedish designer Rolf Engströmer, light floods through a glazed dome upon blackbean veneer and marquetry. The Italianate drawing room and the dining room with ceilings of aluminium leaf are by the Mayfair interior decorator and Italian aristocrat Peter Malacrida. The grounds reflect the Courtaulds' love of horticulture. They left in 1944, taking with them their pet lemur. Until 1992 the palace was home to an army educational unit, before English Heritage took over and began restoration in 1995. The reputed existence of at least three escape tunnels hint at the palace's troubled past.
Court Yard, SE9 5QE. Eltham, Mottingham rail.

④⑧ Crystal Palace Park

Joseph Paxton built the Crystal Palace in 1851 to house the Exhibition of the Industry of All Nations – the first ever 'world fair' and a defining event of the Victorian age. Paxton was head gardener to the Duke of Devonshire, and had designed gardens for Chatsworth, including a lily house, based on the leaves of a giant lily. On a visit to London, he learnt that 245 plans for the main exhibition hall had been rejected, so he dashed off what was essentially a vastly enlarged lily house. It was more than 500m (1,640ft) long and took 2,000 men eight months to build in Hyde Park. By the time the exhibition closed six months later, more than 6 million people had visited.

The following summer a redesigned Crystal Palace was built on Sydenham Hill, where it reopened in 1854, and that area of Sydenham and Upper Norwood had not just a new park and attraction, but a new name and new rail services. Such was its international renown that, in November 1936, *The New York Times* reported: 'Engulfed in a roaring sheet of flames, which towered so high into the night sky that it could be seen almost from the English Channel, the

world-famous Crystal Palace … crashed to the earth tonight, a raging inferno of twisted girders and molten glass.' Churchill called it 'the end of an era'. Touching remnants survive – a statue of Dante, a bust of Paxton, a nymph, sphinxes, a wall of the orangery, the South Basin Pool, steps of the Italian terraces … A museum is situated in the former Crystal Palace School of Engineering, but is open to the public only on Sundays and bank holidays. The historic tea maze reopened in 2009.
Anerley Hill, Crystal Palace, SE19 2BA. Crystal Palace rail.

④⑨ Crystal Palace National Sports Centre

Crystal Palace Park's historical sporting credentials include hosting cricket, athletics, football and motor racing. The sports centre, the work of London County Council architects, was opened by the Duke of Edinburgh in 1964 and was a majestic emblem of early brutalism, emphasised by a huge glass-and-concrete curtain wall. Like the park, for too long the sports centre was allowed to fall into disrepair, but a £17 million investment has enabled it to be brought up to modern international standards. The Olympic-sized swimming pool has a Swiss timing system and touchpads, and there is a new techno gym and refurbished dance studio. The Grade II★ listed centre is more than three times the size of most local sports centres.
Ledrington Road, SE19 2BB. Crystal Palace rail.

⑤⓪ Dinosaur Park

New life has been breathed into the monsters that inhabit the world's first theme park at Crystal Palace, opened in 1854. The sculptor, Benjamin Waterhouse Hawkins worked with palaeontologist Richard Owen to create a series of prehistoric creatures based on what was known at that time. They were displayed on islands, representing a journey from the Palaeozoic to the Mesozoic and Cenozoic eras. The monsters caused a great stir, earning Hawkins notoriety for daring to explore the idea of evolution – five years before Darwin's *On the Origin of Species*. As more was learned about the 'terrible lizards', as Owen called them, the models were mocked for being anatomically incorrect – unfairly since their Victorian makers were visionary. Following meticulous restoration, the sculptures have Grade I listed status and are free for all to see in the wilds of the Penge end of the park.
Thicket Road, SE20 8DT. Crystal Palace, Penge West rail.

LIGHT FLOODS THROUGH
A GLAZED DOME
ELTHAM PALACE

KEY
- Spitalfields
- East End
- Isle of Dogs
- Bow & Hackney
- Farther East
- The Olympic Park

ANGEL ROAD

High Road

North Circular Road

37

TOTTENHAM
HALE

38 Forest Road

WALTHAMSTOW
CENTRAL

Chigwell Road

Eastern A

Clapton Common

Lea Bridge Road

CLAPTON

Stoke Newington Road

36

High Road

Centre Road

High

Gree

47

DALSTON
JUNCTION

HACKNEY
CENTRAL

35

49

48 STRATFORD
INTERNATIONAL

41 STRATFORD

Romford Road

North Circular Road

Ilford Lane

Longbridge Road

33

34

HACKNEY
WICK

42

46

UPNEY

32

50

43 44

40

11 HOXTON

Kingsland Road

Grove Road

45

PUDDING
MILL LANE

Alfred's Way

7

9

10

31

Manor Road

Barking Road

Royal Docks Road

8

OLD STREET

12

BETHNAL
GREEN

Mile End Road

6

5

4

BROMLEY-
BY-BOW

Newham Way

2

3

14

13

30

Commercial Road

East India Dock Road

Royal Albert
Way

1

LIVERPOOL
STREET

ALDGATE
EAST

15

20

21 SHADWELL

WEST
INDIA QUAY

EAST INDIA

28

29

TOWER HILL

16 The Highway

19

22

27

23

CANARY
WHARF

26

Silvertown Way

17

WAPPING

18

Westferry Road

Manchester Road

Thames

25

MUDCHUTE

24

Whalebone Lane

89

Wood Lane

Heathway

TREE

East

Reclamation, reinvention and reinvigoration are the watchwords of London's Eastend. A stroll through thriving markets, squares and barely recognisable docklands to the Olympic park confirms the transformation.

SPITALFIELDS

❶ Petticoat Lane Market

Every Sunday morning around 1,000 stalls set up along Middlesex Street, known as Petticoat Lane, selling everything under the sun. Petticoat Lane has long been a marketplace, beginning as Hog's Lane, which ran by the City wall, and dyed cloth was pegged out to dry in the surrounding fields. By the end of the 16th century it was called Petticote Lane, a name reinforced some decades later by the arrival of Protestant Huguenot weavers in Spitalfields. Fleeing religious persecution in France, they settled in an area that had been depopulated by the Great Plague, and they had silk and lace to sell. By the 1750s the market was thriving. The delineation of the City boundary in 1830 caused the name to be changed to Middlesex Street, although Londoners wouldn't hear of it. They continued to go 'down the Lane' on Sundays, where a newly arrived Jewish community injected fresh vigour into the market. They have now been largely replaced by Asian traders. *Middlesex Street, E1 6BD. Liverpool Street rail or tube.*

❷ Old Spitalfields Market

The old covered market at Spitalfields is at its brightest on Sundays, when innovative fashion, craft and vintage items make it a good place to browse. The market occupies a former artillery testing ground for 'longbowes, crossebowes and handegonnes', according to the diarist Samuel Pepys. He visited the ground in 1669, when a large cannon was being tested. Thirteen years later, Spitalfields gained a royal charter for a flower, fruit and vegetable market. The market hall, built by successful trader Robert Horner, opened in 1893. When the produce sellers moved out to Leyton in 1991, the vacuum was filled by traders in young fashion, and today the tradition continues with regular Fashion Fridays promising items original and new.

Stalls fill the market's centre space, and shops and restaurants are open around the sides. Quotations from Pepys, Charles Dickens, Peter Ackroyd and local resident and author Jeanette Winterson appear on a large square cube, or writing box, and each of four gates has an explanation about the person after whom it is named. The fifth, Spitfire Mk Vb W3311 Gate, is named after a Second World War aeroplane bought for the RAF with money raised by traders. *Old Spitalfields Market, 16 Horner Square, EC1 6EW. Liverpool Street rail or tube, Aldgate East tube. Open seven days a week; no stalls on Saturday.*

❸ Brick Lane

The bricks in this East London street have many tales to tell. When bricks and tiles were first manufactured around here in any quantity, the street's name was changed from Whitechapel Lane, and changes have been going on ever since. A palimpsest of immigration starts with the Huguenots followed by Irish, Jewish and finally Bangladeshi arrivals. Street name plates have been translated into Bengali, the language of the Sylhet region in northeast Bangladesh, where most of the Asian community comes from.

A Sunday market north of the Truman Brewery (see right) brings out all sorts of traders, some laying their wares on a cloth on the ground. Tables for games of chess and carrom – popular in Asia – are put out, too. Since Spitalfields' makeover, Brick Lane has become the place to go for whackier fashion. Sunday Upmarket, just off Brick Lane, has many new designers among its 200 stalls. Backyard Market, behind the Truman Brewery Vat House, goes for young designers and kitsch. In F Block there is a weekly Vintage Market with stalls and pop-up shops. Pearly Kings and Queens, splendid in their glittery outfits, don't mind their pictures being taken, as long as a pound or two is dropped into their charity tins. *Brick Lane, E1. Aldgate East tube. Sunday Upmarket, Elys Yard, Hanbury Street; Sunday 10am–5pm. Backyard Market, U Block, next to 146 Brick Lane; Saturday 11am–6pm; Sunday 10am–5pm. Vintage Market, 85 Brick Lane; Friday–Saturday 11am–6pm; Sunday 11am–5pm.*

❹ Jamme Masjid

The most recycled prayer house in Britain is a fine Georgian building. A modern, silver minaret, rising past the Palladian window and Welsh slate roof, and topped with a crescent moon, marks its corner on Fournier Street. The Latin inscription *Umbra sumus* (we are shadows) is written on a sundial, high on the front wall, together with the date, 1743.

It was built as La Neuve Eglise (the New Church) for Huguenot weavers, with a school in the adjoining building in Brick Lane. The architect was Thomas Stibbs. But by 1809 the congregation had all but evaporated and it was sold to the London Society for Promoting Christianity Among the Jews. Then in 1819 the Methodists moved in. Following the assassination of Tsar Alexander II in 1891, for which the Jews in Russia were blamed, a large influx of persecuted and banished Ashkenazis arrived in the area. A group from Lithuania called

Machzeike Haddas (Upholders of the Law) embellished the prayer house's plain interior and turned it into the Great Synagogue, with a Torah school in the vestry. It became the heart of the Jewish community, open at all hours of the day.

After 70 years the Jewish population had largely dispersed. By this time the building had been listed, and after falling vacant for a while, it was reopened as the Great Mosque to serve the expanding Bangladeshi community. The mosque can accommodate up to 4,000 at Friday prayers. *59 Brick Lane, E1 6QL. Liverpool Street rail or tube, Aldgate East tube.*

5 Old Truman Brewery

One reason Brick Lane is such a honeypot is the 4.5ha (11 acres) of space vacated by London's biggest brewery, which has been turned into the East End's largest area for the arts and media. Creativity resounds through 19 industrial buildings, yards and alleys on both sides of the street, accommodating exhibitions, bars, market stalls and pop-up shops. There is variety in the architecture. Some interiors have serried

ranks of iron columns and girders, some have flagstone floors. Narrow stairs and corridors lead into spaces so large they can put on end-of-term shows for several art colleges simultaneously. Beneath a tall, brick chimney is the Boiler House, a high-ceilinged hall of food stalls that operates from Friday to Sunday. Next door, the Vat House (1803) has the look of a meeting house. Its clock stopped at 10 minutes to 8, perhaps on that tearful day in 1988 when the brewery closed.

Joseph Truman began brewing in Brick Lane 300 years earlier, and the business expanded when the Black Eagle Brewery was built in 1724 under Sir Benjamin Truman. Advertisements for Ben Truman's Pale Ale continued into the late 20th century, showing a jolly, wooden-legged sailor hopping along accompanied by the slogan 'there are more hops in Ben Truman'. Some say that it was the Huguenots who introduced fermented hops into the beer-making process, but although they may have passed on some of their brewing knowledge, hops had been used in Britain for two centuries before their arrival. *91 Brick Lane, E1 6QL. Liverpool Street rail or tube, Aldgate East tube.*

PETTICOAT LANE MARKET

PART MUSEUM,
PART THEATRICAL
INSTALLATION

DENNIS SEVERS' HOUSE

❻ Dennis Severs' House

Flaming lanterns and crimson shutters set this house apart from the other handsome silk weavers' houses on Folgate Street.
Inside, it is part museum, part theatrical installation. The creation of the American artist Dennis Severs, the whole house is made to look as it did when occupied by the Huguenot Gervais family, anglicised to Jervis, from 1725 to 1919. To appreciate the atmosphere, visitors must submit to its proposition. Chipped china, antiques, paintings, drapes, four-posters and candlesticks, chamber pots and rumpled beds are all signs that people are living here, that somebody has only just left. Guttering candles suggest there is no electricity. Sounds of life are emitted from hidden speakers. There is the smell of food; unfinished meals are on the table.

A complete romantic, Severs gave horse-drawn carriage tours around Hyde Park when he arrived in London, before buying this property in 1979 and devoting the rest of his life to reliving its past. Since his death in 1999 it has been kept open with the help of the Spitalfields Trust.
18 Folgate Street, E1 6BX. Liverpool Street rail or tube. Tours, which must be booked, last about 45 minutes and take place on Sundays (12–4pm), Mondays (12–2pm) and Monday evenings, when there is a 'Silent Night' evening tour (6–9pm).

❼ Hoxton Square

Jugglers and fire-eaters can sometimes be seen practising in Hoxton Square, following a tradition in the area from Victorian times. Artworks are often on show here, too. Overlooked by the White Cube Gallery, this is art-student land, and buzzy places, such as the Hoxton Bar and Grill and the Breakfast Club, fit easily into former Victorian premises built for light industry.

Some say it is one of the oldest squares in London – it was laid out by Samuel Blewitt and Robert Hackshaw in 1683. A blue plaque at No 1 on the southwest corner shows where the physician James Parkinson lived and practised, and in 1817 first described the disease that bears his name. On the north side is the primary school and former Augustinian friary of St Monica, now partly occupied by Training for Life's Hoxton Apprentice, a restaurant that takes on the long-term unemployed. The friary church is still active. It has a light and delicate interior, with wooden windows and arches designed, like the whole priory, by Edward Welby Pugin, son of the better known Augustus, the great Gothic revivalist.
Hoxton Square, N1 6NT. Old Street tube.

❽ White Cube Gallery

The showroom that put the East End firmly on the art map has just two gallery rooms – one more than the original White Cube Gallery in St James's, now closed. Dealer Jay Jopling made his name in the West End by putting on one-person shows in which a single work was sometimes the only offering. When he took on the property in Hoxton Square, he employed architects M.R.J. Rundell & Associates to design the galleries and add three upper floors. It opened in 2000 and promoted the group who have come to be known as the YBAs (Young British Artists), plus not-so-young East Enders Gilbert and George. In 2006, Jopling opened another gallery back in St James's, in Mason's Yard and a third is to open in Bermondsey.
48 Hoxton Square, N1 6PB. Old Street tube.

❾ Columbia Road Flower Market

From 4am on Sunday morning, when stalls start to fill with fresh flowers, the most colourful market in London seems little more than a lane. Cut flowers, bedding plants, annuals, perennials, pot plants, bulbs, shrubs, trees, all reasonably priced and beautifully laid out, begin to scent the air. By mid morning it can take up to half an hour to walk its length, although it's only a few hundred yards long. Nobody is in a hurry to pass by, and it gives the diehard Cockney traders the chance to go through their routines – 'Half what you'd pay in Marks & Spencer, which is where I nicked 'em.' 'Here's a big one – everyone likes a big one.' Sellers have their own nurseries, or they import from Holland and elsewhere, and some have been trading here all their working lives.

The market's first incarnation was when the richest heiress in England, the saintly Angela Burdett-Coutts, used her banking family's millions to sweep away slums and build the indoor Columbia Market, which had so many towers, turrets and pinnacles that it was compared to the Houses of Parliament. But it didn't work out. The costermongers were happier out in the streets, their market moving from Saturday to Sunday to take account of the increasing Jewish population. Today, buskers add to the festive atmosphere, pubs and cafés are busy, and on the pavements between the stalls and the chirpy independent shops there is barely room to nibble a cupcake.
Columbia Road, E2 7RG. Bethnal Green tube. Sunday 4am–2pm.

EAST END

⑩ V&A Museum of Childhood

This fact that this wonderful purpose-built museum, which opened in 1872, is devoted to children is something of an accident. Following the popular success of the Great Exhibition and the South Kensington Museums (see page 118), it was decided to educate and enlighten other parts of London with the overflow of treasures. The result was a large, simple museum overseen by Colonel Henry Scott, a Royal Engineer, who had just completed the Royal Albert Hall. Rising to two floors of galleries held up by iron pillars, the building is exceptionally light and spacious. External murals were made with the help of female students at the South Kensington museum's mosaic class, and fish-scale pattern floor mosaics were the work of women prisoners in Woking jail.

In the 1920s, in an attempt to appeal to the large numbers of young visitors, the curator Arthur Sabin began to collect child-related items. Over the years these increased and in 1974 the V&A, under Roy Strong, completed the task by sending all the children's objects from its collection to Bethnal Green, and renaming this the Museum of Childhood. Toys, costumes and games date back several centuries, while zoetropes and computer games also feature. A large 18th-century Venetian puppet theatre, used by the nobility to entertain guests, is among many prized items.
Cambridge Heath Road, E2 9PA. Bethnal Green tube.

⑪ Geffrye Museum

From hall to parlour to drawing room, the story of middle-class Londoners' domestic life is told in the handsome almshouses built by Sir Robert Geffrye, Lord Mayor of London. Many of London's almshouses were created for guild members, and this one was built in 1715 for the Worshipful Company of Ironmongers, of which Geffrye was Master. The striking redbrick building has two wings, and the decorated and furnished rooms show developing customs and tastes. Contemporary paintings and newspapers add to the flavour, and audiophones provide eyewitness accounts of times when domestic skills were thought of as a 'science'.

Two rooms are furnished to show the bare comfort of the almshouse residents in the 18th and 19th centuries. A new section added on the east side has 20th-century living rooms, from Edwardian and Art Deco to 1950s rooms and a 1990s loft, with a temporary exhibition space beneath. The café has been moved here from the Garden Reading Room, an intimate wooden conservatory at the back of the chapel, which has a contemporary mural by Jonathan Early. Outside, by Hoxton station, a series of gardens are laid out chronologically, going back to Elizabethan times. Geffrye is buried in the grounds.
Kingsland Road, E2 8EA. Hoxton rail.

⑫ E. Pellicci

An East End café with a Grade II listing is rare indeed. It followed a visit by English Heritage inspectors in 2005, who waxed lyrical about E. Pellicci's 'stylish shop front of custard Vitrolite panels, steel frame and lettering as well as a rich Deco-style marquetry panelled interior, altogether representing an architecturally strong and increasingly rare example of the intact and stylish Italian café that flourished in London in the inter-war years'. The Kray brothers, who frequented it and were 'always respectful', might have phrased it differently.

The café has been run by the same family since it was opened by Priamo and Elide Pellicci, from Tuscany, in 1900. In 1946, Elide (the E of the café's name), by then a widow, ordered the marquetry to cover the counter and walls, and it still adds to the warmth of the place. When their son Nevio, who was born above the shop in 1925, died in 2008, his horse-drawn cortege brought traffic to a standstill and there was a glowing obituary in *The Times*. His son, also Nevio, now runs the café, where shared tables are a bit of a squash, but everyone is made to feel welcome.
332 Bethnal Green Road, E2 0AG. Bethnal Green tube.

⑬ Whitechapel Bell Foundry

Appropriately enough, a bell rings when visitors step through the front door of the world's best-known bell foundry. What is surprising is that the Dickensian looking Foundry House can have produced such monsters as the 13½-tonne Big Ben. The wood template for the hour bell of the great clock of Westminster hangs like a proscenium curtain over the front door of the Georgian building. A quaint museum room immediately inside gives a history of the company, with cuttings, models, diagrams and examples, including hand bells. *Guinness World Records* lists the foundry as the world's oldest continuously manufacturing company. Since 1570 it has produced St Paul's clock bells, Bow Bells, America's Liberty Bell and, recently, the 9/11 Bell, a gift from the City of London to the people of New York, installed in Trinity Church on Wall Street. The casting is done in the foundry

WHITECHAPEL BELL FOUNDRY

at the rear, where craftsmen shape the moulds and fill them with the molten copper and tin that has been heated to more than 11,000°C (19,832°F). *34 Whitechapel Road, E1 1DY. Aldgate East tube. Free museum, pre-book tours.*

⑭ Whitechapel Art Gallery

A reputation for cutting-edge art and a loyal local following has put the Whitechapel Gallery at the cultural heart of the East End. Canon Barnett and his wife Henrietta were its founders, beginning with an annual art exhibition in a schoolroom. In 1901, more than 200,000 people attended the opening of the idiosyncratic Art Nouveau building designed by Harrison Townsend. Works by Constable, Hogarth and the Pre-Raphaelites were loaned for the first show. In 1939, when Picasso's *Guernica* was exhibited, the price of entry was the visitors' boots, which were sent to support Republican soldiers on the front in Spain. The gallery introduced Londoners to Pop Art and Jackson Pollock, and to David Hockney, who had his first major exhibition here.

In 2009 it almost doubled in size after taking over Whitechapel library, allowing the gallery to stretch over the entrance to Aldgate East station. *77–82 Whitechapel Road, E1 7QX. Aldgate East tube.*

⑮ Wilton's Music Hall

Despite crumbling plaster, a leaky roof and a boarded-up second floor, the shows go on at Wilton's. This delightful old music hall has seen trouble all its life. John Wilton built it in 1850, but fire regulations introduced some 30 years later forced it to close. Methodists took it over, and ran it for the next 70 years. They made it very much part of the community, feeding striking dockers in 1889, providing a safe haven during the Battle of Cable Street in 1936, when local people clashed with police while trying to stop Oswald Mosley's fascist march, and finally turning it into a rag-sorting centre not long before it was abandoned. In 1964 John Betjeman led a campaign for its salvation and it was spared the wrecker's ball, but it wasn't until 1997 that it reopened. Fiona Shaw's rendering of *The Waste Land* was the first performance here in 117 years, a tour de force repeated in 2010 on the theatre's 150th anniversary. Architecturally, it is a 'giant pub hall' with a gallery on three sides supported by spiral, cast-iron pillars thin enough not to interfere with the view. The patina of its history is clearly visible, including scorch marks on the ceiling from the old gas chandelier. *1 Grace's Alley, E1 8JB. Tower Hill, Aldgate East tube.*

The River Thames: waterborne history

A trip on a riverboat in company with a joke-cracking skipper is a good starting point for a look at London. Modern innovation and times past can be viewed in equal measure.

London grew up on gravel banks, and only since Victorian times have the river's meanderings been fully contained. In fact, it twists and turns so much that landmarks, such as Canary Wharf, the Gherkin and the Shard, seem to be at first on one side of the river, then the other as you draw nearer.

Some 210 miles long, the Thames reaches London 40 miles from the sea, yet the water is still tidal and salty here, ebbing and flowing so fast that it's sometimes possible to watch it rise and fall. On a spring day in 1952, when the tide was out, a 6ft 3in peer of the realm, Lord Noel Buxton, attempted to

One of the largest moveable flood defences in the world, the Thames Barrier is closed when the surging river threatens to engulf the city.

THAMES BARRIER

prove it was shallow enough to walk across at Westminster. He was out of his depth before he was halfway there.

Until Westminster Bridge was opened, London Bridge was the only crossing point in the city. It supported houses and was built on piers with narrow gaps between them through which the water would rush. Part of its first stone arch remains on the north side of the current bridge outside St Magnus the Martyr, where there is a 4m (13ft) long model of the old bridge. Downriver from London Bridge the tideway is known as the Pool of London, and this is where the city's maritime history begins. In the Upper Pool, between London Bridge and Tower Bridge, the Romans had their port; for 1,000 years the city's fishing fleet docked at Billingsgate, where golden fish weathervanes sparkle on the old market roof, and the 363m (1,190ft) façade of the Custom House, last rebuilt by Robert Smirke, shines brilliant white. Outside the commercial City, the prized riverside was occupied by monasteries and royal palaces, stretching from Richmond in the west to Greenwich in the east. When the monasteries were torn down during the Reformation, their wealth helped to fund the English Renaissance of Elizabeth I. During her reign, explorers carried letters addressed to 'all, kings, princes, rulers, judges and governors of the earth', and the royal docks at Deptford and Woolwich built the privateers. So began the global plundering that would continue to enrich London for centuries.

As the Empire expanded, so did the docks. By the 19th century, they stretched downriver from Tower Bridge, covering over 24ha (60 acres) and importing everything under the sun. The Industrial Revolution had started it, ending ships' reliance on wind, and harnessing steam to haul up anchors, pump water, build docks and drive cranes and trains. With it came the worst filth and poverty the city had seen. Jacob's Island in Bermondsey, just east of Shad Thames, was as bad as it got. This was where Bill Sykes met his fitting end in Dickens' *Oliver Twist*: '... dirt-besmeared walls and decaying foundations, every repulsive lineament of poverty, every loathsome indication of filth, rot and garbage ...'.

Reinvention and renewal

By the 20th century, London had become the world's largest port – 291ha (720 acres) of water, 35 miles of quayside. 1,000 ships came and went every week. And then came the Second World War. The Thames provided the flight path for German bombers; every single dock was set alight on one night in September 1940, and 250,000 bombs rained down.

After the war what life was left in the docks began to slip away downriver to large container ports in Essex and Kent, but new opportunities opened up for water sports and leisure centres. Today, the Thames Path runs along both banks, allowing walkers to appreciate the river and its past, especially along the South Bank. Riverside pubs, from Strand on the Green to the old haunts of Wapping and Rotherhithe, continue to be among the most attractive in the city.

The emphasis now is on a greener river. Salmon ladders are positioned upstream by the locks. More than 100 fish species have been recorded since the millennium, and seals have reached as far upriver as Richmond. But the great empty stretches of tideway, viewed from Tower Bridge, from the new roof walkway above the O2 Arena, or perhaps from a cable car beside it, seem to be yearning for big ships to be sailing on their waters again.

⑯ St Katharine Docks

Hard by Tower Bridge, with high walls originally built to prevent pilfering and now blocking out traffic noise, this 4.5ha (11 acre) site is the work of the engineer Thomas Telford. Completed in 1828, it took the place of 1,250 homes and the medieval St Katharine's hospital, now a charitable foundation in Limehouse.

Just as Covent Garden reinvented the use of abandoned market space, so St Katharine pioneered the use of docks for modern leisure. The city harbour is an attractive place to visit after the heavy toll taken on the emotions by the Tower of London. Harmonious yellow-brick warehouses stand close to the water in three basins with 200 berths. West Quay is where timeless Thames sailing barges moor. City Quay is the parking lot for gin palaces, overlooked by modern apartments. An 18th-century tea warehouse has been rebuilt on Marble Quay as the three-storey flower-decked Dickens Inn. A lock leading to the Thames provides interest with marine traffic; it also prevented large ships from entering. Vessels would tie up in the river and lighters would fetch their ivory, spices, rum, tea and sugar, marble and indigo as well as apes, peacocks and other exotica that helped to make London a centre for global trade. In 1921 explorer Ernest Shackleton sailed from here aboard the creaky *Quest*, on his last, one-way, Antarctic voyage.

On Fridays there is a food market, and some of the Thames barges are for hire. Every summer they race in a match covering around 40 miles near the Thames estuary.
50 St Katharine's Way, E1W 1LA. Tower Hill tube.

⑰ River Police Museum

After more than 200 years of action, tragedy and adventure, Britain's oldest police force has plenty of material for its small museum. The place is crammed. Uniforms, medals and hardware on show include boarding pikes and cutlasses from early encounters with river pirates.

Around half the cargo that arrived in the highly congested Pool of London was going astray when the West India Merchants and Planters Committee got together with a London magistrate Dr Patrick Calquhoun to set up the river police force in 1798. Recruited from seamen and lightermen, the officers rowed open galleys, patrolling the river day and night, and in those violent times they frequently came under attack.

In 1839, the force was absorbed into the newly formed Metropolitan Police, as the Thames Division. Now known as the Marine Support Unit, it is responsible for policing all London's waterways, and for rescue work: on average, 50 people are found drowned each year. Around 90 officers operate from the original police station among the riverside wharfs of Wapping High

ST KATHARINE DOCKS

Street. The carpenter's workshop, where the wooden boats used to be looked after, has been converted to house the museum. Visits are by written request. Police vessels, mainly inflatables, are now based in a large white boatyard on the east side of Wapping Steps. A small patch of green gives a view of their activity, and of the force's pier behind the police station, where a blue lamp hangs reassuringly over the gangway. *Wapping Police Station, 98 Wapping High Street, E1W 2NE. Wapping rail. Visits by prior arrangement.*

⓲ Prospect of Whitby

From the bowsprit on which the pub sign hangs to the lamps on the terrace, London's oldest riverside pub reeks of authenticity. The whole place is built around massive masts, some with sail hoops still in place. The main room has the original flagstone floor and the bar is clinker-built with barrels, topped with a pewter counter. The views over the Thames are panoramic.

Dating from 1520 or earlier, the pub was at first known as the Devil's Tavern. Following a fire it was rebuilt and named after the *Prospect*, a collier from Whitby that berthed here. There are portraits of former regulars, among them J.M.W. Turner, Charles Dickens and the diarist Samuel Pepys. A gimmicky noose hanging out over the river is a reminder that Judge Jeffries came here to watch his victims swing at Execution Dock. In search of such tales, sawdust and a bit of East End rough-and-readiness, celebrities of the 1950s and '60s made their way here – Princess Margaret, Richard Burton, Liz Taylor, Paul Newman. The sawdust has gone, the rough edges are smoothed over, but the ghosts remain. *57 Wapping Wall, E1W 3SH. Wapping rail.*

⓳ Wapping Project

This old hydraulic power station, a redbrick structure standing alone opposite the Prospect of Whitby, looks much as it must have done when it was built in 1890, but now it stages site-specific installations, photographic exhibitions, music and dance. A restaurant and bar occupy the Engine and Turbine Houses, where tables are set among the dull green hulks of worn-out machinery. Exhibition and performance space, which can be flooded, is provided by the Boiler and Filter Houses beyond. A staircase leads to the roof and there's a bookshop in a greenhouse. The Project sees itself as mixing cuisine and culture, 'an idea consistently in transition'. *Wapping Wall, E1W 3ST. Wapping rail.*

⓴ St George's in the East

'The drug addicts' dream' was how architectural critic Ian Nairn described Nicholas Hawksmoor's church, one of six he built in London, this one around 1730. It was later given a dark side in Peter Ackroyd's 1985 novel *Hawksmoor*, in which a young lad is sacrificed and buried in the church's foundations.

The tower is idiosyncratic, 49m (160ft) tall with an octagon inspired by Ely cathedral's, topped by Roman sacrificial altars. Four pepperpot towers protrude from the roof. Each of the Church's doors was designed for a different class of worshipper – where they entered determined where they sat. During the Second World War the church was bombed and burnt out and now the tower acts as an entrance arch. The visitor steps through into a courtyard, open to the skies. The stairs in the turrets that once led to the upper galleries lead to flats, and a smaller place of worship occupies the east end of the nave, going into the apse, where Venetian glass mosaics from 1880 have been restored. This innovative modification was brought about in 1964 after much effort, the by architect Arthur Bailey. A Montessori School and a ministerial training centre occupy the crypt. The former graveyard, lined with tombstones, is a pleasant park. *16 Cannon Street, E1 0BH. Shadwell rail and DLR.*

㉑ Cable Street Mural

The Battle of Cable Street is depicted as a passionate fracas in this spectacular mural. The turmoil seems to be taking place in a tumble dryer, the figures spinning around the side wall of St George's Town Hall at the entrance to St George's Gardens. Fists fly, chamber pots are emptied from upper windows, leaflets are scattered, marbles roll beneath police horses' hoofs, and Hitler, trouserless, is helplessly out of control.

'They Shall Not Pass' a banner declares. And they did not. The battle occurred one October Sunday in 1936 when Oswald Mosley, leader of the British Union of Fascists, attempted to lead his blackshirts on a provocative march through a predominantly Jewish part of the East End, protected by 10,000 police. Ethnic groups were joined by socialists and communists to halt them in their tracks and a running battle with police ensued. Mosley abandoned the march. War with Germany was declared in 1939 and eight months later Mosley was interned. The conflict continues. The mural was begun in 1976 by a local artist, Dave Binnington. Right-wing vandals have several times caused it to need repainting. *236 Cable Street, E1 0BL. Shadwell DLR.*

ISLE OF DOGS

㉒ St Peter's Barge

London's only floating church is a former Dutch barge moored at West India Quay, opposite the Museum of Docklands. Among all the new developments, no prayer house has been built for the burgeoning working population of around 100,000. Most of the area lies within the parish of St Anne's, the distinctive Hawksmoor church in Limehouse, which began outreach meetings in local wine bars, but had no permanent home in this high-priced part of town. A solution was provided by the 12m (39ft) barge, which was refitted in the Netherlands and sailed here in 2003.
West India Quay car park, Hertsmere Road, E14 4AL. West India Quay DLR.

㉓ Traffic Light Tree

Unsuspecting motorists are liable to hit the brakes when they first encounter the Traffic Light Tree. Set on a roundabout, the 8m (26ft) cluster of 75 traffic lights flashes randomly, creating a crisis between stop and go. The installation is by a French artist Pierre Vivant and might be read as a commentary on the proliferation of street furniture, although he says, 'the changing pattern of the lights reflects the never-ending rhythm of surrounding domestic, financial and commercial activities'. The original idea had been to link the lights with Stock Exchange activity, but this proved too complicated.
Junction of Heron Bank Quay, Marsh Wall and Westferry Road. Canary Wharf DLR.

㉔ *Great Eastern* Slipway

Massive timbers on which the ship *Great Eastern* was launched are a legacy of Isambard Kingdom Brunel, an engineer who always did things on a gargantuan scale. For six years John Scott Russell's Napier Yard on the Isle of Dogs rang to the hammering of iron as the biggest ship in the world was built broadside on to the river – had it launched bow first it would have smacked into the Greenwich bank opposite. Large crowds gathered on both banks and on the water to watch the launch in 1857 – the ship got stuck and a worker was killed in the attempt to move it down the slipway. It was finally floated three months later, bankrupting the shipyard. Two days before her maiden voyage, Brunel had a stroke while on deck, and he died ten days later.

Powered by side wheels, screw propeller and sails, the *Great Eastern* went on to lay the first transatlantic cable before being retired to Liverpool, and used as a music hall. Some of the timber 'ways', excavated in 1984, are preserved between a warehouse and a modern housing estate, along with lengths of hefty chain used to restrain the ship in her final rush to the water. At low tide on the foreshore, more slipway timbers can be seen.
Napier Avenue, E14 3QB. Mudchute DLR.

㉕ Mudchute Farm and Park

The largest of three East London farms has the skyscraping giants of Canary Wharf as a backdrop, yet it still has an out-of-town feel. Mudchute gets its name from the spoils that were dumped here during the excavation of Millwall docks in the 1860s. The area was left to grow wild, or to use for grazing or as brick fields.

In the 1970s, after the docks had decamped, plans were drawn up to build high-rise flats on the site, but a local outcry resulted in the establishment of the 13ha (32 acre) farm and park. Llamas, Oxford Down sheep and rare Irish Moiled cows are among more than 200 animals kept here. A riding school and pony club add to the country air.
Mudchute Farm, Pier Street, E14 3HP. Mudchute DLR. Closed on Monday.

㉖ Canary Wharf Underground Station

Of all the new stations in London, both overground and underground, none is as impressive as Canary Wharf. Like an insect-eating plant, the curved glass canopies at ground level devour around 60,000 commuters a day, swallowing them into the Jubilee Line below. Grey steel pillars, endless moving stairs and an enormous station hall that dwarfs the rush-hour workers, make it seem straight out of Fritz Lang's 1927 expressionist film *Metropolis*. Sir Norman Foster's tube station is a match for Cesar Pelli's nearby building, 1 Canada Square – in fact, at 223m (732ft) long, the concourse is just 21m (68ft) shorter than the tower.
Canary Wharf, E14 4DH. Canary Wharf tube.

㉗ West India Docks

These docks have been overtaken by the 21st century. On one side of the most northerly of the original three is Cabot Square, looking fresh from the architects' drawing boards; on the other, the yellow brick warehouses on West India Quay have been turned into a hotel, cinema, restaurants and bars. The Museum of London Docklands is here, too. Outside is a statue of

MUDCHUTE FARM AND PARK

Robert Milligan, under whose supervision the docks were built in 1802. His father owned a sugar plantation in Jamaica. The story of the docks, their social history and their heyday at the centre of world trade, is told in the museum. Here, too, is a record of the Blitz, and of the docks' decline, when container ports downriver made them redundant.
Warehouse, E14 4AL. West India Quay DLR.

㉘ East India Dock Basin

A rare salt marsh and nature reserve lies by the Thames opposite the O2 Arena. The tide brings both salt and fresh water into the East India Dock Basin, and the dock quay has hides for birdwatchers. Bird boxes are positioned among the trees by the riverfront, from where the panorama takes in the Greenwich Peninsula. A little way to the west is Virginia Quay and the Settlers Monument, commemorating the founders of Jamestown, who sailed from here to start the British colony in North America.

The Basin is a remnant of the East India Docks that once covered 12ha (30 acres). They were built for East Indiamen, the largest vessels using the Thames at the beginning of the 19th century. Owned by the East India Company, they brought high-value cargoes, including silk, tea, wine and spices. These days, the east entrance to the Basin is through the Salome Gates. Crafted by the sculptor Sir Anthony Caro, they are made of steel flats, ladder, chain and shackles from a shipbreaker's yard. To the west, just beyond East India DLR station, is a long stretch of 6m (20ft) high brick wall, built to prevent theft from the docks and now running down two sides of a gated business estate. A prettied-up stretch of canal, with sculptures, is all that is left of the Import Dock, but street names such as Clove Crescent and Saffron Avenue are reminders of its trade. Tower Hamlets Town Hall is in Mulberry Place, named after the prefabricated D-Day floating harbours built here.
Aspen Way, E14 9QS. East India DLR.

㉙ Longplayer

In the former lamp room of London's only lighthouse, at Bow Creek at the mouth of the Lea, a musical composition for Tibetan singing bowls and gongs will play for a thousand years. It began at midnight on December 31, 2009, and is remixed so that no sequence will be repeated until the end of December 31 2999, when it will begin all over again. The whole area is an arts space and has a breezy, seaside air.
64 Orchard Place, E14 0JW. East India DLR. Longplayer is open at weekends.

BOW & HACKNEY

30 Ragged School Museum

Pupils sit obediently at desks on which the names of predecessors have been scratched, writing as they are told with chalk on slates. The straitlaced teacher, in Victorian dress, has a blackboard and easel, and a dunce's cap for anyone who gives the wrong answer. In the kitchen, pupils help prepare their free, if not very appetising, meals. They are lucky to get anything at all. The Ragged School Museum shows what school was like in Victorian times.

Between 1887 and 1908, thousands of children from impoverished homes were educated in these former warehouses beside Regent's Canal. The Ragged School Union had been founded half a century earlier as an umbrella for a number of Christian-based charitable institutions, offering free education to the poor. Thomas Barnardo started this one. He had been on his way from his native Dublin to China to become a missionary when he stopped off in London and saw the appalling conditions that people endured. That was in 1866, when cholera had just claimed 3,000 lives. By the time the school closed, the government had set up Local Education Authorities to provide free schooling. As well as classrooms, the museum has a collection of items from pens and inkwells to letters and storybooks, plus artifacts that would have been found in the home or in the workplace at that time.
46–50 Copperfield Road, E3 4RR. Wednesday and Thursday 10am–5pm; first Sunday of the month 2–5pm. No booking needed.

31 Three Mills Island

The East End's most attractive group of industrial buildings is a welcome and unexpected sight. It occupies part of an 8ha (20-acre) island on the Bow Back Rivers, a complex network of waterways on the River Lea (also spelt Lee) and an ideal spot for watermills – eight were recorded in the Domesday Book, and two survive.

A Saxon mill once stood on the site of the Grade I listed House Mill, perhaps the largest tidal mill in the world. Grain was ground here for flour and for alcohol. Four large waterwheels can be seen, as well as six pairs of millstones and other mechanical parts, in the timber-framed building. The mill trapped the river at high tide so the wheels turned as the water ebbed. New locks on the waterways mean that this is no longer possible, but in 2011 the River Lea Tidal Mill Trust received a Lottery Fund grant that will go towards restoring the waterwheels to generate hydroelectricity with additional turbines. Tours are conducted on Sundays, and entrance is through the adjoining Miller's House, where there is a café.

Opposite, and more prominent with oast cowls and a clock tower, is the Grade II listed Clock Mill from 1817. This is now part of 3 Mills Studios, London's largest film and TV complex, which occupy all of the other buildings and include a mocked-up prison block. In 2010 these came into the hands of the Olympic Park Legacy Company, providing an ideal space for much of the creative work behind the Games.

From Three Mills Green, behind the mill buildings, there is the unmistakable view of Abbey Mill Pumping Station, looking like an opulent Byzantine church. Built by Sir Joseph Bazalgette, it is a match for the one at Crossness (see page 191).
Mill Lane, E3 3DU. Bromley by Bow tube.

32 Victoria Park

'The earth is the Lord's and all that thereon is' – and it is not much to ask for a bit of it on which to breathe fresh air. Some 30,000 petitioners demanded a public park in this overcrowded, unhealthy part of Victorian London. Their demand was met, and other gifts came, too, such as a Chinese pagoda, lumps of old London Bridge and, courtesy of the philanthropic Angela Burdett-Coutts, a sumptuous fountain, with four clocks, to ensure clean drinking water, and the inscription proclaiming the earth as the Lord's.

The 'people's park', or 'Vicky Park' as it is affectionately known, comprises nearly 121ha (300 acres) of dappled, tree-lined avenues, springy grass, lakes, canalsides and sporty corners. Chartists demonstrated here in 1848, three years after it opened, striking dockers came in 1889, but today the park is peaceful, ideal for picnics and summer festivals.

It stretches from Bethnal Green to Hackney Wick, and is cut in two by Grove Road. The smaller, landscaped western side is reached from Bethnal Green up Approach Road to Bonnor's Gate. This part of the park was previously Bonnor's Fields and belonged to the Bishops of London, who were lords of Stepney Manor. Bishop Bonnor burned heretics here. The stone Dogs of Alcibiades inside the gates are copies of a 2nd-century Roman statue of a Molassian hound, ancestor of the mastiff. Colourful barges are moored on Regent's Canal, which runs along the south side and is one reason why this has been dubbed the East End's Regent's Park. The Pavilion café by the large lake is the place to watch the world go by.

The larger area, east of Grove Road, is for concerts and for sport – tennis, cricket and bowls. The three ponds are, traditionally, for paddling, angling and for the Victoria Model Steamboat Club, which has been meeting at the boathouse since 1904. Sunday regattas begin at Easter. *Grove Road, E9. Bethnal Green tube.*

33 The Clowns' Church

'We are fools for Christ' declares a banner in the Joseph Grimaldi corner of Holy Trinity Church in Dalston. On the first Sunday of February each year, at the end of the Christmas pantomime and circus season, clowns gather to pay tribute to Grimaldi and other clowns past. Born in 1778 into a theatrical family, Grimaldi first appeared on the London stage at the age of two, and he is credited with inventing the white-faced clown and the pantomime. Lord Byron was among his many fans. Grimaldi died in 1837 and was buried at St James's Church on Pentonville Road, where the annual clowns' services began just after the Second World War.

In 1978, St James's was pulled down. The churchyard was renamed Joseph Grimaldi Park, and the grave is preserved inside railings. The clowns' service transferred to this Victorian church, 2.5 miles away, where a stained-glass window commemorates Grimaldi's life. Egg-shaped ceramic clown faces are on show, each one registered with Clown International. Once, the faces were painted on real eggs, which were broken on the death of the clown. Around 60 clowns gather each year, putting on their slap in the church hall before the service and entertaining families afterwards.
Beechwood Road, E8 3DY. Dalston Junction rail.

THREE MILLS ISLAND

34 Hackney Empire

'No more the Hackney Empire/Shall find us in its stalls/When on the limelit crooner/The thankful curtain falls/And soft electric lamplight/Reveals the gilded walls.' Sir John Betjeman's sentimental cockney amorist is not the only one with a soft spot for this dear old theatre, although it's surprising that such a name has survived into the 21st century. The Hackney Empire has an undeniable Victorian ring to it, and from its façade, the theatre looks just the place for a Saturday night knees-up with Marie Lloyd, or a chuckle with young Charlie Chaplin.

The work of the theatre architect Frank Matcham, the 1901 building has always instilled local pride – it was voted the landmark to represent the borough for the 2012 Olympics. It has served as a TV studio and bingo hall, and survived threats of closure that were fought by Harold Pinter, Sir Alan Sugar and every comedian from the 1980s alternative comedy set, who made their names here. In 2005, a modern extension added a studio and pub, but at heart it is still a fine Victorian auditorium that can seat 1,300 people who enjoy a laugh on a Saturday night.
291 Mare Street, E8 1EJ. Hackney Central rail.

35 Sutton House

Life in Tudor times seems to have been comfortable for a royal courtier, judging by Ralph Sadlier's redbrick house. The remodelled Georgian frontage hides the Tudor core, the leaded windows, panelled rooms, carved fireplace and paved courtyard that make it a welcoming home.

'In the cellar are the real traces of the past, like the building's flesh and blood,' wrote Hilary Mantel about her research on Sadlier for her novel *Wolf Hall*. 'Tudor bricks, small rosy bricks, made right on the building site from the earth near Hackney Brook.' Examining the marks on the handmade fired earth, she recalls, 'It was when I saw the grass stalk, the dog's paw print, that I began to sense the spring of 1535, when Thomas More was still alive and pearls were still warm on the neck of Anne Boleyn.' The house's fortunes have waxed and waned as it slipped through the hands of clergy, merchants and the headmaster of a boys' school where the politician and author Edward Bulwer-Lytton was a pupil. In the mid 1980s, after being used for 20 years or so by Clive Jenkins' ASTMS trade union, it fell empty and attracted squatters, before being restored by the National Trust.
2–4 Homerton High Street, E9 6JQ. Hackney Central rail.

36 Hackney Marshes

'Wiv a ladder and some glasses/You could see to 'Ackney Marshes/If it wasn't for the 'ouses in between.' Gus Elen's music-hall song explains why the marshes aren't exactly a landmark; now they are hidden behind Olympic buildings, too. But when they can be seen, they seem to go on for ever. The River Lea's marshy valley stretches from Hackney to Walthamstow and Tottenham.

Hackney Marshes are the home of Sunday football – a line of goalpost after goalpost retreats into the distance. On 60 pitches and 121ha (300 acres) more than 100 games are played on a winter weekend. Hockey, rugby and cricket are played here, too, and a kite-flying festival is held in summer. The marshes have long been an area for sport. Leyton Orient and Tottenham Hotspur both started on the road to fame on these level playing fields. Before football there was hare coursing, game shooting and bull baiting. The pitches were made possible by the 19th-century canal system, which tamed the River Lea and ended frequent flooding. The marshes are now part of the Lee Valley Regional Park, which embraces the Waterworks Nature Reserve, a wildlife sanctuary with a visitor centre and hides. More than a quarter of all dragonflies in Britain are found here.

Nearby Walthamstow Marshes are natural wetlands and an important wildlife site where rare-breed cattle graze in summer. The air was first disturbed by the sound of machinery in 1909 when Sir Edwin Alliott Verdon Roe took off in the first all-British powered plane; a blue plaque on the railway arches marks his workshop.
Hackney Marshes, E5. Hackney Wick rail.
Walthamstow Marshes, E10. Clapton rail.

AT HEART IT IS STILL A FINE VICTORIAN AUDITORIUM
HACKNEY EMPIRE

FARTHER EAST

③⑦ Fatwalk, Lee Valley Regional Park

One of the greatest benefits of the Olympic Games has been the creation of the Lee Valley Regional Park, which has opened up East London's waterways to leisure. Its central spine is the Fatwalk, a 26 mile riverside path from the Thames across Three Mills Island, past the Olympic site and the Marshes, to the White Water Centre in Waltham Cross (created for the Olympic river sports), via Ware in Hertfordshire. Its 405ha (1,000 acres) take in Waltham Abbey in Essex, five nature reserves and two farms.

Clearing and planting has been going on all along the way, and signposts have gone up. New and refurbished bridges, and attractive locks and keepers' houses, such as the one at City Mill Lock, add to the walk's interest. A new lock system means that the waterway above Three Mills Island is no longer tidal.

The purpose of clearing the canals had been to allow bulk material to be transported to and from the Olympic site, and in the course of dredging, parts of the monumental Euston station arch, which was demolished in the 1960s, came to light. In the end, land transport was used, but the River Lea navigation channels can now be used by barges for the first time in 50 years, and canal boats can link up, via a broad, straight shortcut known as the Limehouse Cut, to Regent's Canal.
Marigold Road, N17. Angel Road rail, Tottenham Hale tube.

③⑧ William Morris Gallery

William Morris, the great Arts & Crafts pioneer, was a Walthamstow boy. When he was 13, his father died and the family moved from Woodford Hall to the smaller Water House, today set in a park and by no means a modest residence. In fact, the home where William lived with his eight siblings – he was the oldest boy and had two older sisters – is a beautiful Georgian mansion, dating from around 1750. It is not difficult to imagine the young William dressed in armour and brandishing his sword as he galloped about the estate. His boyhood knightly garb is among the possessions on display in this gallery, the only one devoted to the life and work of Morris and his Pre-Raphaelite companions. The large collection includes fabrics, wallpapers, painted tiles, books and sketches. The Gallery was opened in 1950 by the then prime minister, Clement Attlee, 1st Earl Attlee of Walthamstow, and it reopens in mid 2012 after a major overhaul.
Lloyd Park, Forest Road, E17 4PP. Walthamstow tube.

③⑨ Valence House Museum

The best place to learn the story of Barking and Dagenham is in a manor house that is itself a museum piece. The ancient, moated building has undergone many alterations since its first mention in 1269. The Valence estate was the largest in Dagenham and takes its name from Agnes de Valence, who lived here in 1291. Royal blood, both French and English, coursed through her veins; she was a half sister of Henry III. Her father-in-law was John de Baliol, founder of Baliol College, Oxford, and on her death the property passed to her brother, Aylmer, Earl of Pembroke, who founded Pembroke College, Cambridge. The last residents were the May family, farmers from Devon, who were here for 40 years, bred shire horses and grew tomatoes – the first in the district to do so commercially. The house was compulsorily purchased from the Mays just after the First World War, and today the pristine white timber-framed museum tells the story not just of the manor house, but of the whole area.
Becontree Avenue, Essex RM8 3HT. Becontree tube.

④⓪ Eastbury Manor

Local lore has it that the Gunpowder Plot was hatched at Eastbury Manor, and its supporters watched for the explosion at Westminster, 10 miles away, from the top of the tower. However, that may have been a slander on the succession of Catholics who lived here. The brick-built Tudor gentry house is in the shape of an H, with lofty chimneys and a cobbled courtyard. It was completed around 1573 for a City merchant, Clement Sisley, 32 years after the dissolution of Barking Abbey, owners of the property. The last remnant of the powerful Abbey, the Curfew Tower, stands less than a mile away, by St Margaret's parish church.

Outwardly, the house has changed little, although it was in a poor state of repair, and part used for livestock, when the National Trust took it over in 1918. Some frescoes have been restored, notably the fishing scenes in the Painted Room. The spiral wooden staircase to the turret is a rarity, as is the attic, where exposed beams show the construction of the roof. The Great Hall has an original brick fireplace, and is now used for weddings. In the walled garden are bee-holes, from which honey was extracted for the family. There are about 0.6ha (1½ acres) of garden, and the square in which it stands surrounded by modern housing creates a kind of tarmac moat.
Eastbury Square, IG11 9SN. Upney tube. Open Monday and Tuesday.

The marathon route to 2012

The London Marathon turns some 35,000 runners into Olympians. From Blackheath, they follow a route that takes a tour of the sights and finishes in front of Buckingham Palace.

Marathons have been held in London every year since the London Olympic Games in 1908. The long-distance race had become a modern Olympic sport in Athens 12 years earlier. This was an appropriate starting point, since the original race celebrated Pheidippides bringing news of victory over the Persians at the battle of Marathon in the summer of 490 BC. On arrival in the Greek city, the messenger is said to have made his announcement, 'We have won,' and promptly expired. The distance of the first race in Athens, and at the intervening Olympics, had been approximately 25 miles, but it wasn't a finite length until the Games reached London for the first time in 1908. Here Jack Andrew of the Polytechnic Harriers was set the task of working out the course. At the request of Edward VII, it began on the East Terrace of Windsor Castle, and it ended by the royal box in the White City Stadium. Andrew measured the distance as 26 miles and 385 yards, which was to become the Olympic standard.

Courageous performance

The race has never been more dramatic than in 1908, when the leader, Dorando Pietri of Italy, collapsed several times on his final surge through the stadium, way ahead of his rivals. Officials helped Pietri across the finishing line, and as a result the runner was disqualified. The event caught the public imagination and established the marathon as a race for heroes. The Polytechnic Harriers, an all-male athletics club initially associated with Regent's Street Polytechnic, ran the Poly Marathon every year from 1909, breaking several records, until it was eclipsed by the current all-comers' event.

The first of London's three Summer Olympic Games had arrived through Italy's ill-fortune. The 1908 Games had been allocated to Rome but were cancelled because of the disastrous eruption of Mount Vesuvius. As luck would have it, London was getting ready to stage another great event when Vesuvius blew. Sixteen hectares (40 acres) of farmland around Shepherd's Bush had been commandeered for the Franco-British Exhibition, the inspiration of Francophile Edward VII, to confirm an *entente cordiale* between the two countries. It was to be the greatest spectacle in Edwardian Britain. The 20 dazzling white plaster palaces, including the Indian Court rising over a lagoon, plus 120 trade pavilions, became known as the White City. Space

was found for a 130,000-capacity Olympic stadium on the east side of the site. Built by George Wimpey in 10 months, it was completed on April 27, 1908, just three weeks before 'the Franco' opened, to provide the most fantastic Olympic park.

Tug-of-war, cycling, swimming and diving were held in the stadium. Some swimming events as well as the boxing, in which Britain won all five gold medals, took place in the Northampton Institute, now City University London, in Clerkenwell. This is the only host building still standing from the 1908 Games apart from the Queen's Club where *jeu de paume* (real tennis) was played.

London won the Olympic bid a second time in 1939, but the Second World War intervened and the 1944 Games were postponed until 1948. Germany and Japan were not invited, and the USSR chose not to participate. These were the Austerity Games, and participants were put on the same rations as miners and other heavy labourers. The main venue was Wembley Stadium, some 4 miles northwest of White City. It had a capacity of 120,000 and had been built as a temporary structure by Sir Robert McAlpine for another extravaganza, the Empire Exhibition of 1924. No new stadia were built for the Games, and athletes were accommodated in London colleges and military bases. This was the last Olympics to include an Arts competition, which took place in the Victoria and Albert Museum (the art, architecture, sculpture, literature and music all had a sporty theme).

Olympic winners

The area of London chosen as the main site of the 2012 Games lies in Newham, a borough created in 1965 largely out of East Ham and West Ham. In order to build the Olympic park, a big tidy-up of the area and of the industrially scarred waterways of the lower Lee Valley was first necessary. Factories and garages had for a century been leaking arsenic, asbestos, petrol and tar into the environment, and 50-tonne washing machines were moved in to clean 1.4 million tonnes of soil. Landfill sites had to be restored and a number of buildings, including Britain's largest purpose-built housing co-operative, with 450 residents, were demolished. No aspect of the Games was planned without thought for what would happen after everyone had gone home. With new buildings, a park, new waterways and transport links, Londoners are the real winners of the 2012 Olympic Games.

Spectators line the route, encouraging professionals, fun-runners and charity fundraisers alike. The race is followed by a marathon clean-up of discarded water bottles.
LONDON MARATHON

THE OLYMPIC PARK

㊶ Stratford Place

People arriving at the Olympic Games by any train will enter the site through a '24 hour lifestyle street' in Westfield Stratford City, also known as Stratford Place. This is the largest urban shopping area in Europe, covering 18ha (44 acres) and providing employment for more than 8,000 people in 300 shops, three hotels, galleries and a 14 screen cinema. There are performance spaces, public screens and market stalls, and 50 escalators glide the hungry and thirsty up to the top-floor restaurants and bars from where there is a view over the Olympic park and Docklands. With its own gas-fired power plant, the lights in Stratford Place will never go out. Only a couple of decades ago Stratford, now the hub of East London, was just the stop at the end of the line.
Stratford, E15. Stratford rail, tube, DLR.

㊷ The Olympic park

The greenest of green credentials are evident in the olympic park, which has been created for permanent enjoyment. Around 4,000 native trees and 300,000 wetland plants have been installed, and landscaping covers the high points from which live broadcasts can be viewed – much like Wimbledon's 'Henman Hill'. Formal gardens have been laid out around the Olympic Stadium and Aquatic Centre. Trees, flowers and herbs from around the world represent the achievement of Britain's pioneering plant collectors. To retain the festive atmosphere of the Games, this southern area of the park is designed as a leisure destination, with markets, cafés, bars and riverside walks suitable for a day out on sunny weekends to come. Farther from the Games buildings, the quieter northern area is a habitat for birdlife, and there are hopes of introducing otters, which are still found on the upper reaches of the River Lea. It will be worth visiting the Park just to see them.
E15. Stratford rail, tube, DLR.

㊸ The Olympic Stadium

Moated on an island peninsula, the Stadium has a truly Olympian aura. At the southern end of the Olympic park, the 16ha (40 acre) site is enfolded in a waterway, so entrance on three sides is across bridges. Incorporating all the latest that technology has to offer, it is the most eco-friendly Olympic stadium built to date. The venue for field and track events seats 25,000, and the upper tier a further 55,000. After the Games the upper tier will be removed for the next occupants. Gone, too, will be the decorated wrap and the cable-net roof that covers two-thirds of the stadium and reduces the effect any wind could have on a result.

The design is by Pupulous, an architectural firm well used to designing sporting buildings. Based in Kansas City, they have been producing winter and summer Olympic buildings since 1996, and the new Wembley Stadium, Arsenal's Emirates Stadium and Wimbledon Centre Court are in their portfolio. Among this stadium's facilities are 700 rooms and four prayer rooms, the turf was grown in Scunthorpe and the chairs made in Luton. All the facts and figures are enough to keep pub quizzes going for a decade.
Olympic Park, E15. Stratford rail, tube, DLR.

㊹ Arcelor Mittal Orbit

The best view of the Olympic site is from a platform built for that very purpose on Britain's tallest sculpture – the East End's answer to the London Eye. Twisting, dipping and turning upwards to 115m (377ft), the scribble of blood-red steel tubes looks a random act among the linear order of the games. The sculptor Anish Kapoor joined forces with the architect Cecil Balmond to come up with the design, described by Richard Morrison of *The Times* as 'an enormous wire mesh fence that has got hopelessly snagged round the bell of a giant French horn'. For the Orbit, more than 1,000 tonnes of metal were provided by the Indian steel magnate Lakshmi Mittal, whose Mittal Championship Trust funds training for Indian Olympic athletes. The observation tower is on two levels, the lower one encased in glass. Each one holds up to 150 people. Access is by lifts, or via 500 stairs.
E15. Stratford rail, tube, DLR.

㊺ The View Tube and Greenway

Built of recycled shipping containers to provide exhibition space, a café and viewing tower, the fluorescent green View Tube is for spectators without tickets. Opened in November 2009, it stands close to Pudding Mill Lane DLR station, on the south side of the site.

The site can also be seen from the Greenway, a path on high ground leading westwards, then north beside the river. Decorated with rubble from the Olympic excavations – granite cobbles, bollards, manhole covers – the Greenway walking and cycle path links to Victoria Park.
Marshgate Lane, E15 2PJ. Pudding Mill Lane DLR.

THE OLYMPIC STADIUM

㊻ Aquatic Centre

The architectural showpiece and 'Gateway to the Games' is a stunning building by Zaha Hadid. The multi-award-winning Iraqi-born architect is known for uncompromising designs that push back boundaries, and she has certainly done it again here. The Aquatic Centre houses two Olympic-sized pools and a dive pool. On the north side, a bridge, which forms the roof of a training pool, leads to the main pedestrian entrance to the park. It continues across the end of the building over a river to the main stadium.

The Centre's steel roof represents a wave. It is 160m (525ft) long, weighs 3,000 tonnes and is covered with recycled aluminium. Inside, the ceiling is of sustainably sourced South American red lauro timber. The roof elements were put together 20m (66ft) off the ground on temporary supports. Then the whole structure was moved just over 1m (3ft) and dropped on two pillars at one end and a 28m (92ft) wall at the other. It is the most complex architectural element on the Olympic site.

A temporary water-polo arena alongside the Aquatic Centre has shared facilities and will be removed after the Games when the whole place will be turned over to the local community as a leisure centre, and the 17,500 capacity reduced to 2,500.

Olympic Park, E15. Stratford rail, tube, DLR.

VELODROME

㊼ Velodrome

The eco-friendly velodrome has received a great deal of attention, not just because it is green, but because cycling is a sport in which Britain has excelled. The 2008 Olympic cycling team won eight gold medals, and one of its stars, Sir Chris Hoy, was involved in the design and construction of this venue. *The Times's* Hugh Pearman described it as 'effortless class'. The temperature inside is a steady 26°C (78.8°F), and as the 35 miles of Siberian-pine track dried out, the circuit became faster and faster, making it the speediest in the world.

Like the Aquatic Centre, however, attention has been centred on the roof, which has been dubbed 'the Pringle' because it is shaped like the snack of that name. Mike Taylor of Hopkins Architects (who are also responsible for Glyndebourne and Westminster tube station) came up with a lightweight canopy pierced through to allow natural light to enter, and modelled it in a double curve to reflect the shape of the track. Old pipelines and recycled granite from the Royal Docks have been used, and, as in

the handball arena, rainwater is collected and used for flushing toilets. There are 3,500 trackside seats, plus 2,500 seats in upper tiers suspended in the roof. A glass wall allows spectators to look out over the park – and people outside to see in. The Velodrome is part of the VeloPark. After the Games, this will become a road-cycling circuit and moutain-bike course, connecting to cycle paths across London.

Olympic Park, E15. Stratford rail, tube, DLR.

㊽ Olympic Village

The Pantheon frieze on the side of one building will tell future generations what once went on here. Residents-to-be in the 2,800 two, three and four-bedroomed flats in 11 residential blocks, half of them affordable homes, will have many modern features to enjoy, including parks and a school for 1,800 pupils aged from three to 19. The first occupants are expected to move in in 2014.

Olympic Park, E15. Stratford rail, tube, DLR.

49 Handball Arena

An architectural first for this arena is the copper cladding, which was extracted from the polluted earth of the Olympic site. Recycling has proved the cheaper option in sourcing some metals. The cladding covers 3,000 sq m (32,291 sq ft), creating a golden box above the glazed ground-floor level. Sunpipes – glass-ended tubes set into the roof – bring natural light into the building, and water collected on the roof flushes the toilets.

Among games played here will be goalball, in the Paralympics, in which two teams of three visually impaired athletes, wearing eyeshades to ensure equal lack of sight, try to roll a ball with bells into the opposite goal. The game was devised to help rehabilitate soldiers after the Second World War, and is played in silence, so any movement can be detected. Olympic fencing also takes place here, and after the Games the building will become a multi-sports complex.
Olympic Park, E15. Stratford rail, tube, DLR.

50 Forman's

One early winner in the Olympic Games was a long-established salmon smokery. Founded in 1905, it had been doing very nicely, with such clients as Harrods, Fortnum & Mason and the House of Lords. Then the Olympics bid was won, and the greatest powers in the land decided to build a park that would demolish their small patch. A deal was struck, and Forman's vacated its site in exchange for a beautiful new canalside building immediately opposite the main Olympic Stadium, with the best ringside view of the park. The salmon-pink building, designed by architect Phil Hudson, is shaped like a darne (middle cut), and has scales tiling the roof and supporting 'bones'. Forman's Fish Island, run by the fourth generation descendants of the original Russian immigrant smoker, Aaron Forman, has an exhibition gallery and bar, and opens as a restaurant from Thursdays to Sundays.
Stour Road, Fish Island, E3 2NT. Hackney Wick rail, Pudding Mill Lane DLR.

Index

Acknowledgements

Front Cover Getty Images/Gavin Hellier/The Image Bank (The Millennium Bridge and St Paul's Cathedral); **Back Cover** Photolibrary.com/Ellen Rooney (Red tulips and The Orangery, Kensington Gardens); 1 www.arcaid.co.uk/G. Jackson/Marks Barfield Architects (the London Eye and the Houses of Parliament); 2-3 Photolibrary.com/Loop Images/Ricky Leaver (Kensington Gardens and the Royal Albert Hall); 6-7 Photolibrary.com/Martyn Rose (Barnes); 8-9 Photolibrary.com/Lewis Phillips (View from Waterloo Bridge towards the City of London); 10-11 Collections/Oliver Benn; 12-13 Collections/Ray Roberts; 14-18 www.arcaid.co.uk/Richard Bryant; 21 Photolibrary.com/Dennis Gilbert; 22-23 www.arcaid.co.uk/Richard Bryant; 24-25 Photolibrary.com/Eric Nathan; 27 Photolibrary.com/Pawel Libera; 29 www.arcaid.co.uk/Derek Kendall/English Heritage; 32-33 Corbis/© Jon Arnold/JAI (Covent Garden); 35 www.arcaid.co.uk/Richard Bryant/ Pierre Yves Rochon; 36 www.arcaid.co.uk/Peter Durant; 39 www.arcaid.co.uk/Diane Auckland; 40 Homer Sykes; 43 Photolibrary.com/ Eric Nathan; 45 www.arcaid.co.uk/Richard Bryant; 46-47 www.arcaid.co.uk/Richard Bryant/ Foster & Partners; 50-51 Photolibrary.com/Alan Copson (Eros Statue, Piccadilly Circus); 52-53 Corbis/Doug Pearson; 54-55 Getty Images/David Redfern; 57 John Parker; 58 Alamy Images/ David Pearson; 61 www.arcaid.co.uk/G. Jackson/Grey Wornum; 65 Corbis/Tony Latham; 66 Corbis/Sylvain Sonnet; 70-71 Photolibrary.com (View towards Buckingham Palace from St James's Park); 72 John Parker; 75 www.arcaid.co.uk/James Balston/John Miller & Partners; 76 The Royal Collection © 2011, Her Majesty Queen Elizabeth II (See www.royalcollection.org.uk for visiting information); 78-79 Getty Images/Andrew Holt; 81 John Parker; 84 Photolibrary.com/Tim Macpherson; 87 www.arcaid.co.uk/Richard Bryant; 88-89 Photolibrary.com/Pawel Libera (National Theatre and River Thames); 90-91 www.arcaid.co.uk/Richard Bryant; 92 www.arcaid.co.uk/Charlotte Wood/London County Council, Leslie Martin and Peter Moro; 94-95 Corbis/Jane Sweeney/JAI; 96 www.arcaid.co.uk/Benedict Luxmoore/Norman Foster Arup; 99 John Parker; 104-105 www.arcaid.co.uk/Richard Bryant (Albert Memorial); 107 www.arcaid.co.uk/Damian Grady/English Heritage; 108-111 www.arcaid.co.uk/ Richard Bryant; 113 Photolibrary.com/Steve Vidler; 114-115 www.arcaid.co.uk/Roman von Götz/Bildarchiv Monheim; 116 Getty Images/Roy Rainford; 118-119 Photolibrary.com/Bill Varie; 120-121 www.arcaid.co.uk/Richard Bryant (Primrose Hill); 122 John Parker; 125 www.arcaid.co. uk/Nicholas Kane/Future Systems; 126-127 John Parker; 128-129 www.arcaid.co.uk/Richard Bryant/John McAslan and Partners; 130 www. arcaid.co.uk/Morley von Sternberg; 133 Angelo Hornak; 134-135 Photolibrary.com/Jon Spaull; 136-137 Angelo Hornak; 139 www.arcaid.co.uk/G. Jackson; 140 www.arcaid.co.uk/Natalie Tepper; 144-145 Alamy Images/© Prisma Bildagentur AG; 146 www.arcaid.co.uk/Richard Bryant; 148-149 Photolibrary.com/Loop Images/Ricky Leaver (Richmond Park); 150-151 www.arcaid.co.uk/Richard Bryant; 153 Homer Sykes; 154-155 Photolibrary.com/Raf Makda; 156 www.arcaid.co.uk/Martine Hamilton Knight/Building Design Partnership - BDP; 159 Press Association Images/ Joe Giddens/EMPICS Sport; 160-161 www.arcaid.co.uk/Natalie Tepper; 162 www.arcaid.co.uk/Ben Luxmoore/Rick Mather; 165 www.arcaid. co.uk/Richard Bryant; 166 Angelo Hornak; 170-171 www.arcaid.co.uk/Richard Bryant/www.nationaltrust.org.uk; 172-173 www.arcaid.co.uk/ Richard Bryant (Panorama from Citigroup Tower); 175 John Parker; 176-177 Photolibrary.com/Janine Wiedel; 180-181 www.arcaid.co.uk/Peter Durant/Herzog and de Meuron; 182-183 © The Brunel Museum/Bryan Jones; 184-185 Photolibrary.com/Jon Bower; 186 Photolibrary.com/ Jevgenija Pigozne; 188-189 Photolibrary.com/Jon Spaull; 190-191 Photolibrary.com/Eric Nathan; 193 www.arcaid.co.uk/Christopher Simon Sykes/Interior Archive; 194-195 Corbis/Jane Sweeney/JAI (Royal Victoria Docks); 196-197 Photolibrary.com/Eye Ubiquitous; 198 www.arcaid. co.uk/Richard Bryant; 201 Getty Images/Matt Mawson; 202-203 John Parker; 206 Photolibrary.com/Ludovic Maisant; 206-207 www.arcaid.co. uk/Natalie Tepper; 208-209 John Parker; 213 Getty Images; 215 www.jasonhawkes.com; 216-217 Getty Images/David Poultney/ © ODA 2008. **135** quote by Benjamin Zephaniah, *Too Black, Too Strong* (Bloodaxe Books, 2003).

Contributors

Project Editors Penny Craig, Jo Bourne
Art Editors Conorde Clarke, Thomas Keenes
Writers Rose Shepherd, Roger Williams
Sub-editor Marion Paull
Cartographic Consultant Alison Ewington
Picture Editor Caroline Wood
Proofreader Barry Gage
Indexer Marie Lorimer
Maps European Map Graphics Limited

FOR VIVAT DIRECT
Editorial Director Julian Browne
Art Director Anne-Marie Bulat
Managing Editor Nina Hathway
Trade Books Editor Penny Craig
Picture Resource Manager
Sarah Stewart-Richardson
Pre-press Account Manager Dean Russell
Product Production Manager
Claudette Bramble
Production Controller Jan Bucil

Origination by FMG
Printing and binding Arvato Iberia, Portugal

The Most Amazing Places to Visit in London is published in 2011 in the United Kingdom by Vivat Direct Limited (t/a Reader's Digest), 157 Edgware Road, London W2 2HR

The Most Amazing Places to Visit in London is owned under licence from The Reader's Digest Association, Inc. All rights reserved.

We are committed both to the quality of our products and the service we provide to our customers. We value your comments, so please do contact us on **0871 351 1000** or via our website at **www.readersdigest.co.uk**

If you have any comments or suggestions about the content of our books, email us at **gbeditorial@readersdigest.co.uk**

ISBN 978 1 78020 004-0
Book Code 400-524 UP0000-1